T0354335

THE *KENŌSIS* OF GOD

The self-limitation of God - Father, Son, and Holy Spirit

DAVID T. WILLIAMS

iUniverse, Inc.
New York   Bloomington

KENŌSIS OF GOD
The self-limitation of God - Father, Son, and Holy Spirit

iUniverse books may be ordered through booksellers or by contacting:

iUniverse
1663 Liberty Drive
Bloomington, IN 47403
www.iuniverse.com
1-800-Authors (1-800-288-4677)

ISBN: 978-1-4401-3223-0 (pbk)
ISBN: 978-1-4401-3224-7 (ebk)

Printed in the United States of America
iUniverse rev. date: 04/06/09

CONTENTS

PART 4
The *kenōsis* of the Church
"… be with you all"

PART 5
The end of *kenōsis*
"Amen"

The cover:
The parabola symbolizes the process of the *kenōsis* of Christ, reaching its depths in the cross, and succeeded by the process of his exaltation.

Preface

It is not for nothing that I call myself a "Christian", rather than "religious" or "follower of God". Although it would seem that the early disciples of Jesus did briefly experiment with other names for their new faith, such as "the Way" (eg Acts 9:2), a reminder that Christianity must result in a distinct lifestyle, they would seem to have quickly settled on the one which has stuck up to this day. And rightly so; even if Christianity does teach a distinctive manner of life, its essence is not merely following a teacher. That may well be what is taught in many other faiths, but the uniqueness of Christianity lies in its insistence that its heart is not following a Master, but in a continuing relationship with him. Action follows from that. Thus for any Christian, the understanding of the nature of Christ must be of vital importance, because if for no other reason, it affects the understanding of how we are saved.

Christianity must involve *kenōsis*

Who is this Christ? Here there are several key passages of the New Testament to which we may naturally turn; nobody would question that the short passage in Philippians 2, sometimes called a "hymn to Christ" is one of the most important. But right there is a landmine; its main idea is the fact that Jesus "emptied himself", from which is derived the key word *kenōsis*. And it is this that the apostle is holding up as the pattern for a truly Christian lifestyle. So what does it mean?

In the fourth century, in the height of the Arian controversy, Athanasius suffered exile five times because of his belief about the nature of Christ, that he was indeed fully divine. He realised that if Jesus was not divine, then we cannot be saved. Immediately this tells us that whatever else it means, the word *kenōsis* cannot mean that he became any less than fully God.

It is necessary to say this right at the very beginning of the book, because the idea, and particularly the word *kenōsis*, has a history, an unfortunate one. In the nineteenth century the proposal of kenotic Christology was put forward, that the second Person of the Trinity was limited in aspects of his divinity, and in that way could become incarnate. Objections and criticism of the idea were rapidly forthcoming, and after a few decades, the idea was largely abandoned and forgotten. This means that any suggestion of *kenōsis* is likely to produce a bias against it from the very beginning, and it is in danger of not being taken seriously (Dawe 1963:24). Yet, with qualification, some aspect of *kenōsis* is absolutely essential if the incarnation is to be any more than just an idea. It is impossible for God to appear on the world without in some way limiting himself; as the appearances to Ezekiel (Ez 1-3) or to John on Patmos (Rev 1) make clear. People would simply be overwhelmed, and those appearances must in any case not have been of God in total fullness. God in blinding majesty is deadly, but in condescending self-revelation is saving (Horton 2002:320). The "coming down" of God is basic to his nature, and so to his revelation (Oliphint 2004:44). And to be incarnate, not just appear, limitation is even more necessary. Dawe (1963:142) believes that some form of *kenōsis* is essential for New Testament theology. Richard (1982:162) describes *kenōsis* as "the link relating the finitude and sinfulness of man to the love of God". Indeed, there are several modern thinkers, well respected, Jürgen Moltmann being the obvious example, who have espoused the idea (cf Pinnock 2001:12). It must be suggested that the rejection of *kenōsis* in its nineteenth century form, although this is justified in the form in which it was then put forward, was motivated more by the influence of a Greek worldview which stressed the immutability and particularly the impassibility of God. The idea of *kenōsis* had been one of the casualties in the battle with Hellenism (Dawe 1963:53).

This had already given problems to theology in the Christological discussions of the early centuries. In contrast, if reliance had been put more on a Hebraic, a more Biblical world-view, suggestions of *kenōsis* would have been treated more fairly. The idea of change is more compatible with the modern world-view (Pinnock 2001:116). Indeed, the *kenōsis* of Christ, and its attribution to the other Persons of the Trinity, is consistent with the Biblical witness, as van den Brink (1993:245) affirms. This is as long as it is a SELF-limitation, and that God is not believed to be inherently limited, or constrained from without. He is emphatically sovereign, even in his *kenōsis*. Unlike other suggestions, such as in process theology, *kenōsis* does not reflect an inherent limitation in God, so includes the affirmation of God's ultimate control.

Kenōsis through the spirit

The *kenōsis* of Christ is in the context of an appeal; the Philippian passage urges personal *kenōsis* upon Christians. This imitation of Christ must then be an act of will, a voluntary choice, a response to the appeal that the apostle is making. But one of the wonders of Christianity is that it is not simply a human act in response to belief and decision, but is enabled by the Holy Spirit. Without this, it would be impossible; perhaps there are some few individuals who have been able to humble themselves, but at best, they are rare. But for Christians, it is a possibility; Philippians 2 starts with a reference to participation in the Spirit. Thus any imitation of the *kenōsis* of Jesus is empowered by him, just as was the *kenōsis* of Christ himself. God is not overpowering but empowering (Coakley 2001:206). This self-limitation was done from a desire for relationship with the world and in particular with the redeemed. Philippians 2 describes the act of *kenōsis*, done in order to enact salvation. *Kenōsis* is then both the means, and the goal, of salvation; it is therefore a key role of the Spirit. Even when his activity may seem to be spectacular, such as when he enables healing, or speaking in tongues, *glossolalia*, the one who experiences them must, or should, be extremely humbled by the fact that God has worked through him or her.

But the Spirit does not only work in a kenotic manner, but his very nature is kenotic. At face value, it is amazing that God in the world could just be ignored, but this is in fact the case! The Spirit has been referred to as the "self-effacing", or "shy" Person of the Trinity, and certainly this is the case. He does not glorify himself, but Christ (Jn 16:14); this is also an example for Christians to emulate. Such as Congar (1993:5), and Moltmann (1985:102), do not hesitate to speak of the Spirit in terms of *kenōsis*; likewise Gaffin (1996:25) writes that the Spirit "boxed himself in".

The nature of God is kenotic

This suggests something that is most significant. If Jesus acted in *kenōsis*, and if that is the same for the third Person, could it then be that *kenōsis* is an aspect of the very nature of God? What Jesus, and the Spirit, are doing, is simply acting in accordance with their very nature. This then suggests that it should also be a feature of the first Person, of the Father, and this is indeed the case. If the Spirit is "shy", how much more the Father, who is never seen, choosing to act by the Son and Spirit, jealously guarding his transcendence? It is not for nothing that many writers have commented on the hidden nature of God. His action likewise is kenotic; for example many have understood the act of creation in terms of *kenōsis*, God limiting himself in order to give existence, and a measure of freedom, to the creation. Creation and incarnation are understood as two phases of "the one process of God's self-giving and self-expression" (Rahner, in Richard 1997:94). Such self-limitation can provide a ready explanation for such old problems as the existence of evil.

x

This introduces the Trinity, and provides the framework for this book. Our experience is first of Christ as kenotic, but this relates back to the fundamental nature of God. "It is precisely in the kenōsis of Christ (and nowhere else) that the inner majesty of God's love appears, of God who 'is love' (I Jn 4:8) and a 'trinity'" (Hans Urs von Balthasar, in Richard 1997:22). This kenotic love is for salvation, as God desires "new partners for the eternal dance" (Pinnock 2001:30), which is how the *perichōrēsis* of the Trinity has been described. Then it relates forward to its application to Christians by the power of the Spirit. The order, interestingly, is that of the traditional "grace" of 2 Corinthians 13:14, known and used on a regular basis by countless Christians. Here grace, love and fellowship are ascribed to the three Persons, each of which is in nature kenotic. This is obvious in the case of the first two attributes, which involve giving, and implied in the third, where any fellowship involves a measure of yielding to the other. Incidentally, although it may be thought that giving does not diminish the infinite God, it is observable that when Jesus healed, he did feel the loss of power (Mk 5:30). This must bring us back to the key question, which provides the theme for this book. What does *kenōsis* mean, and how does it manifest in the three Persons of the Trinity?

And of course, lurking in the background is another – what does this have to do with us? Theology may well be fascinating, but I can never be content unless it affects my life and that of others round about. If *kenōsis* is fundamental to what God is like, this would immediately explain why Christians are urged to be kenotic themselves, for being a Christian should mean reflecting the nature of God; we should become like him. The essential idea therefore comes frequently in Christian devotion; to give one example, taken from one of Charles Wesley's hymns:

He left his Father's throne above

So free, so infinite his grace -

Emptied Himself of all but love

And bled for Adam's helpless race

'Tis mercy all, immense and free;

For, O my God, it found out me!

Such a conclusion would have far-reaching consequences, but if it is a valid part of the imitation of Christ, must be taken seriously. *Kenōsis* is the pattern for Christian life, simply because a Christian life should be in imitation of God. This book started, as my others, with a study of the implications of Christian doctrine, in this case *kenōsis*, for the Christian life. What happened was that the tail started to wag the dog, and the section of the book dealing with application got so big that it really had to be separated. It then appeared as *Have this mind* (Williams 2007), leaving me to develop the theoretical basis for the application here.

But this step is essential if the appeal to follow a kenotic life is to be taken seriously, and so it is indeed necessary to continue to consider in all seriousness what the emptying of God is all about. What does it mean for Christ to empty himself? What are the implications of the *kenōsis* of the Father? In what way has the *kenōsis* of the Spirit affected his working in the world? And how does *kenōsis* relate to the fundamental Christian message, the means of salvation? And finally, how does the entire process work out in the future? These are the questions that this book seeks to answer.

It will probably be pointed out that the book as it stands is quite uneven, especially in respect of the referencing, where some chapters are liberally sprinkled, while others have almost none. The reason for this lies in the diverse origins of the material. Those with few are usually notes written to help students, supplementing what was covered in lectures, so that referencing was not so useful; how many students take the trouble to follow them up? The ones with many, on the other hand, were prepared for publication in academic journals, and are therefore likely to contain novel or controversial ideas which need to be supported. I hope that there are enough references to enable anybody interested to follow up material quoted or alluded to. I would hope that this book also stimulates further thought, and especially that further aspects of the idea of *kenōsis* will be uncovered. The author would love to hear suggestions; maybe one day the book might be developed further in a more even and satisfactory way.

I need to acknowledge therefore especially the comments of editors and referees. These were always appreciated, even if they were not always agreed with. They often stimulated new lines of thought. My thanks therefore to *South African Baptist Journal of Theology, Old Testament Essays, Koers, Theologia Viatorum, Acta Theologica, Journal for Theology in Southern* Africa for their exposure to, and publication of, various articles reflected in the book. All previously published material has however been extensively revised both to avoid the inevitable duplication between chapters and to attempt some continuity of thought in the book. A few sections are reworkings of parts of my earlier books, and are included here for completeness as they are relevant to the theme of *kenōsis*. Some of my previous books are referred to in the bibliography, and a list is included at the end of the bibliography. A number of colleagues read the entire book before publication, and I am especially grateful both for their patience and comments. I would particularly acknowledge Deon Thom, professor emeritus in Theology, retired from the University of Fort Hare, who has been a constant encouragement to me in my career there.

He writes, "I must congratulate you on a very extensive and thorough discussion of a very important topic, a discussion which is indeed long overdue. One can only hope that other scholars will take up the challenge and enter the debate. For far too long the facts, as well as the many problems connected with God's kenosis, have largely been ignored by theologians." Professor König, formerly of the University of South Africa comments, "I ... find your approach well informed, broadly based, strongly argued, responsible in terms of conclusions - an overall laudable piece of research. I highly appreciate both the exegetical and the systematic aspects of the presentation. You have a definite ability to draw lines together into an overall view. That is Systematic Theology at its best. And added to that, your Biblical basis is very strong." Then Dr. Lubunga w'Ehusha, of the Evangelical Seminary of Southern Africa, says "in dealing with the topic of "kenosis" the writer wants to stretch the mind of the reader beyond the controversy about the divine nature of Christ and Pauline Christology that has fuelled many theological essays and books. The passage of Paul's epistle to the Philippians is not an essay to oppose or compare the divinity of Christ to his humanity but a calling to live out one's Christian faith. The book argues that the kenosis of Jesus is not an isolated act in the history of incarnation but is embedded in the very nature of his divinity. The entire Trinity operates in kenosis, a deliberate choice to self-limitation in order to relate with one another and with the powerless. The book shows that each person of the Trinity, Father, Son and the Holy Spirit, participates and works in a kenotic way in their relation to the humanity. The creator who accepts to give dominion to the people He created, Jesus who limits himself by becoming a human being and the Spirit who dwells in and works through the Church accepting the risk of being grieved by the human fallen nature.

Professor Samuel Waje Kunhiyop, the head of Postgraduate School, South African Theological Seminary, writes that he expected that the book "was going to be an academic book replete with boring, complex and difficult exegetical and theological arguments. On the contrary, I found out after reading that it was very engaging, exciting and very refreshing book on Christian Theology. "What is most refreshing in this book, often lacking in theology is the practical implication of the study. This is surely a plus!" He found that "The major strengths of this book are [that it is] (1) thoroughly biblical, (2) historically and theologically consistent with evangelically Christianity, (3) philosophically logical and coherent, and above all (4) relevant to the Christian life. I enthusiastically commend this book not only to Bible students and academic theologians but to Christians who desire not only to know the truth of Christian Theology but its implications on the Christian life."

I must add, in conclusion to my introducing this theme, that Thielicke (1966:489) observes that any book is a compromise, that between the desire to develop an exact and exhaustive treatment of the subject, and the constraints of time, marketability, and even the demands of prospective readers. He could then have noted that what is necessary for the author is a form of *kenōsis*, seeing that a book is subject to such limitations! The desire is always to continue to develop, read and add, but I have learnt that there must come a day when the line is drawn, and completion is enacted. Always of course a sadness, and regret, for there must remain gems that have escaped the process of mining!

PART 1

The *kenōsis* of Jesus Christ

"The grace of our Lord Jesus Christ"

Chapter 1

The "kenotic" theory of the atonement

The word *kenōsis* has such a history in theology that it is advisable to start with a look at what gave it such a reputation. Ironically, the very term seems to have emptied itself, humbled itself, and "become of no reputation"! If it is to be used in any meaningful way, it must follow the example of Jesus and be resurrected and exalted. But how did that state of affairs come about?

The gospel must be understandable

The centre of the Christian message, so fittingly called the "gospel", the *euangelion*, the good news, is that the means of salvation is available. We do not just have to die, but have the possibility of eternal life, not only after death, but also experienced, to some extent, even in the present. Perhaps the "cherry on the top" is that we are able to experience an anticipation of salvation even in the present, "life abundant". Such a claim, such an offer, is stupendous, and almost unbelievable. When we are confronted on a daily basis with death, the hope of being able to overcome this is simply amazing. It is so amazing that for many people the message

3

just cannot be accepted; it is just too good to be true. This is perhaps a particular problem in the modern world, which has a tendency to only accept something if it can be experienced or proved in some other way. And of course life after death is something that just cannot be proved. Even the experiences that some claim, to have contact with the dead, whether by western style séances or African divination or ancestral veneration, cannot really prove the point as they are subject to delusion, to psychological influence or even fraud. In any case it does not prove that spirits can live forever; maybe they too can live only for a short while longer. Claims of the experience of "abundant life" can also be scoffed at as being all in the mind.

But the same attitude that produces scepticism, and very rightly, can also produce an openness to being convinced even of such a claim that Christianity makes. If it can be shown how salvation may be achieved, then people are more open to accept it. The faith of Abraham, held up as an example of saving faith by Paul in his explanation of the gospel in his epistles to the Romans and Galatians, is totally amazing just because he simply believed the promise that God made to him without any explanation of how God would achieve what he said that he would do. For us, living on the other side of the incarnation, faith should be so much easier to receive, simply because it is possible for us to see the means by which God did, what he promised. We do not have to just trust, but we can, to an extent, understand. It was a common medieval description of theology that it was *fides quaerens intellectum*, "faith seeking understanding". Indeed, despite Tertullian, who said that he believed the gospel "just because it is absurd", we have the privilege, with the rationality that God created us with, to understand, and so to accept. Such a rationality is even, as has often been pointed out, an aspect of the fact that people are created *imago Dei*, "in the image of God" (Gen 1:26).

Of course there is a significant difference between the faith that

Abraham had and the faith that we are called upon to have. He was effectively called to accept that God would continue to create; that is not unreasonable, for as God had created the world, creation of a son for him, even in his old age, was not fundamentally different. We are not called to have faith in creation in the same way, but in a different action, the modification of what already existed. The difference is that God is not just doing something new, but altering what he had already done. This is something that he could not just do without infringing upon what had been already done. As people had already been made, and made with a measure of autonomy, it would just not be ethical to simply override what had been done without the acceptance of the people. So whereas it would have been possible for God to have simply given eternal life to the people that he had made, he needed a mechanism by which this could be done with the concurrence of those that he was in fact benefiting. Otherwise he would in fact be over-riding what he had already done, saying that it was wrong. On the contrary, one of the wonders of the gospel is that God did not go back, that he affirmed the sort of creation that he made, but made a way by which people could be saved, within the terms of that creation.

Salvation necessitated incarnation of full deity

It is the fact of the incarnation, presumably unknown to Abraham, that is at the heart of God's mechanism of salvation. Respecting the creation that he had made, he entered it by means of his Son to make salvation available to people. Perhaps this does not really help the problem of faith, for just as salvation itself, the idea that God had become incarnate is also hard to accept. This is one reason why the faith that saves is of the same order as the faith that Abraham had.

The actual mechanism of salvation, the means by which we are saved, does require that Jesus Christ had to be fully divine.

Salvation had to include a means of dealing with the sin that had caused separation from God in the first place and so death. This was by sacrifice, enacted on the cross, the fulfillment of the Old Testament practices. And if the death of Christ was to be adequate for the sins of the world, he had to be divine. Then if salvation was the granting of eternal life, that also demanded divinity, because this is a receipt of the eternal life that is a divine attribute. Christians live by the life of Christ, received by their union with him. In a sense they are "divinised" (2 Pet 1:4), re-created (2 Cor 5:17), born "from above" (Jn 3:3), all pictures that imply the divinity of the Christ who enabled this. It is hardly surprising that in the Arian controversy of the fourth century, Athanasius, the main opponent of Arius' belief that the second Person, the Son, was essentially less divine than the first, the Father, was so steadfast in his belief because he appreciated that salvation was only possible if the Son was indeed fully divine. In the words of the creed proposed at the conference in Nicaea in 325 AD, called to deal with Arius' ideas, the Father and the Son are *homoousios*, "of the same essence". It was this that Athanasius so staunchly defended, and which has been a central Christian belief ever since.

But how can Christ also be human?

But it is because the affirmation of Jesus' full divinity is so incredible that almost as soon as the Arian controversy was effectively settled, a further dispute arose as to how the divinity in Jesus related to his humanity. A reading of the New Testament, and especially the gospel of John, makes it very clear that Jesus was claiming to be divine, equal to the Father, a claim that several times prompted the Jews to try to stone him for blasphemy (eg Jn 8:59, 10:31). But not only did their staunch monotheistic belief, a result of the realisation, drummed in to them by the experience of several centuries of history, predispose them against any hint that Jesus could be a second God, but he so clearly appeared to be human. It was of course the first aspect that led to the Arian problem, and the realisation that in fact there was no contradiction with the Old Testament stand on monotheism, that God was indeed one, but in three Persons. However, the second problem, that Jesus so clearly seemed to be human, proved, if anything, to be even trickier to understand.

It was quite clear to those at the time that Jesus was a human being. Even if the account of his conception indicated his divinity, a perception reinforced by the event in Jerusalem when he was twelve (Lk 2:41f), the birth was normal, his growth as a boy and young man likewise, and even in the time of his ministry, so much that he did reflected a humanity that was completely normal. Just as we do, he ate, drank, got tired, and eventually even died. Indeed, even the message of salvation itself depends not only on his divinity, but again, as many of the early Fathers, not least Athanasius, realised, he had to be fully human in order to identify fully with us. If he were not, how could he die as an adequate sacrifice? How could he be our representative and substitute? How could we share his life if that life was not really human? How could he be a valid example for our lives, if he did not feel what we do? It is quite reasonable that so many modern attempts to understand the nature of Jesus do not do so in the traditional way, "from above", by first accepting his full divinity, but rather "from below", accepting the evidence of full humanity and trying to understand the Nicene affirmation that he was at the same time fully divine.

It is those words "at the same time" that caused such a problem at the time, a problem that continues up to today. How could a person who was so clearly a human being be divine? The greater conception that there is of the greatness and holiness of God, the greater seems the impossibility that the one who walked the paths of Galilee could actually be the one who created the stars. Yet although

Jesus was truly human, this did not mean that he was merely human (Macleod 1998:65). It is hardly surprising that in theology, Christology has always generated the most heated debate (Erickson 1998:677). However, Erickson (1998:752) also points out that both humanity and deity are most clearly seen in Jesus, so they must be compatible!

The repeated question is how they can be compatible; what explanation can be at all acceptable? Yet, if the gospel message is to be presented successfully to thinking people, there just has got to be a reasonable explanation of how Jesus could manifest both divinity and humanity.

The aspect that has impressed most modern thinkers is that whereas it was clear that Jesus was human, it was not so clear that he was divine. The latter affirmation was a result of accepting his claims, the evidence of his deeds, his quality of life, and latterly his resurrection, but was not obvious just from his appearance. Should not God clearly appear to be divine, as at the transfiguration (Matt 17:1f), or when Jesus appeared to John on the Isle of Patmos (Rev 1:12f)? And even these, glorious though they were, hardly reflect the wonders of who he claimed to be.

How he appeared is the point. This was an early solution to the problem, that God presented himself in such a way that he only appeared, or seemed to be human. This docetism (Greek *dokeō*, "seem") is obviously something that God could do, but at the cost of his real humanity, and especially then of salvation. If he only appeared to be human, we could not really be identified with him. In particular, if he only appeared to die, which was a very attractive solution in a world-view that presumed that God must be impassible, unable to suffer, then his death was not real and could not be a real atonement for our sin. We could not be forgiven, we could not be saved, if Christ's humanity was docetic. The same objection was later raised to a more sophisticated explanation, that of Apollinarius, who proposed that Jesus did not have a human soul, but it was replaced by the second Person of the Trinity, the *logos*. This as well was speedily rejected by the Church; in the course of the Christological controversy it was repeatedly affirmed that "what was not assumed could not be saved". Human beings could only be saved if Jesus was a full human being.

After much discussion and controversy, the affirmation was finally made, enshrined in the famous statement of Chalcedon in 451 AD, that Jesus was fully human, "consubstantial" with us, and that the Nicene affirmation remained correct, that he was consubstantial with the Father, so fully divine. He then had a complete human nature, and a complete divine one, these two natures being in one person, unconfusedly, unchangeably, indivisibly, inseparably (quoted fully in Grudem 1994:557 and Macleod 1998:185).

But this only sharpened the problem; the fact was that he most definitely appeared to be human, but not obviously divine. If Chalcedon was correct, surely he would have appeared to be divine? The answer is in the negative, for if he appeared to be in any way divine, then he would not be human, for part of the features of being human is of appearing to be. This is not applicable to being divine, for "God is spirit" (Jn 4:24), and so there is no divine appearance as such. This was again an Old Testament affirmation, resulting in the stringent prohibition of idolatry, for God just cannot be pictured.

It must be insisted that the attributes of divinity cannot detract from the real humanity of Jesus. This misconception has even resulted in the questioning of the traditional doctrine of the virgin birth, from the mistaken belief that full humanity requires two human parents. Even more significantly, the sinlessness of Jesus has been doubted, just because sin seems so much an attribute of humanity. Such beliefs are in any case contrary to the plain indications of scripture, firstly in the gospel stories of the birth of Jesus, and secondly in the explicit statements of such as Hebrews 4:15 or 1 Peter 2:22.

But those same scriptures also state clearly that on several occasions Jesus just did not manifest qualities that have traditionally been understood as those of divinity. It was not merely that his appearance was not as might have been expected, but also his actions did not seem always to be those of deity. On one occasion (Mk 6:5) he was not able to perform the wonders that might have been expected. Is not God supposed to be omnipotent? Then at other times he professed ignorance, such as of the time of the *parousia*, the second coming (Mk 13:32). Is not God omniscient? Then he was clearly not present everywhere at once, so, for example, had to travel in order to heal Jairus' daughter (Lk 8:41f). Is not God omnipresent? They are clearly consistent with humanity, for people are by very nature limited in power, in knowledge, in location, but not with being God. If these are not just examples of docetism after all, how are they consistent with being divine? Some modern thinkers, such as John Robinson, have persistently argued that traditional Christology has been "predominantly docetic" (Macquarrie 1974:117). If these limitations of Jesus are real, how are they consistent with divinity? Such a question has to be answered if the incarnation is to be understood to any extent, which it must be if it is to be believed, and then, more importantly, if the atonement is to be believed and so able to be accepted on any more than just plain authority, so unlikely in a post-Enlightenment world.

The proposal of a kenotic solution

It was then in the context of the *Aufklärung*, or "Enlightenment", that a novel solution to the problem of Christology was proposed. People were no longer prepared to accept seemingly contradictory affirmations just on the authority of the Church. They just had to be rationally acceptable, and if not, should be rejected. Not surprisingly the new idea stressed the real humanity of Jesus and questioned traditional credal formulations (Dawe 1963:90); it proposed that the exercise of Jesus' divinity was limited. Central to this idea was the text of the Christological "hymn" of Philippians 2:5f:

> Have this mind among yourselves, which you have in Christ Jesus, who, though he was in the form of God, did not count equality with God a thing to be grasped, but emptied himself, taking the form of a servant, being born in the likeness of men.

The key word here is "emptied", *ekenōsen*, a word better known in the noun form, *kenōsis*. Athough this passage most clearly sets out the source of the idea, there are others which are most relevant, such as Hebrews 2:9. In particular, 2 Corinthians 8:9 was felt to lend support:

> For you know the grace of our Lord Jesus Christ, that though he was rich, yet for your sake he became poor.

Even if it had also become fashionable to question scripture and its authority, again on rational grounds, the theory proposed was scripturally based. Such as Thomasius, Ebrard and Mackintosh found the *kenōsis* theme widespread in the New Testament (Dawe 1963:27). They saw it present not only on the inferences of the life of Jesus, but also in a couple of very explicit references, such as John 3:13, 16:28, 17:5, and Romans 15:3, which however could well be dependent on Philippians 2 (Dawe 1963:28). Essentially, what was suggested was that in order to become incarnate, the second Person of the Trinity "emptied" himself of the attributes that are characteristic of being God, such as omnipotence and omniscience, so that the aspects of power and knowledge manifested in Christ were just those of an ordinary human being. However, it was believed that while the metaphysical attributes were curtailed, the moral ones, such as love and holiness, were unaffected (McGrath 1997:260).

This idea was immediately attractive to the Enlightenment world-view, for it meant that Jesus could share the understanding of the Bible of the "unenlightened" world of his time. It also reflects the Biblical assertions of Jesus' ignorance (eg Matt 24:36, Mk 9:21), and growth (Lk 2:52). He would therefore accept the stories of the creation and of Jonah as historical, and ascribe the authorship of the Pentateuch to Moses and the Psalms to David, all of which traditional beliefs were increasingly questioned at the time. Gore had particularly emphasised this point (Macquarrie 1974:118). What kenotic Christology was doing was starting from a definite affirmation of Jesus' humanity and laying the old docetism to rest (Richard 1982:160). Most importantly, it was an attempt to make sense of the incarnation; Martin (1959:100) notes that Christ's self-limitation was absolutely necessary for him to become human at all. Feinberg (1980:46) feels that the *kenōsis* of his divine power is necessary to be truly human. Relating to humanity renders *kenōsis* essential; Calvin even speaks of God's "baby-talk" in order to communicate with us (Horton 2002:324). Erickson (1998:754) comments that while it is impossible for a human being to become God, for God to become human is a possibility.

The "kenotic theory" was popular in Germany between about 1860 to 1880, and then in England from about 1890 to 1910 (Grudem 1994:550). On the continent, the Lutheran, Gottfried Thomasius was the most significant presenter of the idea in his *Christ's Person and Work* (Richard 1982:158). He taught that the Son had abandoned the metaphysical attributes (McGrath 1997:355). Gess went further, including the other aspects of divinity, and also the idea of generation and the exercise of his cosmic functions, such as upholding the universe (Macleod 1998:206). The theory in this form quickly came under attack, for it implied that God had in fact changed, so contradicted the idea of divine immutability. Then a Christ who was kenotic in this sense was no longer God (Pannenberg 1968:320). Moreover, the lessening of one Person then destroys the unity of the

Trinity (Richard 1982:160). Later development avoided this problem by arguing that the attributes were not abandoned, but rather either "hidden" or that Jesus abstained from using them. Admittedly, this then has similarities to the old docetism, so that while he was fully God, he did not appear to be. It is subject to the same objection, that what is portrayed is not real (Pannenberg 1968:305); indeed there could even be said to be hypocrisy. The former is often called the theory of *krypsis* (Greek "hidden"), and was advocated by the University of Tübingen, the latter, referred to by *kenōsis*, by Giessen (Ward 2001:155).

In England, the idea of *kenōsis* was espoused by Gore, who saw it as a way of reconciling Anglo-Catholics and liberals (Macleod 1998:206). As in the early Church, it was hard to separate theological discussion from more worldly concerns! He sometimes spoke in terms of "refraining", sometimes of "abandoning"; it is notable that he accepted the definitions of Nicaea and of Chalcedon without reservation (Macleod 1998:206). P T Forsyth is also associated with the idea, especially as he saw the aspects of such as omnipotence not so much as attributes of deity, but rather as functions of those attributes. He pointed out some of the problems with the traditional views, such that it is hard to see how there could in fact be two wills in Christ if one was divinely omniscient while the other was human and fallible (Macleod 1998:208).

Objections to *kenōsis*

Of course, an immediate objection to the idea is that the Gospels do indicate that Jesus did know and claimed that he was indeed the Son, and that the disciples also recognised his divinity. He also is recorded as having performed significant miracles. The explanation of the time, in keeping with the Enlightenment understanding of the Bible, was that these could well not be factual or original, but the result of later belief, inserted in editorial revisions. However, it must also be observed, with more respect to the text and authority of the Bible, that all of this could well be attributed not to the divinity of the Son, but to the action of the Spirit, who empowered him at his baptism, then inspired him and his disciples. The very word "Christ", "anointed", indicated the source of his power. Paradoxically, the ministry of the Holy Spirit was largely neglected at the time of the development of the kenotic theory, but if it had not been, the self-limitation of Jesus may perhaps have met with fewer objections.

Thus the theory was attacked from a Biblical perspective. Martin (1983:171) comments that any metaphysical "laying off" of attributes is foreign to Paul, or, he suggests, to reality. Then the respected New Testament scholar Lightfoot noted that the term used in Philippians 2:6, that Christ was in the *morphē*, "form" of God implies the essential attributes (Thomas 1970:143), but at the same time observed that the schema of Philippians 2 was of the outward and accidental (Macleod 1998:216). The use of *morphē* was not based on Greek philosophy, but on the Septuagint; it implies outward appearance and change, the accessibility of what is there. Thus Bulgakov interprets it as God's glory, which is given up (Gavrilyuk 2005:260). A further significant observation that he made was that the humility that he expressed in the incident where he washed the feet of his disciples was in the immediate context of his coming from the Father (Jn 13:2f). "It is his very form to forgo his rights"; so he felt that it was inherent to the very nature of God to humble himself. This point becomes clearer with the realization that the *kenōsis* of Philippians was in relation not to humanity in relation to deity, but to the lordship which Christ refused to use (Martin 1983:175), but later, after the cross and resurrection, was clearly granted. Thus *kenōsis* is a self-limitation, a rejection of the use of power and authority that is still available.

The idea of *kenōsis* was attacked for other reasons as well. J

M Creed cites the admission of Thomasius himself that there was little support for the notion in the Fathers; and that the closest was a comment in Apollinarius that "incarnation is self-emptying" (Baillie 1956:94), but Dawe (1963:60) points out that this is "by way of limitation, not of change". Apollinarius was of course condemned as a heretic for his Christological views! This in itself is not too serious; in fact many of the Fathers would have been condemned by later standards. All theology must be seen in its own context. Thinkers such as Apollinarius were trying to understand and had no intention of being heretical or of denying what had previously been accepted. Grudem (1994:550) also asserts that no recognised teacher taught the idea for 1800 years, including native Greek speakers. Dawe (1963:9) however suggests that the idea is ancient, even pre-Paul; he cites Origen, who rejected Celsus because of his assumption that God had to be unchangeable, or he could not remain divine; he cites also Tertullian. Feinberg (1980:21) notes that the term *kenōsis* was first found in Patristic literature, "and is used thereafter almost as a synonym for incarnation". Erickson (1991:78) asserts that it has featured in Christologies from the earliest days. Philippians 2 played a crucial role in Patristic Christology (Gavrilyuk 2005:259). For Irenaeus, the *logos* was quiescent in the temptations and crucifixion; For Athanasius there was no emptying of the divine, simply because, for him, salvation was deification (Dawe 1963:63). Dawe (1963:53) comments that the idea of *kenōsis* only fell away in the early centuries as it was incompatible with Hellenism; this was exacerbated by the rejection of Arianism as heretical. This then really demanded a denial of any real *kenōsis* in Christ, as if he was one substance with the Father, it was felt that there could be no changeableness. However, if immutability is seen not so much as an aspect of a divine attribute, but as consistency or faithfulness (eg König 1982:89), this problem is resolved, and also explains such problems as the repentance of God as in the story of Jonah (also Pinnock 2001:85f). H R Mackintosh accepts *kenōsis* as the only immutability is that of love (Macleod 1998:218).

A common criticism of kenotic Christology was made by Archbishop William Temple, who voiced an objection based on Hebrews 1:3. He could not see that a kenotic Christ could fulfil his function of upholding the universe (Macleod 1998:209). As with the problem of immutability, *kenōsis* would be in conflict with the traditional teaching. However, providence does not in fact need the constant involvement of Christ, but his overseeing the process; this need not then be Deism (cf Sanders 1998:10). Many open theists, while respecting free choice, so seeing a limitation of God's control, speak of God intervening if his overall intention is threatened (Nicholls 2002:629f); the same can be true of a kenotic God. Of course, the upholding of the universe could also be done by other Persons, especially as the three are involved in all actions of God. This had been Gess' solution, seeing the Spirit as taking over this function (Dawe 1963:100). Likewise if the attributes were not curtailed, but hidden, this is again no problem.

Although Macquarrie (1974:119) asserts that kenoticism was determined to retain the traditional framework of Christology, Macleod (1998:209) adds that *kenōsis* in the original sense would seem to go against the formulation of Chalcedon, as Jesus would not be fully divine for a while. There is also a problem with the continuity between the incarnation and the pre-existence of Christ, and therefore between the divine Christ and the human Jesus. Very significantly, in the extreme form, *kenōsis* affects salvation, for, as Athanasius pointed out, a Christ who is not fully divine cannot save. A kenotic Christ is not even worthy of worship (Ward 2001:156). Bulgakov insists that *kenōsis* cannot involve abandoning deity, which would go against the traditional understanding of Christ (Gavrilyuk 2005:254).

Because it seemed to demand a change in the actual divinity of Christ, the theory did go out of favour, and the very word *kenōsis* gained a measure of notoriety. Baillie (1956:97), in his study of Christology, feels that it presupposes that divinity and humanity cannot be united. In fact, it is often felt that the statement of Chalcedon is not so much an explanation of the incarnation but a statement of its parameters, even of the problem. Küng points out that the Christological debate is not yet over, as all attempts to define Chalcedon have failed (Richard 1997:3). The kenotic theory is at least an attempt to probe a little into the mystery and not just to ignore it.

Meeting objections

However, if *kenōsis* is understood not as a removal of attributes but as their restriction, these difficulties to some extent fall away. God, as omnipotent, is quite capable of doing this. Even if he limits himself, God is quite free to transcend his self-limitation (Peacocke 1993:208). Thomas (1970:150) goes so far as to assert that this is the only possible way to understand Philippians 2. This is not a *krypsis* in the sense of a hiding, as this would be docetic, even deceptive, but rather a restriction; Jesus did sometimes "manifest his glory" (Jn 2:11). It was a veiling, which was absolutely essential (Macleod 1998:106). Augustine can of course be relied upon to make at least some comments relevant to the issue; for him "Jesus emptied himself 'not by changing his own divinity but by assuming our changeableness'" (Macleod 1998:216). The self-emptying is rather a self-adding (Turretin, in Oliphint 2004:49). The emptying is explained by the taking humanity and becoming human (Martin 1983:170); this was the view of Origen (Dawe 1963:55). Bockmuehl (1997:134) however points out that this point is not recognised by the original kenotic theory. For Thomasius, *kenōsis* was not a renunciation of use, but a real renunciation, thus challenging impassibility (Dawe 1963:94). A more modern belief is that of Calvin, who said that whereas Jesus could not divest himself of his Godhead, he concealed it for a time (Macleod 1998:218); *kenōsis* did not affect "what Christ was, but how he conducted himself" (Dawe 1963:72); this is more in line with the *krypsis* idea. Thomas (1970:147) comments that God's attributes are not possessions that can be laid aside, but part of his very being; he notes that Philippians 2 actually says nothing about attributes at all (1970:149). In fact, if *kenōsis* is not seen as an essential change, but a voluntary self-limitation, it does not imply any change in God. As Thomasius stressed, "self-limitation is nothing else but self-determination" (Dawe 1963:94). Macleod (1998:219) writes that "it is perfectly possible to speak of real renunciation without defining it as renunciation of deity". Bulgakov says that the Word retains his divine nature, but divests himself of his glory and his foreknowledge, becoming temporarily subordinate to the Father and even to the Spirit (Gavrilyuk 2005:251,263). There is then no conflict with pre-existence, as Temple feared (Macleod 1998:210). Smith, in the article on *kenōsis* in the *Evangelical Dictionary of Theology* endorses it as orthodox (Grudem 1994:550, who however finds this assessment surprising). Martin (1983:171) is insistent that there is no contradiction between *kenōsis* and the affirmations of later dogma. As to the objection that after the glorification of Christ, when *kenōsis* would have ceased, and so Jesus would have stopped being human, the reply could aptly be made that he is only then what humans should be, that it is sinful humanity that is defective. As our resurrection, we become really human for the first time!

With all the background of controversy, it is not surprising there has been great diversity as to the understanding of Philippians 2, enough to produce "intellectual paralysis" (A B Bruce, in 1876, cited by Richard 1982:101). However, more modern thought has expressed some sympathy with the idea of *kenōsis*. For Hegel, *kenōsis* was the pattern of all reality; the generation of the Son was the limitation of pure being (Dawe 1963:118). Küng then develops this; the being of God is essentially becoming, the medieval *acta pura*; hence he can empty himself without losing himself (Richard

1982:171). For Barth, Christ's self-emptying was the expression of God's will to love (Richard 1982:163). Naturally Pannenberg objects to this, saying that Barth loses a personal unity in Christ, seeing only functional harmony between the natures; nevertheless he also understands Jesus' unity with the Father in kenotic terms, as full dedication (Richard 1982:164). Moltmann is particularly noteworthy. For him, the depth of *kenōsis*, the cross, "becomes the general criterion of theology" (Richard 1997:85). Modern Christologies try to understand transcendence in the light of human self-emptying and suffering (Richard 1982:190), so "from below". Thus Moltmann is concerned to relate his view of God to the current situation in the world, especially, writing as a German who participated in the second World War, that of human suffering. Certainly a suggestion of God's self-limitation can provide an explanation for suffering, and if for no other reason, can justify a re-examination of *kenōsis*, especially against the background of the Trinity. As in other areas of his thought, he expresses an appreciation for the insights of Eastern Orthodoxy, for which *kenōsis* is a vital part of piety and its understanding of God (Dawe 1963:149,155). Kenotic motifs are common in Russian thought (Gavrilyuk 2005:252), such as in Bulgakov (*the wisdom of God*), who has used the idea in respect of creation and the Trinity, not just in Christology (Baillie 1956:98). This is close to Moltmann, who has described the act of creation as a limitation in God, insofar as it was the result of a choice to create an entity which has an existence outside, and therefore to an extent independent of, God. God therefore suffers with, and therefore for his creation, hardly the traditional impassibility. He participated in the cross (Bulgakov, in Gavrilyuk 2005:264). Perhaps Moltmann, as a Lutheran, saw some affinity with the teaching of the "two kingdoms"? Indeed Luther had questioned the traditional exegesis of Philippians 2 for the first time since Arius; for him, Christ was not so much a judge, but shares our griefs (Dawe 1963:68); the essence of the *logos* was retained, but the form of God set aside (Dawe 1963:73). Not surprisingly, Bonhoeffer is also noted for similar views, which must also be seen in the context of his historical context in the Germany of the second world war. For him, the ultimate meaning of Christology is self-emptying. His successors however, go much further in the kenotic idea, adopting the radical view of the "death of God" (Richard 1982:164).

Even more recently, the "open theism" movement (cf Pinnock 2001) has stressed human free will, but their belief in God's limitation has incurred the wrath of many Calvinists. This allows the world to affect God (Pinnock 2001:12). This has obvious affinities with "process theology"; Erickson (1998:307) sees it as midway between this and traditional Christianity. It is also attractive especially as it is in keeping with the preferred modern approach to Christology "from below", to start from the evidence of Jesus' humanity, and to seek to understand him in the context of that. This is in contrast to early kenoticism, which was really "from above", so tried to relate it to an assumed immutability; this certainly contributed to its downfall. A recent approach is rather to try to understand God from the experience of Christ's *kenōsis* (Richard 1997:84).

Acceptance of *kenōsis* becomes more reasonable when it is suggested that the traditional view of God's attributes is actually foreign to Christianity, but is imported from Greek philosophy (Horton 2002:317). Moltmann (2001b:140) believes that the attributes of infinity, such as omnipotence, derive from Aristotle, not from the Bible. It must be observed here that a similar accusation is often made about the doctrine of the Trinity. Nevertheless, it is not necessary to deny the traditional view, as do the process theologians; centuries of Christian thought have accepted these attributes. What the idea of *kenōsis* does is to retain this affirmation, while accepting that God in practice does not use them, so does not do what he could.

Limitation as good and necessary

Here it may be highlighted that the context of the Philippians passage is that Paul was urging the Christians there to limit themselves, taking Jesus as the example in this respect, as indeed he always should be. Thus Grudem (1994:550) sees this as the point of the passage. For Bernard of Clairvaux, *kenōsis* and exaltation were the path of mysticism (Dawe (1963:64). Kenotic thinking was common in pietism, as in Zinzendorf (Dawe 1963:18), and, not surprisingly, in Wesley:

"mild he lays his glory by"

This does emphasise the point that theology should never simply be academic but should have practical implications for Christian life and practice. This example of Jesus may then be seen to be particularly relevant in a world that has almost totally accepted the capitalist ideal and sees self-interest as a valid and reasonable motive for life's activities. In fact any relationship, whether in the act of creating, or with other people, must necessitate a self-limitation (Dawe 1963:99).

There is a natural inclination to view limitation as inherently bad, and so inappropriate to God. Part of the reason for this is that many of the limitations that are experienced by human beings are not inherent, but on the contrary have been received by choice, but to sin, and so are indeed bad. Boyd (2001:251) suggests that Jesus' power was what people would have had if unfallen. The connection of human limitation with sin is certainly implied in the Genesis account of the fall. Quite apart from the Genesis account, the limitation of humanity follows as an inevitable consequence of the nature of sin itself. This may be understood as a breakdown in relationship; Boyd (2001:346) suggests it to be self-centredness, so closedness. It was because of this that humanity lost the ability to live forever, as they lost access to the tree of life. They lost eternal life. Because of the breakdown of the link with God, his life is not enjoyed by people and death occurs. It will in any case result as the inter-relationships enabling bodily life deteriorate. Then, in the Fall, human beings certainly lost their power to affect the environment because of the curse that was laid upon it (Gen 3:17). In any case, as the power that humanity has over its environment is largely enabled by cooperation between people, any breakdown in this results in a diminishing of that power. They also lost an aspect of the freedom of movement in their exclusion from the garden. Perhaps it is even the case that although the first sin is described as due to eating from the tree of knowledge, this was specifically "of good and evil" (Gen 2:9). Certainly their knowledge was also affected. As human knowledge is also due to interaction, both with other people and in the internal brain processes, this is also affected.

However, even if sin, and so the limitation due to it, is wrong, the choice that enabled sin is not. In fact, the ability to choose is part of the human role as in *imago Dei*, being able to choose because God has himself chosen. And such choice can be to self-limit. The Philippians passage (2:5f) indicates the free choice of the second Person in this regard. Christ chose, but choice does not have to result in sin; the New Testament witness is of his sinlessness. Likewise, whereas the choice to sin restricts relationship, Christ's choice to self-limit was in order to enhance it. Incidentally, of course, it is the absence of sin in the Trinity that enables the possibility of the full inter-relationship of *perichōrēsis* between the Persons, and between the two natures of Christ.

For Balthasar, *kenōsis* reflects a "genuinely human act of trusting self-abandonment" (Macleod 1998:219). In this case the humility and willingness to be a servant that is exemplified in the incarnation shows what real humanity is like. Humanity becomes as God intended it to be when it is fulfilled in the imitation of Christ, which includes his *kenōsis* as a fundamental part of his nature. Real fulfilment comes not in seeking to benefit oneself, often at the expense of others, but in seeking to serve. This then highlights the Christian message, that Jesus did come to help people to salvation. This salvation is not just the forgiveness of sins, not even the attainment of eternal life, but so that people could become as fully human as God created them to be.

Chapter 2

Kenoō: what does "emptying" mean?

As well as trying to clear away negative connotations attached to the word *kenōsis*, so that the idea can be employed without prejudice in theology and in application to the Christian life, the meaning of the word itself must be understood. This may be done from a consideration of its use in the New Testament and related literature. Here, it must be insisted that the ascription of *kenōsis* to Jesus must be without any hint of docetism (Bulgakov, in Gavrilyuk 2005:262, Best 1985:99); until more recent theology, there has always been a tendency to so stress the divinity of Jesus that an incipient docetism has never been far from the surface.

Related words

The noun *kenōsis* is derived from the verb *kenoō*, of which the verb in Philippians 2:7 is the third person singular aorist indicative active form. Here the RSV translates as "emptied himself", and the older KJV (AV) as "made himself of no reputation". The verb occurs in just four other places in the New Testament, but it also occurs as a noun, *kenos*, once as an adverb, *kenōs*, and in two compounds, *kenophōnia* and *kenodoxia*. It is these, especially the verb, which should be a guide as to the meaning in Philippians 2, and therefore what the experience of Jesus was.

Real loss or self-restriction?

The essential issue is whether the emptying is metaphysical or metaphorical (Feinberg 1980:40). It is the understanding that the verb means to "empty" which led to the former, the idea that the Son of God "emptied" himself of the attributes of Deity. Although this was the usual early Church belief (Coakley 2001:195), modern translators have rarely favoured that particular nuance. Elsewhere than in Philippians 2, Paul uses it figuratively (Richard 1997:59). In particular, a metaphorical interpretation would be consistent with 2 Corinthians 8:9, which is often cited to support an idea of *kenōsis*. Moreover, neither the verb nor the other contentious word *harpagmon* have an object, something that is emptied or grasped (Fee 1995:210). Fee (1999:95) comments that the verb regularly means powerlessness or emptying of significance. It does have a literal sense in the Old Testament Septuagint (eg Gen 24:20, 2 Chr 24:11), although Martin (1983:165) notes that it is metaphorical in Jeremiah 14:2 and 15:9. Of the four occurrences of the verb, apart from the key one in Philippians 2, the RSV only takes actual "emptying" as the meaning in one place, 1 Corinthians 1:17, where the phrase *hina mē kenōthē ho stauros tou Christou* is rendered "lest the cross be emptied of its power". Here it is followed by the NIV. It may be immediately observed that the word "power" is not actually present, but is an interpretation. In contrast, the old KJV (AV) translates "should be made of none effect". The verb is rendered in various ways in the other three occurrences. Romans 4:14 says that "faith is null", and 2 Corinthians 9:3 "may not prove vain" (both RSV). The idea of "in vain" is common in other instances of the root. The only other instance of the verb, 1 Corinthians 9:15, is bedevilled by textual variations, in most of which the root *kenoō* does occur, except in one admittedly significant manuscript, A, which reads the similar sounding *kainosei* instead of *kenōsei*. Here AV prefers the idea "make void"; other versions give various possibilities for a difficult text.

Best (1985:58) also notes that "being in the form of God" is in the present tense, which would indicate what he still was in the incarnation, so not less than God at that time. Erickson (1998:751) also draws attention to Colossians 2:9 "in him the whole fullness of deity dwells bodily". He has eternal existence, as indicated in the "was" of John 1:1. It may also be observed that as spirit and so immaterial, or infinite or "boundless", God does not need to empty himself in order to be incarnate. In any case, he has to retain full deity, or he could not be a mediator between God and humanity (Best 1985:82). There is no "emptying" as such; *kenōsis* does not affect God's essential being.

Certainly the idea of emptying is not a common understanding of the verb. It is a little more accepted for the noun, but again the idea of "in vain" predominates. KJV and RSV translate it as "empty" in only four places, three of which are the same incident, where those sent to the vineyard were beaten and sent away "empty" (Mk 12:3 = Lk 20:10,11). However, although their hands were indeed literally empty, so that they returned to their master without what they went for, the implication is surely that their mission was in vain, or ineffectual. The only other place is Luke 1:53 in the "Magnificat", where "the rich he has sent empty away". Here a similar consideration can apply; they had not achieved what they expected that their riches could do for them. In this case the idea of ineffectiveness is consistent, and a literal emptiness is not demanded by the word.

Two occurrences of the root which are more important for the understanding of Philippians 2:7 are those which occur in close proximity to it. The first is the compound, *kenodoxia* (Phil 2:3), which RSV renders "conceit", the second is the double occurrence *eis kenon* (Phil 2:16), usually rendered "in vain" so again meaning "ineffectual".

The idea of ineffectiveness is supported by Isaiah 53, which Jeremias (1965:86) feels has a plain connection with Philippians 2. Martin (1983:182) indicates the considerable support for this view; in particular, Dodd "would therefore boldly translate the latter [Is 53:12] as 'he emptied his soul unto death'", rendering the key verb as *exekenōsen*, identical to Philippians except for the prefix. Such a translation does reflect the Septuagint use of the Hebrew "poured out" in other places, although not in Isaiah 53:12, where it renders it as *paradothē* (delivered). Indeed there are reflections of *kenōsis* in other servant songs as well (eg Is 49:4, 50:6), and in Wisdom 3 & 4 (Richard 1997:61). Particularly Isaiah 53:12 can well be rendered as *kenōsis*; in this case it is the surrender of life, not so much of incarnation (Jeremias 1965:98). Although the key word in the Septuagint is *paredothē*, Feinberg (1980:39) notes that many of the fathers cite Philippians when commenting on Isaiah; he suggests that *ekenōsen* was chosen as closer to the Hebrew. Martin (1983:185) can affirm that the meanings of the Hebrew verb in Isaiah 53:12 and the Greek verb of Philippians 2:7 "are not far apart". but that the latter preferred *ekenōsen* over *paradothē* as the former added the nuance of humility. It is probable that Jesus understood his death in terms of Isaiah 53 (Jeremias 1965:103). Some hesitation about the connection comes from the observation that the Septuagint of Isaiah 53 interestingly uses the word *pais* rather than the *doulos* adopted in Philippians. Elsewhere the Septuagint uses each about equally as a translation of *'ebed* (Jeremias 1965:37); the words would seem interchangeable (Bockmuehl 1997:135). Other translations of Isaiah, notably that by Aquila, which Paul often seems to use, do use *doulos*, and its verb form is used in the Septuagint in the previous verse (Martin 1983:188). This possibly reflects an earlier Greek version (Feinberg 1980:37); Martin (1983:188) observes that Paul often agrees with Aquila against the Septuagint. Here Jeremias (1965:86) notes that *pais* is a term of honour where applied to David; it is then perhaps surprising that later Judaism never refers to the Messiah in this way (1965:51) although he notes that Isaiah 53 can support a Messianic interpretation (1965:43). In this case, the writer of Philippians 2 probably wanted to avoid the idea of dignity, so opted for *doulos* (Feinberg 1980:37); it also contrasts with lordship (Martin 1983:175).

Perhaps the easiest understanding is of Jesus as a personification and fulfilment of Israel. This is then a direct extension of the Jewish apocalyptic belief that Israel is the last Adam (Richard 1997:58). Interestingly it was a dove that descended on Jesus as his baptism, as this was not only explicitly identified as the Spirit, but is a common symbol for Israel (Williams 2003:48). It may then be observed in passing that other connotations of a dove, such as its use as a peace symbol, are very appropriate in a reference to *kenōsis*. It then of course follows that Jesus then personifies the Church, as this is a continuation of Israel (Gal 6:16), albeit that membership is by faith and not on the basis of biological descent. In any case, Paul refers to the Church as the "body of Christ" (eg 1 Cor 12:27, Eph 1:23).

Thus the understanding of the key word of Philippians 2:7 need not be taken as "emptying", but rather as ineffectiveness. "All modern continuations of the nineteenth century kenosis have emphatically excluded even a partial renunciation by God of his divinity ... thereby the idea of self-emptying loses the radicality of self-relinquishment" (Pannenberg 1968:319). This means that the second Person did not empty himself of the attributes of deity, but that they were rendered ineffective. Whereas the word *kenoō* in secular Greek does mean "empty", this by inference, means "to make of no effect" (Martin 1983:165, Best 1985:96); it is this latter which is relevant to the experience of Christ in Philippians 2. He did not then divest himself of divine attributes either absolutely or relatively (Best 1985:77), but rather rendered them ineffective. There is no hint that Jesus gave up equality with God (Bockmuehl 1997:133). Therefore Christ, although fully God in the incarnation, did not appear as such. Augustine suggests that his divinity did not change, but he adopted human changeableness (Macleod 1998:216); likewise for Aquinas, emptying is not laying down divinity but taking up humanity (Richard 1982:186). This was the common view among the fathers, a humble bending down to humanity (Pannenberg 1968:310). He was indeed "of no reputation" as the KJV renders the phrase. Gore constantly pointed out that the "self-emptying" of God in the incarnation was no failure of power, but a continuous act of self-sacrifice (Macquarrie 1974:118). It may just be commented here that the incarnation was not so much a loss, but a gain, of humanity; there is a parallel in that in humility, people gain in relationships. Certainly *kenōsis* adds to God in this way (Ward 2001:156). Pinnock (2002:214), affirming this, feels that any *kenōsis* in God is balanced by a *plērōma*, a fullness. It is clear that the seventeenth century translators of the Authorised Version (KJV) struggled with the text, but their rendering does have value; Macleod (1998:215) feels that it is a good translation, especially in the context of the image-conscious Philippians (1998:216). If Christ was not known as God, having that reputation, he would not be treated as divine. Calvin feels that although Christ could not divest himself of deity, he could hide it (as in the old view of *krypsis*) (Macleod 1998:217). God retained his omnipotence; there is no need to say, with Vanstone (1977:59), that God emptied himself completely, leaving no reserves. What this means is that the people with whom he had to do were not compelled to respond to him as God, and so retained their free will. The nature of love is that it does not control (Vanstone 1977:45). In the Magnificat, the rich were not rendered poor, but still sent away.

Refusal to grasp

This suggests that the previous words, which have also engendered considerable discussion, *ouk harpagmon hēgēsato to einai isa theō*, be understood similarly. "Ruling" is the usual understanding of the verb *hēeomai*, especially in the noun form, although it can also be understood in the sense of "esteeming" or "considering". The sense is clear from the previous word, which although is a hapax in the New Testament, does occur in related forms. The discussion has centred upon whether *harpagmon* has an active force (*res rapta*), or passive (*res rapienda*) (Feinberg 1980:30f). In the former, it then has the sense of despoiling, robbery (cf KJV), or grasping (RSV), all of which carry the nuance of a forced action, that Jesus wanted to acquire divinity; however, there is no expressed object for the verb. The latter sense also seems to imply adoptionism, that he was caught up to divinity. However, the text indicates that Christ originally had equality with God; Käsemann indicates that Hellenistic religion sees the "form" of God and equality as synonymous (Silva 1988:114); did he then lose it? Best (1985:68) believes that there is no indication that *harpagmos* means "to retain in possession". Martin (1983:152) then has proposed a third idea, that of *res retinenda*; Christ, although he was equal with God, yet did not exploit his position, so did not rule on that basis. Although Christ was God, he did not insist on his rights (Macleod 1998:214). Hoover writes that Jesus already possessed equality with God; "the question ... is not whether or not one possesses something, but whether or not one chooses to exploit something" (in Feinberg 1980:35). Bruce (1989:77) comments that Alexander the Great saw his conquest of Asia Minor as an *harpagma*, but done not for his advantage, but to spread civilisation.

Thus Jesus, because he was in the form of God, had his authority, but rather emptied himself of this to the exact opposite, taking the form of a servant. Certainly he did not treat his deity as grounds for avoiding incarnation (Silva 1988:113). Here the word "form" is *morphē*, which in traditional Greek thought indicates equality with God (Dawe 1963:36), although the Arians sought to interpret it is as "only" in the form of God, so less than full deity (Richard 1997:74). Chrysostom said that it implied there was nothing inferior to the Father (Thomas 1970:143). It is used interchangeably with *eikōn*, "image" in the Septuagint and New Testament (Feinberg 1980:28, although he cautions against treating the two simply as equivalents). This latter must remind the reader of Genesis 1:26, and the creation of the first human beings in *imago Dei*, which is generally understood as indicating dominion. It is this right of dominion that Jesus refused to use. Martin (1983:163) observes striking parallels between the Adam narrative and Philippians 2. The two figures have been contrasted since the time of Irenaeus (*Adv Haer* 5.16.2-3) (Bockmuehl 1997:131). Here Hall (1986:98) understands the concept of "image" relationally; the incarnation, and the sin of humanity therefore involve no loss of attribute, but rather a change in relationship.

Self-limitation

This interpretation then sits very well in the context of the hymn as a whole. The meaning of the *ekenōsen* of Philippians 2:7 should in any case come from the next phrase "taking the form of a servant" (Macleod 1998:215). The influential scholar James Dunn, for example, in keeping with his advocacy of an "Adam Christology", views the *kenōsis* as explained by Jesus accepting the powerlessness of a slave (Dunn 1989:116). Martin (1983:170) also has this view. It may be commented that this is indeed part of Christ's *kenōsis*, and in fact that crucifixion was a punishment reserved for slaves and for insurrectionists, even if the accusation of the latter was the official justification for Jesus' execution. If however a more traditional Christology is accepted, especially in keeping with Chalcedon, such an idea can be a part of the whole picture. Here John 17:5, also a "kenotic" verse, implies a glory in his pre-existence; Dunn (1989:31) however simply rejects this testimony to Jesus' self-consciousness. A servant, more accurately "slave" (*doulos*), is not one who compels obedience, but the reverse, so is obedient to his or her master. At that time a slave had no rights (Best 1985:103), not even being able to own any property. Nevertheless, Philippians 2 states that Jesus was in the "form" of a slave, one of several instances in the hymn where stating direct identity is avoided. Here, whereas most slaves are forced into service, Jesus is different as he does it voluntarily. This is of course so that we can be freed. A slave refers always to his master, which is what Christ did, proclaiming not himself, but his Father (Martinez, in Richard 1997:213); in itself this is an act of *kenōsis*. Incidentally the slavery must be understood as to God, not to the "powers"; this again indicates that the reference must be to Isaiah 53 (Fee 1995:212). Slavery to powers would be a Gnostic idea (Bockmuehl 1997:135).

There is then also a meaningful contrast with the exaltation of Christ where he is given the name of "Lord". This is a common understanding of the name given to him (Phil 2:9) (Fee 1999:99), but the result is in any case clear in the bowing of every knee to him which follows. Hawthorne (1983:93) notes that "Jesus is Lord" was the earliest creed. It again indicates his divinity; Bruce (1989:73) draws attention to Isaiah 42:8, which indicates that this title is unique to God. So whereas in his humiliation, the deity of Christ was not clear, and so did not compel a response, at his exaltation his lordship was evident and obedience will be compelled. "Every knee shall bow" (Phil 2:10). Unlike Adam, who tried to grasp at deity, Jesus accepted the honour of it as a gift (Best 1985:69).

The *kenōsis* or emptying is then not substantive or ontological, but relational, and therefore the word is freed from many of the problems that those who suggested a kenotic Christology had burdened it with. It is not an emptying of attributes, but the

33

way in which they are exercised (Ward 2001:160). There was no emptying of attributes; indeed, as Spirit, there was no necessity for any removal of divinity to occur for the second Person to become human. Such a self-limitation is in any case not incompatible with the idea of infinity. God is without boundaries, filling a human frame as easily as the universe. Similarly, as omnipotent, he is able to restrict his power; otherwise he would not be almighty, able to do all things (cf Erickson 1991:81). In fact it is only by God's power that he is able to accept powerlessness (Richard 1997:71). Martin refers to him as "not drawing on his divine might and energies but denying himself their exercise" (Macleod 1998:220). This implies that the act of emptying was an act of choice, of free will; the New Testament stresses the voluntary dimension of Jesus' death (eg 1 Thess 5:10, Col 2:20, Matt 20:28). For Thomasius, Jesus was not almighty "because he did not want to be" (Pannenberg 1968:310). Such limitation, emphatically, was by the free choice of the second Person, as such as Käsemann has emphasised (Martin 1983:216); Martin feels that the main emphasis of the hymn falls on Christ's freedom. Likewise Hawthorne (1983:85), who notes the emphasis in Philippians 2:7 is that he emptied himself; the emptying was then also not just of attributes. Ward (2001:160) however comments that it is not so much an act of will, but an expression of God's nature. Indeed it flows from his love, which as Vanstone (1977:42) points out, is unlimited, or it would be just kindness. In fact the original proposal of *kenōsis*, by such as Thomasius, understood attributes such as love as not limited.

Richard (1997:99) comments that *kenōsis* is a personal act, that the main revelation of the nature of God was in a Person. In fact any revelation is necessarily kenotic. Thus in Hebrews 1, Christ is the image of God revealing the nature of God of whom he is the image. This does not of course mean that Christ is essentially subordinate to the Father, but is the image as incarnate, and in that state must be less than God (Jn 14:28). Indeed, the better that an image is, the more attention is given to the original, so it follows that an image must essentially have to be limited itself to glorify that of which it is an image. Moltmann (1981:159) asserts that it is the crucified Christ who is the image, so as suffering for others. The idea of *kenōsis* is even implied by the famous reference to Jesus as the *logos*, the word (Jn 1:1), for a word delimits to one meaning rather than another; likewise he is called *sophia*, wisdom, which again says that one thing is correct, another is not, so is excluded. Hegel wrote that it is the essence of a person to acquire an identity by losing it in and for the other (in Richard 1982:285).

Cullmann indeed points out that the New Testament does in general reflect a functional rather than an ontological Christology (Martin 1983:171); these were indeed the earliest interpretations of what it meant for him to be the Christ (Richard 1997:44). P T Forsyth saw the limitation described in Philippians not of attributes of deity but of functions of those attributes (Macleod 1998:207). Indeed, Martin (1983:175) points out that *kenōsis* is reflected in the text not by taking humanity, but by being a slave, a functional term. But because it is relational, it then includes, almost inevitably, suffering, especially when that relationship is changed, as in abandonment (Richard 1982:199).

Continual *kenōsis*

It may be added at this point that one of the difficulties of the old kenotic theory is that it predicated change in the essence of God. The hymn must imply Jesus' pre-existence (Talbert, in Richard 1982:106), so therefore in some sense a change. However, *kenōsis* is rather a constant factor in God's nature. It is not an event, which is how Thomasius understood it, but an eternal process (Dawe 1963:200), an "*uninterrupted* self-emptying" (Bulgakov, in Gavrilyuk 2005:260). His nature is to be constantly giving, so emptying. The *kenōsis* is not a "dimming down", a curtailment of God's nature, but a positive expression of it (Richard 1997:104). The Hebrew equivalent means to make bare by revealing contents (Martin 1983:184), so indicating what God is like. Jesus reveals completely, in his emptying, what God is like; his *kenōsis* is then no change in God (Vanstone 1977:58). Hawthorne (1983:85) suggests that Philippians 2:6 be translated not "though he was in the form of God", but rather "because he was..." (also Bockmuehl 1997:133). His very sovereignty is expressed in his suffering servanthood (Hall 1986:151). *Kenōsis* indicates his act of salvation, which, as Athanasius insisted at the time of the Arian controversy, demands full divinity (also Pannenberg 1968:308); but this is seen in *kenōsis*. Jesus' equality with God is seen not in *plērōsis*, fullness, but in *kenōsis* (cf Col 2:9) (Bruce 1989:77). In fact, *kenōsis* is actually *plērōsis*; indeed it is fitting that on the cross he was "lifted up" (Macquarrie 1974:123). The Spirit makes present the powerful powerlessness of God; Hans Küng writes that he shows God's spirituality confined in the flesh, his vastness in his limitation, his eternity in temporality, his omnipresence in being here, his immutability in growth, his infinity in privation and his omniscience in silence (in Richard 1997:117). It is in the Passion that Mark most clearly shows Jesus' divinity (Richard 1982:112). Barth says that *kenōsis* is no loss of divinity, but an indication that Jesus is Lord even in his humiliation (in Richard 1982:162); he affirms that for God it is just as natural to be lowly as to be high (Macquarrie 1974:120). Dawe (1963:165) comments that Barth's rejection of natural theology includes a rejection of the Greek categories of unchangeability in God. The idea of the "servant" lies behind the title "Son of God" (Jeremias, in Richard 1982:125); it indicates "unique fidelity" (Richard 1967:83), although it must of course mean more than this (cf Matt 14:33). Although the deity of Jesus is not just the acceptance of God's purpose, as is sometimes suggested, for example by Baillie, it is demonstrated by it. It is "precisely because he is truly in the form of God (or God's image) ... he is prepared to take the form of a slave ... his very action in becoming what we are is a demonstration of what he eternally is" (Hooker, in Richard 1997:60). Richard (1997:60) thus comments that the emptying of Jesus actually indicates his deity; it is the very nature of God to give. Fee (1999:96) notes that Philippians 2:6 refers to the emptying as due to being in the form of God. "Grasping" is entirely opposite to God's character (Fee 1995:210). Incidentally, how appropriate it then is that we celebrate the incarnation of Jesus at what is basically the lowest part of the year (at least in the northern hemisphere), even if it is unlikely to be the correct date from an historical perspective. And how appropriate that we celebrate by giving!

Indeed, it is often pointed out that God's immutability cannot be seen in static terms. This idea was favoured in the Greek worldview, which rejected change (and suffering) in God (Richard 1997:75); if God is perfect, any change must be to less perfection. However, it is clear that the Biblical presentation of God is that he does change, such as when he is described as "repenting" (eg Jnh 3:10). Likewise, he must suffer, otherwise the work of Christ loses its divine aspect, becoming simply a human act (Richard 1997:76). This suffering, which demands change, is of course an act of love; true love must involve suffering (Fiddes 1988:16). Indeed, unless he changes, God cannot show constancy of love to a people who change. Not only because he himself lives, but also because he is in relation, he must change. In fact, he must change in order to be unchanging! It must just be noted here that we are saved by faith, which is a trust in God's faithfulness, or constancy. The Biblical example of this is of course that of Abraham, as Paul explains in Romans 4. Abraham was also the key actor in another example of God's repentance, in the incident of the destruction of Sodom and Gomorrah (Gen 18). For Abraham, that change was not a denial of God's reliability, but an example of it.

Seeing the *kenōsis* as an eternal process also removes another of the objections made to the kenotic theory, that it is incipient Arianism

(Pannenberg 1968:311); if this is taken as at a point in time then it had a start, and an Arian interpretation of the subordination of the Son follows naturally. Arius had liked the expression "in the form of God" (Phil 2:6) (Dawe 1963:29). However, Origen's understanding was that the Son was generated eternally from the Father and not at a point in time; this meant that they are equal in divinity. The sonship is eternal (Macleod 1998:127). In this case neither Father nor Son essentially changes, and neither can be seen as subordinate in essence. This eternal generation is an aspect of the *kenōsis* of the Father. At the same time, the fact that all the Persons are kenotic reflects their essential equality in the Trinity. Athanasius is of course famous for his opposition to Arius; his motive was that as he understood salvation as divinisation, this demanded the full deity of the Son. For him therefore, *kenōsis* was veiling (Dawe 1963:30,56). It was in fact one of the results of the Arian problem that any kenotic understanding of the incarnation became problematic (Dawe 1963:66). Nevertheless, it is then not surprising that just as Eastern theology has always had a tendency to subordination in the Trinity, that self-limitation is an integral aspect of the Eastern Orthodox understanding of God (Dawe 1963:155); hence, of course, Moltmann's interest in the idea.

It must be stressed that the *kenōsis* of the second Person need not be thought of as affecting his fundamental nature. The Fathers constantly applied Philippians 2 to the incarnation, seeing no change in the eternal *logos* (Richard 1997:75). Emphatically, it is not something imposed from outside, which would indeed be contrary to the sovereignty of God. It is a voluntary self-limitation, so does not imply any change in the essential nature of God. Richard (1997:38) then stresses that redemption occurred because Jesus positively accepted death; it was by his choice of love, not something forced on him. As omnipotent, he is freely able to limit his own omnipotence, and his omniscience; in fact to say that God cannot limit himself is itself a limitation (Erickson 1991:81). In this regard, a useful distinction has been suggested between omnipotence, being able to do anything, and almightiness, being able to do all that is wanted (van den Brink 1993:215). Pinnock (2001:96) therefore criticizes Wright as believing that God's sovereignty demands that he actually controls everything.

Similarly, the open theists commonly assert that far from compromising God's power, their stand rather enhances it (Boyd 2001:147). A fixed, so known future, effectively limits God. On the contrary, self-limitation enables a real gain for God, enabling relationships with free agents that would otherwise not have been possible (Pinnock 2002:216). Again, an open future means that God is open to being affected by it, while opening to relationships involves being affected by them. In fact, God is so great that he is able to cope with the uncertainty generated by the freedom of others. The point is also made that he would have been limited if he could not have created free agents; indeed, although there are things that God cannot do, such as sin or die, these are in fact negations of limitation (Highfield 2002:286).

Finally, the recognition of *kenōsis* as voluntary self-limitation means that the human nature of Christ is not lessened by being taken up into the divine, but rather given its fullness, becoming totally authentic (Metz, in Richard 1982:287). The full expression of humanity is in its own humility, its *kenōsis*; the essential nature of Jesus is as the "man for others", and in this he is fully human (Richard 1982:304). God is nowhere more present than in humanity (Pinnock 1996:73); in their humility, their *kenōsis*, he is most clearly seen.

Chapter 3

Kenōsis: two aspects

A careful look at the key passage relating to the emptying, or *kenōsis* of Christ, reveals that there are actually two things happening, not just one. One the one hand, there is the famous one, *kenōsis* proper, the refusal to grasp at equality with God, the choice of incarnation, assuming the slavery to God that is inherent in being a human being. How could very God partake in, and identify with, humanity except by the curtailment of at least some of the attributes that were rightly his as divine? It is only in this way that he could be "born in the likeness of men" (Phil 2:7). It is understandable that interest has centred in this aspect of what is described in Philippians 2, for an emphasis on Deity has been the general characteristic of western theology. This has traditionally favoured an approach "from above", assuming the Nicene affirmation of full divinity, and then trying to squeeze the humanity of Jesus into that presupposition. It has only been recently that an approach "from below", asking how affirmation of deity can be reconciled with the humanity of Jesus that was evident to the disciples and witnessed to in the New Testament, has become more fashionable. Obviously the former, which is the approach of the New Testament, so of Philippians 2 (Macleod 1998:22f), immediately interprets *kenōsis* as applying to divinity, and so it is often overlooked that the process of self-emptying did not stop with the incarnation, wonderful though that would be, but it continued in the human life that the second Person had adopted, being again a refusal to grasp at what he could have by right, but on the contrary, "he humbled himself" (Phil 2:8). Indeed, this is clear from Philippians, where the *kenōsis* is explained by being in the form of a servant. This is what P Henry has called a "double kenōsis" (Martin 1983:199). Thus many, such as O'Connor, have observed that it is also the humanity of Jesus which is the subject of the emptying, in his humiliation (Richard 1997:57). Such humbling immediately meant that he adopted an attitude of humility in his humanity, so becoming obedient, an obedience which he carried to the uttermost to death, and a death which in itself was the epitome of self-denial, the agonising torture of crucifixion. In his proposal of *kenōsis*, Thomasius had made a distinction between these two aspects, which is reflected in Philippians 2, saying that the humiliation belongs to the *logos ensarkos,* the emptying to the *logos asarkos* (Macquarrie 1974:120,123).

Kenōsis as humility

In this case, the passage must be read as a basis not for Christology, but for the Christian life, and it must be asked what can be learnt about this from Philippians 2. If the *kenōsis* was only of the deity of Christ, Christians could legitimately say that his experience is not directly relevant to them, but a location in his humanity makes it supremely applicable. It must then be an example for humanity. Nevertheless, of course, this is not to drive a wedge between the two, for the simple reason that the Church continues the ministry of Christ in the world, so must reflect his nature. As Irenaeus of old put it, the Church works as the two "hands of God", Son and Spirit. Carson (1979:565) has stressed that even the work of the Spirit convicting people of sin (Jn 16:8) is through human agency.

In fact, does this not reveal even more of the *kenōsis* of God in that he humbles himself so much that he is willing to use even fallible human agents to do his work?

For us, the real experience of Jesus' emptying is not of divinity, which is rather hidden, but in the humility in his humanity (Best 1985:96), identifying with the lowest of the low. This interpretation of *kenōsis* is exactly what humility is; it can never be a removal of human ability or attributes, but is a restricting of them for the sake of relating to others. It could then more aptly be referred to as *krypsis* (hiding). In fact, it is in humility that full humanity is expressed, just as the limitation of the divine presumes and demonstrates full deity (Fee 1999:97). Thus the Philippian passage recounts firstly that the second Person emptied himself, *ekenōsen*, then he humbled himself, *etapeinōsen*. The first word is then explained by the phrase that follows it, "taking the form of a servant" (Martin 1983:170); in this case, the humility is also best explained by the words that follow it, "and became obedient unto death", where this rendering actually obscures the parallel, in that "became obedient" should rather be rendered, like "taking", a participle, so "becoming obedient". Martin (1983:212) draws attention to the similarity to the Septuagint rendering of Isaiah 53:8. In this case, the humility consists in his obedience, and in fact there is a close parallel with the assumption of servanthood, as a "slave" is necessarily obedient to the master. Both aspects, although a result of the choice by the second Person, are then a subjection of that ability to choose. In particular, obedience is a yielding to the will of the master, so indeed itself a *kenōsis*.

Communicatio idiomatum

Quite rightly, these two are often seen as parts of one process; the term *kenōsis*, even if it strictly should apply only to the curtailment of the divine, is appropriate also for the choice that the power of

a human being also limits itself. However, they are distinct; Fee
(1995:197) writes that as God, he emptied himself, but as a man, he
humbled himself. It would have been possible for the second Person
to have become human, but for the Christ not to have lived a life of
humility. Indeed, that was expected; it was a scandal for the anointed
king, the Messiah or Christ, to limit himself, and an especial scandal
to die. Isaiah 53 brings in ideas which naturally are very hard to
accept. However, the very nature of the incarnation means that the
two must be connected, that if the divine nature in Christ experiences
self-limitation, then also the human. The fundamental reason for
this is the old idea of the *communicatio idiomatum*, the mutual
interplay of the two natures. This idea is first cousin to another, that
of *perichōrēsis*, the mutual interaction of the three Persons of the
Trinity. If the divinity of the second Person experienced *kenōsis*,
then the other nature of his humanity is also affected. The sixteenth
century Reformer, Zanchius wrote, "Christ the Mediator never did
or does anything according to his humanity, in which the divinity
too did or does not cooperate, and achieved nothing according to His
Deity, which His humanity did not subserve or agree to" (Macleod
1998:195). It may be observed that there is an implication here
for the view of scripture, where any idea of infallibility has often
been felt to involve the denial of the freedom of the writer (Wellum
2002:265); rather a "concursive" theory can accommodate both, a
type of *perichōrēsis*.

In this case, an even more astounding result suggests itself, which
is that the process of *kenōsis* is actually of the essence of being divine,
while humility is of the essence of real humanity. The Philippian
hymn parallels Jesus' taking the form of a servant with being in the
likeness of men (Bockmuehl 1997:126). It is in an attitude of self-
negation that full human nature is expressed, and that once it is not,
as happened in Eden, that is an act of sin, and humanity is marred.
But if humanity is in *imago Dei*, then this action of self-negation is
also fundamental to the divine; the *kenōsis* of the second Person was

then not an extraordinary event, brought on by the demands of the situation, but is natural to the nature of God.

Impartation of humility

Indeed, in the original proposals of a kenotic Christology, it was suggested that it was the attributes specific to deity that were limited, while others were not. This enabled the divine to be incarnate, for the incarnate Son does not have the attributes that made him divine. Hence omnipotence, omnipresence, and of course his omniscience, were not part of the nature of the Christ, but had been emptied in *kenōsis*. On the other hand, attributes such as his love and holiness were not affected. Some, such as Berkhof (1958:55f) have distinguished between these two groups of attributes in that the first group, being specific to deity, are never communicated, but attributes of the later group are communicated to people. These are a part of what it means for humanity to be in *imago Dei*.

One attribute specific to deity is God's independence, part of which is his aseity. He is not dependent on anybody or anything for his existence and its continuance. As incarnate, this was also limited, and Jesus became a being dependent on others and on the environment for his very existence. After all, he now had to eat, got thirsty and so on, aspects that have convinced people of his full humanity. He was also dependent upon God for very existence, and also for knowledge and for the power manifested in his work, specifically his miracles, he relied on the Holy Spirit. In this regard, the essence of sin is to seek to usurp the nature of God, which includes a rejection of dependence, specifically on God, and the ambition to be totally independent. Essentially there is a refusal to acknowledge a reliance on God.

At the same time, self-limitation, or *kenōsis*, is one of the communicable attributes, so is given to people. Therefore the human nature of Christ was necessarily kenotic. As human, and therefore in *imago Dei*, he was already the person most like God (Erickson 1998:753): his humbling makes his humanity an even better image of his kenotic divinity. His humility was not something subsequent to the *kenōsis* of the incarnation, but an integral part of it. Simply because he adopted ideal humanity, that humanity was humble. Again a refusal to be humble is then a perversion of what it means to be human: it was in his humbling that he was most human.

It is just because of the nature of humanity that *kenōsis* was necessary at all. In order to relate to a fallen humanity, it was absolutely essential for the second Person to limit the expression of his divinity. It is this point which is reflected in the *communicatio idiomatum*. The two natures in Christ, his humanity and divinity, mutually affect each other. Both are essentially kenotic, and relate to each other.

Impartation of sinlessness

On the one side of the causal effect, the divinity of Christ means that although he was fully and totally human, "consubstantial with us" in the terms of the Chalcedonian definition, that humanity was sinless. This aspect is indeed reflected in the Biblical material (Heb 4:15, 1 Pet 2:22). As the holiness of God is not touched by *kenōsis*, it is therefore part of the humanity of Christ as fully in *imago Dei*. The holiness of Christ's deity affects his humanity and renders it sinless. This is possible because of the effect of the divine will upon the human; even though Christ, as fully human, had a human will, this was in total harmony with the divine. Although it has been suggested (eg Pannenberg 1968:358) that this sinlessness means that Jesus could not be fully human, sin is surely not part of the essence of humanity, but rather renders a person less than human. It is sin, not its absence, that adversely affects human nature! Because the normal human being is sinful, Weiss suggests that the Philippian hymn uses the phrase "likeness" of man; the same is present in Romans 8:3. Lohmeyer also observes that Jesus chose to die, something foreign to normal humanity (Martin 1983:203,217). Jesus is "truly man but not merely man" (Michel, in Martin 1983:205). His humanity "is both continuous with and discontinuous from that of the rest of mankind" (Moule, in Macleod 1998:221). Moltmann (1985:218) distinguishes the similarity of "likeness" from the essence of the image; the distinction between the "likeness" and "image" of Genesis 1:26 has commonly been made (eg Pinnock 1996:174). Martin (1983:206) comments that the hymn does not unequivocally declare Jesus' full humanity; but as Vincent Taylor points out, this is clear elsewhere in Paul (Martin 1983:204).

Divine *kenōsis* due to human limitation

The other side of the causal effect then explains why *kenōsis* was necessary in the first place, for if the deity of Christ is affected by human nature, which is limited, that means that the divine also is limited. Thomasius' understanding was that limitation was communicated from the human to the divine (Erickson 1991:80).

It is obvious that the limitation of human nature is inherent, a function of simply being human. If this were not the case, human beings would not be what they are, but would effectively be divine. Nevertheless, specific acts of self-limitation are made by choice. It is this point which can clarify one of the contentious issues relating to *kenōsis*, for is this not a change in the nature of God, specifically a loss of the very nature of being divine? However, it has rightly been pointed out that it would be a change, a diminution in God himself if this were imposed on him, but it is no essential change if it is a freely chosen self-limitation. This aspect meets what is a common objection to the concept of Christ's *kenōsis*. The limitation of the divine, the *kenōsis*, is by choice. The Philippians passage (2:5f) indicates the free choice of the second Person in this regard.

Indeed, much of the limitation of humanity is by free choice; it is due to human sin, which is not a matter of compulsion. Thus Philippians does put the *kenōsis* of Christ firmly in the context of atonement; it was because of sin that this was necessary. It is also evident there that *kenōsis* deepened as the drama of the atonement progresses, with the most complete emptying occurring in the actual crucifixion.

The connection of human limitation with sin is certainly implied in the Genesis account of the fall. It was because of this that humanity lost the ability to live forever, as they lost access to the tree of life. They lost eternal life. Then they certainly lost their power to affect the environment because of the curse that was laid upon it (Gen 3:17). They also lost an aspect of the freedom of movement in their exclusion from the garden. Perhaps it is even the case that although the first sin is described as due to eating from the tree of knowledge, this was specifically "of good and evil" (Gen 2:9). Certainly their knowledge was also affected.

Quite apart from the Genesis account, the limitation of humanity follows as an inevitable consequence of the nature of sin itself. This may be understood as a breakdown in relationship. Incidentally, of course, it is the absence of sin in the Trinity that enables the possibility of the full inter-relationship of *perichōrēsis* between the Persons, and between the two natures of Christ. In humanity, however, it is also the breakdown in relationship that leads to limitation. Because of the breakdown of the link with God, his divine life is not enjoyed by people and death occurs. It will in any case result as the bodily inter-relationships deteriorate. As the power of humanity is largely enabled by cooperation, any breakdown in this results in impotence.

As knowledge is due to interaction, both with other people and in the internal brain processes, this is also affected.

Reversing *kenōsis* from the wholeness of salvation

Once atonement is achieved through Christ, sin is, at least potentially, dealt with, and therefore the active humiliation of Christ ended; he commenced the process of resurrection and glorification. Then, the effect of this reflects back on the divinity of Christ by means of the *communicatio idiomatum*. The vision to the seer of Patmos reflects something of the reversal of this *kenōsis*. Incidentally, these effects are progressive both in human sanctification and in the glorification of Christ.

There is ultimately the full expression of his deity, when "he receives the name which is above every name, that at the name of Jesus every knee should bow, ... and every tongue confess that Jesus Christ is Lord" (Phil 2:9-11). The *kenōsis* of the other Persons also passes away, such as the transcendence of the Father, when "the dwelling of God is with men" (Rev 21:3). The limitation of humanity is also finally transcended. In the immediate there is a possibility of relationship with God, again received by free choice, and therefore the life of God is received. A Christian, in relation with Christ, has eternal life (Jn 3:36 etc), which is, incidentally, an expression of the continued *kenōsis* of the Son, insofar as the life of the Christian depends on it being received from the union with Christ.

Chapter 4

Kenōsis on the cross (Phil 2:8d)

Even a cursory reading of Philippians 2:5-11 gives the distinct impression that the phrase "even death on the cross" does not really fit in the passage. This impression is reinforced if the passage is a hymn, either original to Paul, or incorporated by him into the epistle. Martin (1983:24f), who is so convinced of this that he calls his study of the passage *Carmen Christi*, "hymn to Christ", and reviews several proposals as to its structure. Dawe (1963:33) comments that the tight style of the passage contrasts with the tone of the rest of the letter. Sanders (1971:9f) adds that it would seem to be liturgical, so more than a poem. However, Lohmeyer and Käsemann suggest that the phrase breaks the rhythmic structure of the passage. Then particularly if the passage is an incorporated hymn, the question must be why Paul inserted it. Or alternatively, the question may be why a passage of this nature was composed with such a phrase deliberately breaking the structure. Of course, if he had taken it over, the question could be not just of its origin, but also why Paul felt it important enough to retain it, presuming that he was sensitive enough to the structure to recognise it as an insertion; it is also more than possible that two versions, one with and the other without the phrase, would be known.

Kenōsis demanded the cross

The answer to this must be that Paul considered the phrase so significant that it just had to be there. There are two aspects to this. Firstly, the shock to the reader of the phrase must emphasise the point that is being made; it was not just death that was being experienced by Christ, but specifically death on the cross. It is easy to appreciate why both Jews and Gentiles would have been happier not to have the insertion, and therefore perhaps why it was not in the original. For Gentiles, crucifixion was abhorrent; Cicero declared, "let even the name of the cross be kept away not only from the bodies of the citizens of Rome, but also from their thought, sight and hearing" (in Moltmann 2001a:28). It was so terrible that it was reserved only for slaves and for political offenders (Moltmann 2001b:138). In this regard, of course, the hymn had already identified Jesus as a *doulos* (for which thirty pieces of silver was the ransom price (Stott 1986:57)!), and the following verses would affirm him as *kurios*, a title which was always prone to political implication. Indeed, the reason given by Pilate to justify the crucifixion was the supposed claim of Jesus' kingship.

For the Philippians, the cross was especially an object of degradation (Martin 1983:221), and for Jews, as Paul points out in Galatians 3:13, the physical horror was added to by the belief that a hanged person was especially under the curse of God, a belief based on Deuteronomy 21:23. The Rabbis were concerned not just with martyrdom but with the manner of death (Martin 1983:227). The incredulity of the Jew Trypho to the apologist Justin on this point is understandable (Stott 1986:24), but the apostolic preaching stressed not only the cross, but also the curse (Stott 1986:34); Paul could even boast in the cross (Stott 1986:36).

Then secondly, the horror of that insertion would only reinforce the fundamental reason for it, that it is central to the gospel, as it was to the mission of Jesus (Stott 1986:17). It was in his dying that he wanted to be remembered (Stott 1986:68), a wish which Christians indeed honour in the communion. Stott (1986:28) remarks on the seven references in John to Jesus' "hour", a comment on the fourth evangelist's love of such symbol. The insertion therefore emphasises, even adds to, the message that Paul is seeking to convey in the passage; the progressive humiliation and subsequent exaltation of Christ is fundamental to the gospel. The cross is then a further stage in the process of Jesus' self-emptying, a stage without which the *kenōsis* would not have been complete; it may even be seen as the heart of the process (as Robinson, cited by Martin 1983:182). In opposition to Lohmeyer, who omitted the phrase as adding nothing to the humiliation of Jesus (Sanders 1971:11), Dibelius retained the phrase just because it was the last stage of the process (Martin 1983:31).

At this point it may be suggested that there is in fact a further possible reason for the phrase actually to be omitted. Paul is using the example of Christ as a motivation for Christians, specifically the Philippians, of whom there are several referred to in the epistle who especially needed the message. They are being urged to imitate the example of their Lord in an adoption of humility, of self-abasement, of *kenōsis*. Here it might just be pointed out that even if the earlier stages of Christ's experience were open to fairly literal imitation, this would not apply to the actual cross. However, the writings of Paul are full of exhortations to take up the cross, a metaphor also present on the lips of Jesus himself; it is fundamental to the Christian life. Such a reason for omission must also be considered unlikely as it depends on the function of the passage in the overall context; if the passage were ever independent of the rest of the epistle, this reason would naturally fall away. The passage could be a recitation of the humility of the Christ, with the aim of prompting adoration, but without suggesting imitation.

The phrase may then be taken as an essential part of the *kenōsis* of Christ, and so essential that its place in the structure of the passage draws especial attention to it. Even if it was the death that was the essential means of salvation, the point being made is then that the specific mode of death was such as to indicate that the *kenōsis* of Christ was total. He could have died in other ways, but the actual form of crucifixion expressed an even more total emptying than other methods could have done. *Kenōsis* is then expressed in the very act of crucifixion, and this conclusion is then reinforced in the words expressed by Jesus while on the cross.

Kenōsis of act

The exact manner of Jesus' death has occasioned a great amount of Christian comment as to its meaning, much of which is speculative in the extreme. An example of the latter is the explanation of Cyril, that Jesus stretched out his hands to embrace the ends of the earth (Moltmann 2001a:213). What is significant here is that the very act of crucifixion is a *kenōsis*, a yielding in many ways. It is an acceptance of powerlessness, the heart of suffering (Soelle 1975:11). Graphically, it immediately means a restriction of freedom in the fixing of hands and feet to the cross, a loss of the ability to move. It may just be observed that one of the major effects on the environment is caused by the western thirst for mobility, and travelling for often trivial reasons, even taking cars over short distances where walking would not only be cheaper, but would have health benefits. Jesus, in contrast, willingly accepted the limitation of his mobility by being nailed to the cross. Indeed, there has been a strand of Christian devotion, seen in the monasteries, and especially in the hermits, who limited their mobility as part of their imitation of Christ; the ultimate was Simon Stylites, who lived for forty years on the top of a pillar. However, even if these are rejected as extreme, it must be asked if the western fascination with transport is not equally wrong as at the other extreme.

The cross was then a surrendering of personal privacy and respect, the acceptance of shame, in that despite artistic portrayals of the event, the sufferer was usually stripped naked (McGrath 1992:14). There was even a giving up of one of our most basic experiences in the removal of contact with the earth, and at the same time, the acceptance of the effect of gravity that generated such intense suffering. Such should perhaps not just be taken for granted in the light of the experiences of such as Elijah, Ezekiel, and even Jesus himself at the ascension.

Jesus' acceptance of the effects of gravity on his body involved a progressive yielding up of the abilities of life. Breathing became harder, thirst became intense, and therefore as the life processes ceased, the pain which indicates a breakdown in the activity of life became unbearable. I have suggested elsewhere (Williams 2004:199) that life may be seen as the inter-relationships of the elements of the body, and it is these that are then given up as *kenōsis* proceeds. The dignity of a quick death is given up, as the process could take a considerable period (Stott 1986:23). The very waiting is itself exquisite pain (Soelle 1975:83). Jesus even refused the mercy of the drug, experiencing the "fullness of the emptying". The experiences of his suffering have recently been graphically portrayed in the film *The passion of Christ*, which has brought home the reality of these to many in a fresh way. It is then interesting to read the remark of Goguel, that the earliest gospel does not dwell on Jesus' physical agony, but on the spiritual (Morris 1976:48). Johnson comments that Jesus' death included all that makes death terrifying (Placher 2001:128).

More than this, external relationships also break down; death is to become relationless (Fiddes 1988:200). Jesus gave up the relationship with his mother, entrusting his disciple with her care. Even the closeness of the bond with his Father is removed in the cry of dereliction, "My God, my God, why have you forsaken me?" Jeremias points out that Jesus always addressed God as Father except here (Macleod 1998:95). At the same time, the manner of death implied the curse of God (Gal 3:13), also a step of emptying that death by another means would not imply.

Finally he yielded up even his spirit. This act of *kenōsis*, as the others, was by his choice (Wiersbe 1997:117). Ironically the last deliberate act was then the surrender of the will to act. Tasker (1960:217) observes that his giving up of the spirit can have a variety of interpretations. At the most basic it simply means his life, frequently in the Bible symbolised by the breath (eg Gen 2:7); it may be noted that the actual cause of death in crucifixion was suffocation (McGrath 1992:14). Then it could mean the giving up of the immaterial, or more positively the bestowal of the Holy Spirit onto the disciples. It could then, as the later incident in the upper room (Jn 20:22), be a symbolic anticipation of Pentecost. Tasker feels that this last idea is unlikely; it may be noted that John 7:39 connects the giving of the Spirit with Jesus' glorification, so not naturally linked with the cross. In this case it does form an aspect of Jesus' *kenōsis*, in its reversal.

It goes almost without saying that his sufferings and death were real, that there was no docetism; the thirst was real (Sanders 1968:409). The sufferings are then totally part of the nature of God. This contrasts with the common early view, informed by a Greek world-view, that Jesus could not suffer; the council of Chalcedon even deposed from the priesthood those who believed that the Godhead of the only-begotten is passible (Fiddes 1988:1). Hilary, for example, believed that even if Jesus ate, it was not because he suffered hunger (Richard 1982:141)! He actually wrote that it was a concession to us that Jesus did this; but how much more a concession in that his actions were real! However, the tradition that God cannot suffer is not Christian (Soelle 1975:42). Any impassibility falls away, meaning that we worship a God who can indeed sympathise with the depths of human experience. He must suffer, just because he loves us (Moltmann 2001a:237). Moltmann (2001a:213) can refer to a death in God, not of God. Peacocke (1993:127) notes that a rejection of the impassibility of God has been a feature of recent theology. Fiddes (1988) provides a major study of the theme; importantly, he stresses that God does not suffer because he is powerless to stop it (1988:1).

It must be stressed that Jesus submitted himself to the process of crucifixion. The whole process was voluntary (Stott 1986:60). It is commonly remarked that he gave up the spirit, not that it was taken from him (Westcott 1958:278, referring also to Gal 2:20, Eph 5:2,25, 1 Pet 2:23, and Acts 7:59). The taunt of the rulers (Lk 23:35) was quite accurate for if he was indeed the Son of God, he could have come down from the cross. He was submitting to what held him, even if he did not have to. Interestingly Jesus referred to his coming death as a "baptism" (Lk 12:50), which is a rite that is, at least normally, undergone as a result of a deliberate choice, but involves an action which is done to the one being baptised. It is this aspect of voluntary submission that answers the accusation made to the proposals of kenotic Christology made in the nineteenth century in Europe by such as Thomasius, and then later in Britain by Gore. The *kenōsis* of Christ was not an essential limitation, but on the contrary, an act of omnipotence; as almighty, Christ had the freedom to limit his own freedom. It is not surprising that any hint of limitation in God is resisted: a modern comment on this is that of Berdyaev, who remarks that the natural person always prefers an almighty God, one who is able to provide help (in Moltmann 2001a:220).

It remains a matter for debate as to the extent of Jesus' awareness of what was about to happen as his steps drew even closer to the cross. How far did *kenōsis* embrace his knowledge of the future? Did he die forlornly, having tried to force God's hand, as Schweitzer suggested? He must have been aware that he would suffer, and if the narratives are to be taken at face value, also of the reason for that suffering in human redemption (eg Mk 10:46). John's account of the crucifixion in particular emphasises the expression of the majesty of God even present there (Sanders 1968:410); he stresses the fulfilment of scripture. The acceptation of *kenōsis* does not compromise this, even the opposite, as it flows from, and demonstrates, the love of God. Indeed, there is a sense in which the Father also participated in the *kenōsis*, withdrawing himself from his Son, and even light from the world; in this regard, Wiersbe (1997:91) comments that the darkness then reflects the darkness in the holy of holies, behind the curtain, the place of atonement. The full deity and majesty of God are still present in Jesus, but are voluntarily curtailed in his experience for our sake. There is a contrast here between the belief of the "open theists", who hold that the future cannot be known as it has not happened, and the idea of *kenōsis*, in which God limits himself only in those areas which he specifically chooses. This allows some aspects of the future to be pre-determined, which the open theists also want, albeit inconsistently.

Kenōsis of word

Many churches use the "seven words" from the cross as a basis for their Good Friday worship. These form a good basis for understanding what was happening on that cross outside the walls of Jerusalem. Westcott (1958:278) suggests that the order of utterance was as follows. It will not be surprising to find them reflecting the features of the suffering that enabled atonement, but then also the *kenōsis* that was being accepted by Jesus at that time.

Father, forgive them (Lk 23:34). The words of Jesus in the act of crucifixion have been made much of, although perhaps not enough. Even if the immediate subject of his prayer was those who had the specific task of physical crucifying, the driving in of the nails and the raising of the victim, they must surely encompass more than these. Such is at the heart of the gospel, that in the dying of Christ, forgiveness is enabled. Morris (1976:69) quotes Jeremias, who remarks that while later Judaism included an expiatory prayer as part of the ritual of the execution of a criminal, Jesus turned it around to a prayer not for himself but for others. Indeed the whole motive for his *kenōsis* was for others, hardly for himself; he did not grasp at equality with God (Phil 2:6).

The reason given for the prayer of Jesus was the ignorance of the perpetrators (Lk 23:34); Marshall (1978:869) comments that motive is a particular interest to Luke. It is a frequently overlooked aspect of the Old Testament sacrificial system that it provided atonement for accidental and unwitting sins, but not for deliberate transgression (Num 15:30). This of course does not mean that ignorance saves; Wiersbe (1997:58) comments that this would counter-motivate evangelism!

Can this be extended to those who ordered them, both Pilate and the Jewish leaders? On the one hand both clearly accepted responsibility, Pilate in the famous hand-washing incident (Matt 27:24), and Caiaphas in the celebrated and prophetic remark that it is good for one to die instead of the people (Jn 11:50). But even there, it can hardly be doubted that nobody was really aware of what was actually being done. Even if they knew that wrong was being perpetrated, the extent of that wrong was hardly appreciated. They were guilty, but not of what was actually being done. Such must be even more true for the Jewish people, despite the fact that they actually accepted the blame (Matt 27:25). There cannot be any justification in Jesus for antiSemitism. Nevertheless, Stott (1986:59) points out that Peter was bold enough to blame them in his preaching, and that they agreed.

The possibility of forgiveness on the basis of ignorance is not a removal of guilt. The perpetrators were not hapless puppets in the hand of God. It is this that indicates *kenōsis*. If creation is, as many have suggested (eg Richard 1997:139), a withdrawing of God to give freedom to the creation, and specifically to humanity, then its pain and suffering cannot be blamed on God, who most definitely did not cause it, and can even be argued to have been ignorant of its specific manifestation.

The corollary of this is that God himself suffers when things happen in his creation which he does not want, even if he is not directly affected himself. Once the choice to create was made, creator was restricted by it (Vanstone 1977:64). This becomes more intense when he is rejected and scorned; as the Jewish commentator Heschel has stressed, the Old Testament in particular is full of the pathos of God, but also of his willingness to forgive such injury (eg Hos 6:1). And the same holds to a greater degree in the cross, where in his *kenōsis*, God incarnate allows his direct suffering, but again is willing to forgive, to empty himself of his right to blame. And incidentally to keep on doing it; Wiersbe (1997:53) comments that the Greek implies a repeated event.

Today you will be with me in Paradise (Lk 23:43). This word of comfort was only possible as Jesus was crucified with the two thieves, which could be seen as anticipated by Jesus' comment at the close of the last supper "he was reckoned with transgressors" (Lk 22:37), although Jesus' words may have a more general application to the atonement, since all have sinned (Rom 3:23). As identifying with sinners in his *kenōsis*, his death and resurrection effected their justification. Jesus' comment was that this fulfilled scripture; the reference was certainly to Isaiah 53:12, which Christians, since the time of the New Testament, have understood as referring to Jesus. Even more significantly, the previous words in Isaiah say that "he poured out his soul to death", where the verb has been seen as the equivalent of the "emptied" of Philippians 2:7 (Martin 1983:182).

Even if chronologically these words were not the last, in a sense they should be. On the one hand, they reflect not so much the *kenōsis* of Christ, but the start of the reversal of the process, as Paul depicts it in Philippians 2:9-11. The sufferings of Christ would be over, and the well-deserved rest commenced. The word "paradise" is a Persian word and means a garden, being used in the Septuagint for Eden (eg Is 51:3) (Marshall 1978:872). The placement in Eden must have been intended to be the start of a ministry, the exercise of the role of humanity as given to them in creation, specifically the dominion of the created order. As the death on the cross was the turning point that leads to Jesus' dominion over all, as graphically rendered in Philippians 2:9-11, it enabled the restoration of "Paradise lost", and of human dominion over the creation.

Part of this dominion is of things "under the earth", and without seeing this in crass materialistic terms, the understanding must be of the world of the dead, and here it is most likely that the enigmatic reference to Jesus' preaching to the dead is part of that total dominion starting to be exercised at his death. In this case, it does indicate something of the nature of the rest that is to be entered into, about which the early chapters of the book of Hebrews makes so much. As in the garden of Eden, rest is not inactivity, but the refreshment of service, but without the frustrations that occurred as a result of the "fall".

On the other hand, the entering of Paradise is also a continuation of the process of *kenōsis*. Whereas Jesus promised that the dying thief would be with him that very day in Paradise, it is clear that the body of Jesus remained on the cross after his death, and had to be taken down. It was not the body of Jesus that was in Paradise, but he was there spiritually. The next step of *kenōsis* was the loss of the body, which would only be reversed at the resurrection. This is consistent with Paul's explanation of the state of "unclothing" immediately after death, and the waiting to be "reclothed" (2 Cor 5:4), and also with Jesus' admittedly parabolic description of the state of the rich man and Lazarus after their death (Lk 16:19f), where the possibility of preaching to the brothers of the rich man indicates that they are still in the present life. It is also an indication that justification is not achieved by the action of *kenōsis* as such, so by incarnation and humiliation, but in death, as *kenōsis* proceeded further even than death in the loss of the body and the entry into the afterlife.

It is then particularly striking that the thief was justified, but his faith was not directed to a God exhibiting power, but to one in the depths of *kenōsis*, displaying no obvious power to help (Wiersbe 1997:69).

Woman, behold your son (Jn 19:26). Again there has been much made of the words of Jesus to his mother. One issue has been why Jesus gave the responsibility to John, seeing that he did have brothers. One natural suggestion, probably partly from dogmatic motives, was that Jesus was actually the only son of Mary, so that possibly these brothers could have been of Joseph by another wife (Sanders 1968:408), and that they did not want responsibility for her. What is remarkable was the selflessness of Jesus when it might have been expected that his own suffering would have been enough to fill his consciousness (Soelle 1975:69). Perhaps this is even more remarkable in the light of the attitude toward his mother that comes out in a number of other incidents, where it would seem that he valued the adopted relationships of those who had put their faith in him above the natural relation with his mother and brothers.

The experience of death is the end, the *kenōsis*, of natural relationships, which naturally cease with the extinction of human life. Westcott (1958:276) observes that he addresses her not as a parent, but just as a "woman". It is noteworthy that his natural mother plays very little recorded role thereafter, although that is of course partly a result of the cultural attitude to women, even if the latter observation must be read in the context of the emancipation of women as a result of the salvation available in Christ (Gal 3:28).

It was one of the first objections to kenotic Christology to suggest that if Jesus emptied himself of divinity then providence would be undermined and the universe collapse (Heb 1:3). Even if it were the case that existence depends on continual divine action, which is by no means certain, we have in this instance an indication that *kenōsis* is not the abandoning of responsibility. Of course the issue does not arise if *kenōsis* is understood not in the sense of emptying, but of hiding. There is, in any case, no reason why a divine activity must be restricted to one Person; the Augustinian affirmation is *opera Trinitatis ad extra indivisa sunt*.

My God, why have you forsaken me (Matt 27:46, Mk 15:34)? The quotation of the first line of Psalm 22 can be taken as a reference to the entire psalm (Richard 1997:67), which contains a number of verses which have been taken as fulfilled in the events of the cross (eg Ps 22:18 in Matt 27:35). At face value, however, the cry is expression of the feeling that Jesus had lost even the appreciation of relationship to his Father, the ultimate *kenōsis*. Soelle (1975:85) comments that all extreme suffering gives a feeling of being God-forsaken. This is especially significant in the light of the Trinitarian belief in the relationship of eternal generation of the Son from the Father. Interestingly, and perhaps significantly, the cry was heard as a call to Elijah (Matt 27:47), on the one hand the precursor of the Messiah, but on the other, one who also felt a loss of the relationship with God in his experiences. Perhaps it is valid to say that in the tearing apart of his very being he did even doubt, experiencing an even deeper aspect of *kenōsis*; in this case his identity with this all too common human condition adds basis to the affirmation of McGrath (1992:92f) that the cross and resurrection are a solution even to this. Nevertheless, Morris (1976:43) can suggest that even here, the use of the possessive "my" is an indication that his faith was still strong.

Moltmann (2001a:148) points out that the death of Jesus was not something that was welcomed, not even something that was, as the death of Socrates, accepted stoically, but in extreme distress; he cites Mark 15:33 and Hebrews 5:7. There is in no sense any acceptance of the sin that made his suffering necessary.

Perhaps a key issue here is whether the cry was just a result of the perception of Jesus due to the intensity of his suffering. If so, it mirrors a common human reaction to pain in a feeling that God is silent, uncaring, or even just does not exist. It may be remarked here that the affirmation of the *kenōsis* of God in order to give real freedom to humanity is a possible solution to the old problem of human pain in the context of an all-loving but also omnipotent God. The Philippian hymn itself refers to Jesus, who in the incarnation "did not count equality with God a thing to be grasped" (Phil 2:6), indicating that he did not use his position to enforce action.

More probably, the cry of Jesus was not just a perceived breakdown in relationship, but that the break was real. He was experiencing the separation due to sin, so that it could be atoned for. The *kenōsis* of the Father was now extended to his Son. What may then be suggested is that this resulted in a further aspect of the *kenōsis* of the Son, but even more, that the interplay of these is an aspect of the *perichoresis* between the first two Persons. Even more than this, insofar as it is the Spirit who bonds the Father and Son as *vinculum amoris* (cf Williams 2004), the third Person also experienced a *kenōsis*. (Perhaps here one should say, as with the other two Persons, a further *kenōsis*, as it has been suggested that he limits himself in his relationships, so specifically in the exercise of personality). The entire Godhead suffers, so it is understandable that sin and salvation are cosmic acts, and that the atonement was accompanied by effects such as the darkness and the earthquake.

I thirst (Jn 19:28). Again, this is an indication of *kenōsis*, Jesus' voluntary self-limitation. The experience of extreme thirst was one of the effects of the process of crucifixion. Not only did the sufferer experience the effects of exposure to the elements and consequent dehydration, but the body posture resulted in the collection of fluids in the stomach. When the soldier pierced Jesus' side with a spear, naturally going into the heart from below, it first entered the stomach, releasing the water, before stabbing the heart, releasing the blood. The flow of the two distinct fluids occasioned the remark of the fourth evangelist (Jn 19:34), and a plethora of suggestions as to the meaning. What is however clear is that the body was releasing the water that is the essential means of the inter-relation of the different organs of the body, and so this is an effect of the gradual emptying of the life process from Jesus.

This was in addition to the normal loss of water from the body through breathing and perspiration. Overall the body rapidly experienced dehydration; the effect of this was a thickening of the blood and its decreasing ability to carry oxygen and nutrients throughout the body. At the same time this caused the heart to work harder, so absorbing more of the decreasing amount of available energy. The sum total was growing weakness, increasing emptying of strength.

This sees the thirst as a natural effect, not just to fulfil a scriptural prophecy. The latter phrase can in fact be taken with the preceding as well as what follows (Westcott 1958:277); John's style is to imply both (Morris 1971:813). In the latter case, Westcott suggests that the scripture could well be Psalm 69:21, although Tasker (1960:211) opts for Psalm 42:2, and Sanders (1968:409), although he opts for the former, also notes the possibility that the reference is to Psalm 22:15, already alluded to by Jesus. What is hard to see why these are relevant just to a physical experience. However, in the former case, it was the predicted atonement which was fulfilled. It is not just irony (Brown 1970:930), that the source of living water, the expression of deity, experienced thirst. The word "fulfilled" is not the one which would be more usual, as the *plērōthē* of Matthew 4:14, but is *teleiōthē* which immediately links to the "accomplished" of two words previously (*tetelestai*), which is the same word used in the cry "it is finished", just two verses on (Jn 19:30). The interpretation in terms of *kenōsis* however brings the two views together, as thirst is then part of the process of atonement. Wiersbe (1997:102) comments that thirst is an aspect of punishment for sin (eg Lk 16:24), so part of Jesus' suffering as atonement for us. Westcott (1958:277) indeed links Psalm 69 to the Isaianic Servant; Driver (1986:88) indeed comments on the clear link between the cross and the servant passages.

The thirst is also the only indication of the physical pain of Christ; Temple (1963:351) suggests that relief from it was sought to prepare for the cry which followed. This again links the two. Temple also links it to the "cup". This metaphor for the whole suffering of Jesus has a number of Old Testament precursors, such as Psalm 75:8 and Ezekiel 23:31f; interestingly its use in Gethsemane (Jn 18:11) is in the context of Jesus' renunciation of physical force.

It is finished (Jn 19:30). The single word in the Greek bears the sense of being accomplished, or achieving a goal, not merely of coming to an end. In the context of Jesus' role, it was commonly used when a slave completed a job, when a sacrificial victim was accepted as perfect, or when a business transaction was finalised

(Wiersbe 1997:107f). Again, this is commonly understood as referring to the atonement, of the suffering necessary for the sins of the world, not just to his life (Morris 1971:815). He did not say, "I am finished" (Wiersbe 1997:104). This quantifies something that cannot really be amenable to measurement; if Jesus had died five minutes earlier, would some sin remain unatoned for? And how is it possible to balance an amount of sin with an amount of pain? Could his experience of pain be quantifiably greater than that of another human person? In any case, unless God knew exactly what would happen until the end of time, which indeed some Christians do believe, it would be impossible to know when it had been dealt with.

And again, in view of the fact that "the wages of sin is death" (Rom 6:23), it was not actually the suffering and pain of Jesus that was the penalty for sin, but his death, and this was effective as he summed up in himself those who were saved. There is a sense in which death is indeed the penalty for sin, and those who were saved died in Christ, and by their death sin is atoned for. So why did Jesus then have to suffer; why did he not just die? Suffering is always an enigma, but more especially inexplicable suffering.

Perhaps the answer lies again in the idea of *kenōsis*, which could indeed be said to come to an absolute state, when no further emptying would be possible. Effectively pain is the complaint of the body when it is not functioning as it should, so when the inter-relating of the various parts is disrupted. There then comes a point when interrelation effectively stops, and at that point death occurs. If indeed life is understood as interrelationship, that can be said to stop. Then of course the body starts to experience the process of decay. This would indicate that Jesus was saying that the process of emptying had come to completion. Even if physical emptying, a vacuum, is an impossibility, interrelation can cease in the dynamic sense. All that remains is physical closeness of the parts of the body, but with the dynamic ceased, even that would start to come apart.

Into your hands I commit my spirit (Lk 23:46). This is yet another quotation from the Old Testament, most likely Psalm 31:5. Bernard comments that this is also reflected in Isaiah 53:12, where the Servant pours out his soul (Morris 1971:815): it is a positive action. Marshall (1978:976) comments that the words are a part of the Jewish evening prayer; they reflect the yielding up to sleep, and so the need to rely on God. Significantly Psalm 31:5 is an expression of trust in God as distinct from "vain idols" (Ps 31:6), where the expression reflects the emptiness of those in which people are so often tempted to put their trust. What this means in practice is that the motive for action, the "spirit" is aligned with that of God, that there is an "emptying" of desires contrary to those of God to be replaced with his, a positiveness in distinction to the emptiness of idolatry. This understands "spirit" in the sense of motive, rather than as a supposed constituent of a human being. Here, once atonement had been completed, Jesus' purpose for living had been completed, so he could give up that "spirit". It is also not a direct reference to the third Person, except insofar as the Spirit should be the means by which the human spirit is aligned to that of God (Williams 2004:140).

Here death must be the end of personal ambition and goals, as nothing else may be achieved. It is a *kenōsis* (Peck 1997:180). This is a necessary aspect of dying, and actually may be the cause of death, when a person loses the will to live. However, it is a common human reaction in the face of the inevitable to seek the survival of one's personal spirit, but executed by the hands of others. In the case of Jesus, there was now a complete surrender of a personal spirit in the *kenōsis* of death, that even though there had been a conformity of human with divine wills in Christ through the *communicatio idiomatum*, the extinction of the human life meant that this was no longer necessary, and that the will or spirit could be unreservedly that of the Father.

This aspect would then be more significant that the physical death, which is really a step in the overall physical process. Morris (1974:330) points out that the word in Luke is not the normal one for dying; the choice of *exepneusen* puts an emphasis on the yielding up of the *pneuma*.

At the same time there was indeed a surrendering of spirit to God insofar as the ongoing work of God on earth would no longer be done by the human Jesus, but by God himself in the enabling and motivating of the disciples through the Holy Spirit. In itself this is a *kenōsis*, insofar as God is surrendering the possibility of direct action to the agency of fallible people, with the perhaps inevitable prospect of results not in keeping with the preferred will of God.

Why the stress on *kenōsis*?

If it is accepted that the phrase is there to draw attention to a facet of the *kenōsis* of Christ, it may then be asked why such *kenōsis* was needed. It may well be thought that the essential point could well be made without such a dramatic demonstration, such as, for example, by the foot-washing incident of John 13:2f, a passage which is indeed often seen in relation to Philippians 2 (eg Hawthorne 1983:98). Chrysostom, indeed, illustrated the meaning of Philippians 2 by that incident (Bockmuehl 1997:137). Eastern thought did appreciate hyperbole, but was it necessary to go to such lengths?

Primarily, the *kenōsis* of the cross must be seen in the context of the atonement. It is hardly remarkable that the cross has become the major symbol of Christianity, albeit paradoxically adorned and beautified, although Bockmuehl (1997:139) comments that it was comparatively late, so awful was its implications. It is however, at the heart of the message of Christianity (Richard 1997:85). Paul centred his message on the cross, determining to know nothing except Christ, and him crucified (1 Cor 2:2).

But the atonement can only be understood in the context of Christology. It was only the fact that Jesus was totally human and totally divine, as the statement of Chalcedon affirms, that makes salvation possible. What must then be striking is that the divinity of Jesus is not only demonstrated in his miracles, his claims and teaching or his resurrection, but also in his cross. For Barth, his divinity is most clearly seen, not in his resurrection, but on the cross (Richard 1997:107). This was ultimately the reason for the incarnation: he was born to die. Strikingly, "the incarnation of the Logos is completed on the cross" (Moltmann 2001a:211). It is significant that it was the manner of his death that brought forth the exclamation of the presumably pagan centurion, "truly this man was a son of God" (Mk 15:39). This affirmation must remind us, as in the cross-referencing of the RSV, of the voice from heaven at his baptism and transfiguration, also events that are related as finding their meanings as they anticipated his suffering and death. It was then his dying that demonstrated his divinity and so indicated the sort of God that he is.

As has been noted, crucifixion was the punishment for rebellion, and going right back to the Old Testament (eg Is 1:2), sin may be seen in that context. The cross was the emptying of any political hope for the disciples (McGrath 1992:33), and yet again it proved to be the only real basis for their future confidence. It must empty people of any confidence in humanity. The cross, in its extreme cruelty (Stott 1986:23), must be the total antithesis of human love, also of any sense of justice (McGrath 1992:33). Paradoxically, Christians have seen in it these two qualities expressed in fullness, and moreover rendered compatible. Without the cross, it is impossible to understand how God can show both at the same time.

What is seen in the cross was the end of the exercise of Jesus' activity on earth. Even if he did continue for the forty days after the resurrection, effectively the ministry had come to an end. Not only his life, but his work experienced *kenōsis*; which is linked with his role as a servant in Philippians 2. But this puts the onus for God's work onto the shoulders of the disciples. There is no justification in the cross for quietism in the face of human need, particularly as the union of the disciples with their Master continues with his experience of exaltation. They can exercise the authority of the risen Son of God, through the enabling of his presence in the Spirit.

But seemingly contrary to this, it was an indication of the way in which the ministry of the disciples would be exercised, which would be in imitation of the submission of Christ on the cross. Certainly it is evident that the effect of those few hours on the cross achieved more in the history of the world, and affected more lives, than any other act.

Paul brings in the hymn as an example for the disciples of what is meant by a Christ-like mind. The passage is an example for his followers. Here it may be noted that there is a strand of opinion that sees the action of Christ not as effecting salvation, but of providing an example to follow. God is then able to forgive such repentance. The parable of the Prodigal Son (Lk 15:11f) is often appealed to here, but interestingly, P T Forsyth (1910:110) has suggested that the son would have sold himself into slavery, and that the father would have paid a price to redeem him. This aspect of the cross is especially appropriate, as the whole purpose of the punishment of crucifixion was not just to be as cruel as possible, to inflict the maximum amount of pain, but to present a public display of the result of rebellion against the authority of Rome, or in other words, of the "wages of sin" (Rom 6:23). The example of those crucified was intended to be a deterrent, so motivating any tempted to rebellion towards more acceptable behaviour. Such was the intention of Paul, motivating the followers of Christ towards a lifestyle acceptable to God.

Specifically, it has motivated *kenōsis*, self-sacrifice for others, acceptance of martyrdom. Examples are not hard to find, from Anthony the hermit, through Francis of Assisi, and in more recent days, the missionary, C T Studd, all of whom saw their own self-sacrifice as the only appropriate response to that of Christ. The call to follow Jesus is, as often in the New Testament, a call to suffering, to participate, in a degree, in his (Moltmann 2001a:54). As with Jesus, that is the path that leads ultimately to glory (Moltmann 2001a:56). The insight of Hebrews 12:2 is that the way to Jesus' glorification lay through the experience of the cross, and it is therefore through our experience of the cross in Christ that we also receive life and glory.

It is beyond question that the example of the cross has indeed been a powerful attraction to Christ, as indeed he said it would be. "If I am lifted up from the earth, I will draw all men to me" (Jn 12:32). Is it pressing the example too much to see an effect similar to that of the emptiness of a vacuum, drawing into itself? Indeed, how can we remain detached if we were the cause of the cross (Stott 1986:12)?

Certainly it has proved an ongoing fascination to me. Since becoming a Christian, I have always found reading the gospel accounts of the crucifixion an emotional experience, and certainly thinking about those events as I wrote this article has been moving. To add to this, it was while I was researching for this that I had the opportunity to watch Mel Gibson's *The passion of Christ*, which became very meaningful, and added more context to my thinking. I also found in the writing a greater sense of inspiration than I usually do, so was moved in a different way as well. All of which of course served to reinforce my belief in the centrality of the event of the cross, and deepened my desire to understand it more fully.

PART 2

The *kenōsis* from the Father

"… and the love of God"

Chapter 5

Kenōsis and the Trinity: *perichōrēsis* and *kenōsis*

Any discussion of Christology naturally has reference to the doctrine of the Trinity, and this is especially the case here. Even if the concept of *kenōsis* itself is striking, it becomes especially so in the context of the affirmation of the full deity of the second Person of the Trinity, and for this reason has attracted a vast amount of scholarly attention as to its meaning. The theory of *kenōsis* was put forward as an attempt to make sense of the incarnation, to explain how it could be possible for Jesus to be at the same time fully human and fully divine, particularly as he would have appeared just to be human. But, although it is not always done, any discussion of Christology should take cogniscence of its implications for the Trinity. *Kenōsis* applies not only to the incarnation, but also to creation, and indeed to the inner life of the Trinity (Bulgakov, in Gavrilyuk 2005:253). Indeed, Philippians 2 has distinct Trinitarian implications. Likewise, the doctrine of the Trinity must reflect back on any idea of *kenōsis*; the Trinity shows how this is related to God's power (van den Brink 1993:230).

Full deity of the second Person

The debate that eventually resulted in the formulation of the doctrine of the Trinity started from similar observations to that producing the idea of *kenōsis*. In his earthly life, Jesus did not generally manifest the attributes that are associated with deity; there was obvious limitation. So could he then be divine? And how did he relate to the Father?

It was in the fourth century that the legalisation of Christianity by the emperor Constantine stopped the persecution that had often been the experience of Christians for three centuries, and so relieved the external pressure on the Church. This enabled attention to be given to other things than mere survival, notably the deeper understanding of the faith. It was only five years before the notorious Arius, seeking to understand what had happened in the incarnation, proposed an understanding that was to lead to decades of strife. He said that because Jesus obviously did not exhibit the full characteristics of deity, he must then be essentially less than the Father. His suggestion included the statement that as the second Person was a Son, his origin must have occurred at a point of time; "there was when he was not". The "battle" for the Trinity was bitter, and finally led to a strong affirmation of the full deity of the second Person. Indeed, so strong was it, that it has often been the fear of any hint of Arian subordination which has influenced many against a view of *kenōsis*. However, far from contrary to the idea of *kenōsis*, the understanding of the Trinity can rather be seen to contribute to a fuller realization of what *kenōsis* is

Kenōsis of the Father

Ironically, Arius' theology had been strongly influenced by a fellow Alexandrian of several decades previously, the brilliant Origen, who as common in his day, did believe that the second

Person was essentially subordinate to the first. But in the wealth of other ideas that he produced, many of which did not stand the test of time, was included one which we know as "eternal generation". This simply means that the generation of the Son from the Father should not be understood as an event, but as a process. Unlike the production of human life, where the parents do impart life to their offspring in specific events, the divinity of the second Person is received constantly. It is an eternal process, and therefore has no beginning. The second Person is therefore co-eternal with the first, and in this regard, as in others, they can be equal.

But this means that the Father is always bestowing divinity on the Son; effectively he is constantly emptying himself (Gavrilyuk 2005:255); Richard (1997:108) sees the processions as aspects of *kenōsis*. The eternal nature of the Father is then kenotic. At the same time he limits the exercise of his own divine abilities; instead of acting himself, he delegated all authority to the Son (Matt 28:18). Of course, the fact that led Arius astray, that Jesus was not fully manifesting deity during his incarnation, has exactly the same explanation, that although the second Person was fully divine, he was limiting himself as well. Both the first and the second Persons were manifesting *kenōsis*.

This is hardly surprising, as a fundamental aspect of the idea of the Trinity is of the total equality of the three Persons. In this case *kenōsis* would be a feature of all three of the Persons (Balthasar, in Coakley 2001:199). Thus if the second Person manifests *kenōsis*, it might be expected that this is an aspect of the nature of the other two Persons as well. Indeed, recent suggestions, such as put forward by Moltmann, have indicated that a form of *kenōsis* is actually characteristic of divinity. Along with Barth, Rahner, Küng and others, Moltmann claims that Jesus' death on the cross shows the very nature of God (Murphy and Ellis 1996:175, Fiddes 1988:135). McClendon translates Philippians 2:6 as Jesus "mirroring God on earth" (Murphy and Ellis 1996:177).

Sanders (1998:225f) then notes that God must inherently have limited himself. He notes that any decision God that has made is a limitation, just because it is a rejection of alternative possibilities. More obviously, he must be limited if people have real free will, and indeed, if God cannot allow human free will because his goals would then be frustrated, he is clearly limited. He cites Barth's view that God is the sort revealed in Jesus, which means he is not any other sort, and that of Brunner, that creation implies limitation. He does however stress that this self-limitation is restraint, not an abandonment of power. Likewise, a self-limitation of power is not an abrogation of responsibility; God, unlike the deity proposed by process theology can fulfil his obligations (van den Brink 1993:264). God did not create because of an inherent limitation, to fulfil a need, but in so doing did limit himself. Vanstone (1977:69) uses the illustration of a family that is sufficient in itself, but in adopting a child finds it also develops a need for it; likewise the Trinity is complete, but has developed a desire to relate to the creation and so limits itself so that this is possible. Sanders (1998:170) sees the goal of God that people reflect the Trinitarian love; perhaps better, share in it. This does not mean that God had to create or that he gained by it; Anselm observed that God would not be less if creation ended (Highfield 2002:294). In fact, as God is spiritual, the existence of the world cannot add to him.

In the words of the Apostles' Creed, the Father is almighty, or omnipotent. Yet it is just this ability that he has limited. In the act of creation, humanity was given dominion over the creation, which must mean that God's own power was restricted. Indeed, as creation and redemption are so closely related, the latter being seen as a "new creation" (2 Cor 5:17), it should not be a surprising suggestion that the act of *kenōsis* is not just a feature of the incarnation, so of the second Person, but is a feature of creation as well. The *kenōsis* of the redeemer points to the *kenōsis* of the creator (Vanstone 1977:59). The basis of creation is the self-differentiation of the Son from the Father (Pinnock 1996:59) Then the Father certainly restricts himself in the expression of knowledge, seeing that he is essentially transcendent, hidden, expressing himself through the Son. His transcendence also means that he must inevitably be limited in relationship, choosing to relate to the world rather through the third person, the Spirit. Augustine saw him as *vinculum amoris*, the bond of love between the other Persons of the Trinity. Urs von Baltasar comments that the cross was a separation between Father and Son, but in fact the two were separated from all eternity; but this separation was bridged by the Spirit (in Richard 1997:108). He is then also the one who relates the atonement to the Christian, giving him or her the eternal life that is Christ's by nature.

Thus both Father and Son are limited. After all, the Nicene affirmation is that the three Persons are *homoousios*, of the same nature, which refers to the essence of divinity. Thus if the Son, the second Person, limited himself, it is reasonable that all three do. Paradoxically, the very *homoousios* that has tended to convince so many that the Son could not experience *kenōsis*, indicates that actually all three limit, so that *kenōsis* is a fundamental attribute of being divine.

The Trinity as kenotic

Biblically, the doctrine of the Trinity emerged from the need to reconcile the realization of the oneness of God, particularly seen in the Old Testament, with the revelation of the divinity of Jesus, and of course the Spirit. But the oneness of God is itself there presented as a limitation. The milieu of the Old Testament, and indeed also of the New, outside of the Jews, was of a belief in a great plurality of deities. Into this came the revelation by God, limited, so characteristically, to one particular people, the children of Israel. And that revelation

David T. Williams

was that their God was not just one of a number of gods, but that he was unique, in fact that there was only one God. He was limited in number. A major part of the Old Testament then deals with the establishment of this idea, the demonstration that the other so-called gods were nothing (eg Is 44:9f), that the major sin was in fact the denial of this idea, the accepting of other gods.

Of course, as the history of the people of God unfolded and progressed through the experiences of incarnation and of the sending of the Holy Spirit, there came the realization that this limitation was more complex, that God was in three Persons. Nevertheless, even there, there was still a limitation, as there was no hint whatsoever that the number of Persons was more than three. Christianity has never suggested that Jesus was one in a line of deities, let alone of prophets, but has always insisted that he is the only begotten Son (Jn 1:14). Likewise there is only one Holy Spirit, even if there is just a hint of internal plurality in the seven spirits of the book of Revelation (Rev 4:5). It is of course not possible to state categorically that there are not more Persons in the Godhead, but it can be firmly stated that in his relation to this world, God is limited to three (for a development of this suggestion, cf Williams 2001:97f)).

It was when the emphatic oneness of God was proclaimed in a Greek environment, that this very uniqueness had generated problems for the idea of the Trinity (Pinnock 2001:28). It is the same presupposition that negatively affects the idea of *kenōsis*. Oneness tended to become associated with the idea of his perfection, and then, as any change would be to a state of less perfection, to God's immutability. In this line of reasoning, *kenōsis* is impossible, and out of this context were generated many of the objections to it. Indeed, such a God is effectively unknowable; anything that we affirm of God is in fact a limitation (Sanders 1998:32); if we say that God is good, we deny that he is bad. Thus, many of the objections to *kenōsis* can largely be met through an appreciation that God

82

is not a Platonic unchanging Deity, but is involved in the world. Again, this immediately involves reference to the Trinity, as this is how God manifested to the world. For example, the argument from immutability is weakened in the context of the fact that the second Person did become incarnate; König (1982:86) insists that as the Word became flesh, this involved change. Then the objection that a limited second Person could not fulfill his role of the upholding of the universe is also met by reference to the Trinity, as this could also be done by other Persons, especially as all three are involved in all actions of God.

The problem that generated the Arian challenge was met by the insistence that all three Persons are totally divine, so equal by nature, *homoousios*. The incarnation did not involve a change in divinity, but the second Person remained fully divine in essence. In the same way, the *kenōsis* of the second Person is not a change in his essence, not an inherent limitation. Nevertheless, it remains the case that the second Person, in his incarnation, was not manifesting the attributes of divinity. Jesus could indeed affirm that "the Father is greater than I" (Jn 14:28), for that was the case at that time. This is not just his humanity, as often believed by the Fathers, but due to the *kenōsis* of his deity (Bulgakov, in Gavrilyuk 2005:262). What would be wrong is to understand this, with Arius, as inherent subordination, but nevertheless, at that time, the second Person was indeed actually less than the first. At least during the period of the earthly incarnation, the second Person limited himself. Indeed, even after the consummation of all things, when God is "all in all" (1 Cor 15:28), when *kenōsis* as a process has ended, the Son continues to subject himself for the sake of humanity.

It was the second Person who became incarnate and so had to do this in order to relate to humanity and especially to relate to them, to be able to act as representative and substitute, so that atonement could be achieved. But this *kenōsis* on the part of the second Person, was not an action out of character, but of his very nature as divine. The incarnation and atonement were not God's reaction to the Fall and sin of humanity, but on the contrary were inherent in the very act of creation. As God gave free will, he was well aware that this could be abused, so that with the creation went the initiation of redemption. After all, the acts of creation and of redemption, which can aptly be referred to as a new creation (2 Cor 5:17), are not separate events by God, but aspects of one. In both, *kenōsis* was done for the sake of salvation, as acts of love. God created people, especially people with free will, from a motive of love; it was the most loving way to create. Then, and equally, he acted in redemption from that same motive, for that was the most loving way to free people from the effects of the abuse of their God-given freedom.

So God's nature is kenotic. Specific acts of *kenōsis* are then expressions of his nature, and so do not constitute change, and so are not diminutions in God. But at the same time, they are then also acts of will, by deliberate choice. Being kenotic, he acts kenotically, such as in creation or in incarnation. These are acts of will reflecting his nature. Thus the creation is definitely an act in response to God's deliberate choice to do it; it is an act of *kenōsis*, as such as Moltmann (1985:86) have argued, but at the same time it was an expression of his nature, that of essential creativity. When we apply this to the incarnation, this is then a specific act, by choice, but it is also an expression of the essential *kenōsis* of the Father. Fortman (1982:73) therefore records the opinion of Athanasius that the generation of the second Person was by nature, but the actual incarnation was an act of will. Likewise, of course, the *kenōsis* of Jesus was a natural part of his nature, the incarnation and humility of Jesus were acts in time, and by will. It may be observed here that as in *imago Dei*, humanity reflects his nature and so is then also kenotic; then as God reflects his nature by his kenotic action, it follows that correct human action, also by will, is to act kenotically. Moltmann (1981:132) thus comments that it is in this example of self-limitation that Christ becomes a valid example for us. In fact, God's desire is that people reflect the love within the Trinity (Sanders 1998:170); that resulted in incarnation and *kenōsis*. God desires new partners "for the eternal dance" (Pinnock 2001:30).

Economic and immanent Trinity

If God acts in the world by limitation, an act that does not affect his essential nature, this does imply that the Trinity manifested to the world is not the same as it is in itself (Sanders 1998:30). Thus what the concept of *kenōsis* can be taken to imply is a difference between the so-called immanent Trinity, God in himself, in which there is total equality, and the economic, God as manifested to the world, where there is *kenōsis*, and so subordination. This is a distinction that Bulgakov makes (Gavrilyuk 2005:261). The distinction between economic and immanent was an idea which had been proposed by Joachim of Fiore, but which was condemned by the Fourth Lateran Council (Gresham 1993:331). Certainly many would dispute this distinction, and insist that the revelation of God in the world is a reflection of what he really is, so that there is no real distinction between the two. Rahner (1970:22) in particular is well known for his insistence that the economic Trinity is the immanent Trinity. His view would certainly seem to be more in keeping with the character of God; it seems more logical to see the revelation of God as reflecting what he really is.

Nevertheless, a distinction is often made in the modern period; it contrasts the "processions" of the second and third Persons in the inner being of God, and the "missions" of Son and Spirit to the world (cf Thompson 1994:27,35). Torrance (1996:7) describes the latter, the "economic", as the "evangelical" Trinity, an apt designation! These are appropriate terms, as *kenōsis*, as an aspect of the incarnation, is part of the "mission" of the Son, and the source of the "evangel", the "good news". Indeed it has been suggested, as in the "social Trinity", that the very idea of the "processions" pertains only to the economic, that the immanent relations are simply eternal states (Hodgson 1943:102). Pannenberg notes that texts referring to Jesus' Sonship, although they need not rule out the idea of eternal generation, do not demand it (cited in Erickson 1991:305). While the *kenōsis* of the second Person actually demands that he be generated, at least in that period, this need not pertain to the immanence, where his full divinity really excludes it, because as equal to the first Person, he is in himself *autotheos*. Whether this is indeed so, it is clear that relationships in the immanence and economy need not be the same, as is the case in life, where a person may present a picture to the world which is greatly different from that of the real self.

A distinction between immanent and economic Trinities may in fact even be demanded by the nature of God. LaCugna (1993:219) remarks that God's self-communication in himself must be different from his communication to the world. Molnar (1989:398) comments, particularly referring to Barth, that a theology based on revelation must separate the two. For example, the incarnate Son came from the Spirit, while the traditional understanding is that the second Person was generated from the Father (LaCugna 1993:220). Thompson (1994:27) points out that if the economic and immanent Trinities were the same, God would have been forced to act in a particular way, which would deny God's freedom (Molnar 1989:367); this point is particularly significant in the current debate concerning "open theism". Congar (1983:13) points out that although the economic Trinity is the immanent, this is not reversible, as Rahner alleges; there is more to the immanent Trinity than has been revealed to us. As Athanasius observed, they must be distinguished, but must nevertheless be related (Torrance 1996:7). Gollwitzer is effectively saying the same thing by insisting that God's "being for us" should not overshadow his "being in himself" (Bracken 1979:53). The eastern Orthodox, since Palamas (1296-1359), therefore distinguish the incommunicable "essence" of God from his expression in his "energies", which are what we experience; incidentally, this means that they can say that the essence of the Spirit is from the Father alone, while his energies are through the Son (Gaybba 1987:55). In fact even Rahner in effect distinguishes between the immanent and economic Trinity. It is not consistent to refer to "modes" within the immanent Trinity, but respect real personal distinction in the economic (Bracken, in Hill 1982:219). There then must be distinction in both the immanent and the economic, but there need not be the same distinction, even if they are related. It is quite possible to understand that God's inner being is far more complex than has been revealed to us, and indeed it ought to be. What is necessary is that the economic Trinity must be consistent with the immanent, even if it is only a part of it. Any person is a mystery to others, and God far more. The Trinity as we understand it can well be a single facet of the richness of his full being. "... the economic Trinity is the immanent Trinity, but not the whole of the immanent Trinity" (Boff 1988:215). This is because the Persons in the economic Trinity manifest *kenōsis*, although it must be stressed that as it is a self-limitation, this does not affect their essential natures; there are not two Trinities (Richard 1997:109)! This need not be a loss of perfection, as Greek theology assumed, therefore putting God firmly outside time (Peters 1993:129). Of course, they must not be excessively separated; Peters (1993:8,39) points out that God in immanence must be affected by the world, a belief particularly associated with Moltmann's thought. Of course, this pertains especially to the cross (Olson 1989:218). Many, such as Moltmann and Jenson (Peters 1993:24,133), then suggest that the economic Trinity not only reveals the immanent, but then becomes it at the end of time, when "Rahner's rule" becomes really true (Peters 1993:16,177). At this point, as salvation is fully completed, *kenōsis* comes to an end. It passes away, when "the dwelling of God is with men" (Rev 21:3).

Perichōrēsis

The recognition of the Trinity means that even if the three Persons are absolutely equal in their divinity, yet they are distinguished. These are effective limitations, as each Person is limited by the existence of the others. In any case, the very fact of the Trinity must indicate *kenōsis;* the nature of each Person must be affected simply by relating to the others. As an example of this, because of the existence of the second, the first is the Father. He could not be the Father unless there was also the Son. But this is a limitation; the Father is limited to Paternity, so is neither Son nor Spirit. Likewise the other Persons. Even the Son is not only kenotic in incarnation, but in submitting himself to being begotten (Gavrilyuk 2005:255)! Likewise the third Person, as the *vinculum amoris*, bond of love, between the other two, only has this nature because of them; this would not be the same if even one of them did not exist.

But then each Person manifests limitation by their actions as well. Thus just as the Son is limited in his incarnation, the *kenōsis* of the Father is seen in his transcendence. Then the acts of *kenōsis* of each Person are also different. In the incarnation, a three-fold limitation, of omniscience, omnipresence and omnipotence, was experienced by the Son. But most characteristically, he shows the restriction of omniscience. The theology of the fourth gospel refers to Jesus as *logos*, the word, which means communication, rationality, knowledge; paradoxically, indeed, the most obvious aspect of the *kenōsis* of the Son is that he just does not exhibit omniscience, but on the contrary was often ignorant. In a similar way, the other attributes are associated with the other two Persons. The Father limits himself in the exercise of his power, the Spirit in his presence. We then have the three Persons, who are each particularly associated with the three attributes of deity that were specifically limited in the incarnation. Nevertheless, even if limitation of particular attributes is characteristic of each Person, each of the three do experience the limitation of all three.

Trinitarian theology, while insisting on equality, has made a distinction between the three Persons in a number of ways. At the extreme, Augustine, concerned for the unity of God and the equality of the Persons, stressed that *opera Trinitatis ad extra indivisa sunt,* the external actions of the Trinity are undivided. At its extreme, this has been taken to mean that the only difference between the Persons is in their distinct relationships, so that the Father is different from the Son as Begetter is distinct from Begotten. Richard (1997:95) speaks of a *homopraxis*, a unity of action, rather than of being, *homoousios.* Even in this view however, the actions of God have traditionally been "appropriated" to the distinct Persons, so that the Father created, the Son redeemed and the Spirit sustained. It however has often been felt to be more reasonable to accept that these appropriations are in fact real, that works of God can be attributed to the distinct Persons. After all, it was actually only the Son who became incarnate. What however may be stated is that the three Persons are involved in every action in the world. All three suffer, as Bulgakov insisted (Gavrilyuk 2005:264), or otherwise the Trinity is divided. In this case, the action of the three have characteristic features, which, if *kenōsis* is true, are each limited in their own ways; it is in their limitations that the Persons are distinguished.

The doctrine of the Trinity is then not incompatible with the idea of *kenōsis*; but more than this, it can then contribute to its understanding. This follows from the late suggestion of *perichōrēsis,* part of the commonly accepted formula of the Trinity.

I have on the noticeboard in my office a poster put out by what was then London Bible College (now London School of Theology), where my wife did her theological training, and which I had the privilege to visit for some months in 1975 as I completed preparation for my BD. This poster comprises words commonly connected with theology. Words like "highbrow", "torture", "difficult", and "stifling" are prominent on the display. Are these descriptive of the average Christian's perception of theology? Probably so! Even in a university, mention of the subject can produce fear among Christian students. The study of theology is complicated, and can even be destructive of faith; what we need is to know God, not to think about him! We need experience, and if we try to think about that experience too much, the one certainty is that we will kill it.

It must be admitted that it is very easy for theology to be of such a sort that it is guilty of all of those accusations and very many more. It can become detached from the real world of Christian living, and if so it must deserve to die. It is said that at the eventual end of the Roman empire in the East, a millennium after Rome had fallen in the East, the Moslem besiegers were about to breach the walls of Constantinople, while in the city, in the cathedral of St Sophia, the theologians were intensely debating how many angels could dance on the head of a pin!

But theology does not have to be like that. All it really is can be encapsulated in the Latin phrase, *fides quaerens intellectum*, "faith seeking understanding". It comes from the realisation that if we understand something, we are much more likely to be able to accept it as true. And certainly the heart of the Christian message is incredible; how can it be that God himself has come to earth and become a human being, then died for us? Certainly that needs a lot of explanation before a thinking person is able to accept it.

It is here that those complicated theological words that comprise the theme of this chapter come into play, for they are all intimately linked to the concept of the incarnation. *Kenōsis*, on the one hand, is the "emptying" of the second Person of the Godhead, just so he can take human nature and associate with us, while *perichōrēsis* is the inter-relating of the Persons of the Trinity, even while one is incarnate. But perhaps even more important here is the little word that comes between them, that we are so used to that we hardly notice it is there, the copulative "and". I want to suggest that these two ideas can be connected, and that by this connection, the concept of the incarnation can be clarified.

This is really what theology is all about, or should be. The big danger of religion is to take an idea, and rejoice in it, but to lift it right out of context, and so to get it wrong. This is exactly what happened in that most theological of concepts, that of the Trinity. Many Christians, and even theological students, are secretly convinced that the doctrine of the Trinity is just an idea dreamt up because it is complicated, a mere theological conundrum, a product of human ingenuity and philosophy, especially the Greek sort of the fourth century. However, it is really only a theological synthesis, an explanation of what God must be like if the various pieces of information about God that are found in the Bible are to be reconciled. Over the first few centuries, Christian thinkers battled to understand how such aspects as the uncompromising monotheism, particularly of the Old Testament, but also definitely present in the New, could possibly be consistent with the realisation that Jesus Christ was divine, totally divine, equal yet distinct from, his Father. The fascinating account of how this was worked out in the context of the seemingly inevitable personal and political wranglings, is a part of the history of theology. And also of the Church, for it is always worked out in a social context, and its particular expression and emphasis will be affected by it. Again, theology is an expression of relation, this time of concepts to the context of the day.

The concept of *perichōrēsis* was brought in to explain what was otherwise quite a fundamental difficulty in understanding the Trinity. How could the three Persons be totally equal, yet distinct, for once they are distinct, they can surely not be equal? *Perichōrēsis*, or in its closest

English equivalent, "interpenetration" is the idea that the Persons are mutually involved in each other to such a degree that they are equal. In the Trinity, each Person is limited, but the limitations are overcome by the interrelation between them in *perichōrēsis*. They are fully open to each other (Torrance 1996:153, Moltmann 2001b:140). The distinctiveness of Jesus is not so much his teaching and acts, but his total openness to God (Peacocke 1993:316). This means that every action of God, even if it is through one of the Persons, has the total involvement of the other two. This was not just put forward as a neat theological idea, but, as with the idea of *kenōsis*, was believed to be based on the Scriptures, in this case especially John 14:11. The Fathers were always concerned to develop their theology in accordance with the scriptures.

It must be noted here that the context of John 14:11, so of *perichōrēsis*, is of the nature of Jesus in the incarnate state. This is the same point that pertains to Jesus' remark that "the Father is greater than I" (Jn 14:28), which is true only for the economic Trinity, so in the incarnation, and does not refer, as Arius thought, to the immanence, the essential nature of God. What this then means is that even in the incarnation, even in a state of *kenōsis*, Jesus remained true and essential God, due to the complete relation to the other Persons through *perichōrēsis*.

But then the theology reflects back on the understanding of the texts. That reference in John 14:11, "I am in the Father and the Father in me" can now be understood more fully, just because of *perichōrēsis*. It is then possible to go to the other key concept, *kenōsis*, and to suggest that this term, which has in the past been very contentious, is better understood because of the idea of *perichōrēsis*. It must be stressed at the beginning that it is not just a matter of bringing together two unrelated concepts, but that they are connected through the idea of Trinity. Thus Moltmann (2001b:141) affirms that the inner-trinitarian *kenōsis* is part of the inner-trinitarian *perichōrēsis*.

Whereas *perichōrēsis* is the means by which the Persons of the Trinity relate to each other and so maintain their essential natures, this demands the self-giving, the *kenōsis*, of each Person. *Kenōsis* is then naturally the means by which the Persons, especially the second, relate to the creation, especially humanity, and again, so that both the humanity and the second Person maintain their essential natures. It is just because of the nature of humanity that *kenōsis* was necessary at all. In order to relate to a fallen humanity, it was absolutely essential for the second Person to limit the expression of his divinity. Both *kenōsis* and *perichōrēsis* imply mutual interaction, so openness, in that each of the elements of the relationship affects the other.

Understanding God primarily in the relational category of *perichōrēsis*, rather than in substantively, strengthens the acceptance of the idea of *kenōsis* as a real self-limitation of especially the second Person. Seeing it in these terms, as a restriction in relation, may well be more satisfactory than as the removal of attributes, which need not be affected. Indeed, a constantly recurring criticism of traditional theology, particularly pertinent to the Trinity, is its expression in terms of substance. It is this which generates so many of its difficulties. Modern thinking is however generally more sympathetic to seeing the nature of something in terms of relation (Pinnock 2001:79). A human being is such as he or she relates to others and the environment in a human way; a solitary person is effectively less than human. God is divine not just as he has divine attributes, but because he relates divinely. It is of course the case that *perichōrēsis* is a relational term, and, as suggested above, the same is basically true of *kenōsis*.

Such an approach is especially pertinent to the Christian concept of God, for the Trinity is fundamentally relational. Indeed, there is a strand which sees the difference between the Persons simply as differences in relation. This means that these relations in the immanent Trinity are not essentially changed by the addition of other relationships, which are however limited. More pertinently, the essential relationships to the other Persons did not change when the second Person became incarnate, relating to humanity, even though they must be affected. A man does not change his basic relationships to other people, so his humanity, when he becomes a father, even though they must be affected. Nevertheless, the relationship to his child undergoes considerable alteration over time, and, significantly, must always involve self-limitation.

This mutual influence is reflected in the parallel to *perichōrēsis* that applies in the case of the incarnation. The two natures in Christ are believed to mutually affect each other, an idea known in this case as the *communicatio idiomatum*. Thus the humanity of Christ also experiences limitation. Such an appreciation of *kenōsis* in the wider sense makes the acceptance of the *kenōsis* of the Son easier, and then strengthens the assertion of Paul in Philippians 2 that this should be a fundamental characteristic of real humanity, for this is part of being *imago Dei*. This immediately means that Christians should be more fully motivated to imitate what is then a fundamental characteristic of Christ as God, in their own divinisation (2 Pet 1:4), or adoption as children of God, partaking in his nature.

Chapter 6

Creation as *kenōsis*

It has been suggested that *kenōsis* is not just an act of the Son in his incarnation, but it is an act of all the Persons, so of the Father, which implies that creation is kenotic. There must be some hesitation here which arises insofar as the New Testament portrays the Son as the agent of creation (1 Cor 8:6); however it does identify the Father as the creator, as held in traditional theology. Moltmann (1981:112) explains that the Father created the universe out of love for the Son, and therefore through him. It is also often said that the action of God even in the Old Testament is that of the Son, in a pre-incarnate state; this is because it is the nature of the Father is to be apart and transcendent. It may also be observed that the Philippian passage does not in fact see creation as one of the steps of the *kenōsis* of the Son. Nevertheless, Moltmann (1981:114) links the two in that creation was a necessary precursor for the incarnation. Macquarrie (1978:27) then says that if creation is indeed a sharing and a limitation, then incarnation is actually a logical development of that. In this case, the *kenōsis* of the Son in incarnation is done in parallel to the *kenōsis* of the Father (Pinnock 2001:58); the same would be true of creation.

Creation as self-limiting

Simply by creating an entity with a measure of independence, God has restricted his own freedom. He withdrew, becoming fully transcendent (Bulgakov, in Gavrilyuk 2005:259). Brunner (1952:20) writes that, "He limits Himself by the fact that the world over against Himself is a real existence." As Tillich points out, if God does not include the finite, he is limited (Fiddes 1988:252). Moltmann (1985:79) also points out that the act of creation is necessarily kenotic, as by choosing one form of creation, God rejected other possibilities; Moltmann (2001b:145) in fact suggests that God's prior determination to create is already a *kenōsis*. Creation is then not an act of expansion by God, but his limitation (Pinnock 2001:31, Richard 1997:138). Moltmann (eg 1985:86) in particular has popularised the understanding of creation as kenotic. He cites the *zimsum* (sometimes written *zimzum* or *tsimtsum*) idea of Isaac Luria, a sixteenth century Jewish mystic of the Kabbalah (Richard 1997:139), that God concentrates himself, as in the *shekinah*. This may be seen as a contraction of his omnipresence, giving space for another entity (Taylor 1992:193). Harries (1991:2) cites the delightful old Jewish metaphor that "God picked up the skirts of his clothing to create a tiny space where he was not, in order that there might be a space where free creatures could live". Whether this is a real parallel is however debatable; because God is Spirit, he can be present everywhere (Ps 139:7), while at the same time his total being may be present in a limited space, as in the incarnation. Fretheim (1984:62f) prefers to speak of God's omnipresence, while being specially present as in the Temple, and also relatively absent, but without absence being total. Nevertheless, Moltmann's point is that in the establishing of an entity apart from himself, God has curtailed his own freedom; it is such a limitation that Fretheim (1984:36) affirms. Thus the real limitation is not spatial, but volitional.

Peacocke (1993:308) points out that modern science supports the connection between *kenōsis* and creation. The very nature of the world demonstrates a fundamental unpredictability in many systems of the world; they are simply uncontrolled by their context. At the same time Fiddes points out that the structure of the world involves suffering, which he relates back to the suffering of God himself (in Peacocke 1993:127). Such suffering is a direct result of God's self-limitation in creating a world of that nature.

The *kenōsis* of Christ was a voluntary act, by his free choice. Similarly, Moltmann (1981:105) emphasises that Christian doctrine has always been that creation is an act of God's will, so by his free choice, and not a necessary aspect of his nature. It is interesting that the Hebrew word *bārā'* is very similar in sound to *bārāh*, which means choice. The Fathers, notably, of course, Athanasius, contrasted generation as an act of God's nature, so eternal, with creation, which is not eternal, and an act of will (Richard 1997:220). Simone Weil explains that "creation is abdication. But he is all-powerful in this sense, that his abdication is voluntary. He knows its effects and wills them" (in Taylor 1992:193). Creation is not so much an act of power, but of love and generosity (Richard 1982:260). This means that it must be kenotic, for any expression of love, whether in incarnation or creation, is necessarily self-giving. Interestingly, in Russian Orthodoxy, which has influenced Moltmann, it is not God's power but his love that is almighty (Moltmann 2001b:149). God's restriction in creation, as his choice of Abraham and Israel, is for the ultimate benefit of all.

Emphatically, God's creative act is not an inherent limitation, so meets the objections raised against the earlier proposals of kenotic Christology made by Thomasius and Gore. On the contrary, it is quite consistent with the traditionally held divine omnipotence, for if God is free to do everything, he is also free to limit his own freedom. Kierkegaard felt that only unlimited power could limit itself; God never appears mightier than in limitation (Moltmann 2001b:148). In contrast, process theology treats limitation as necessary, not voluntary (Barbour 2001:12). Here Sanders (1998:226) reiterates that God's limitation is in no way a contradiction of divine sovereignty, but even observes that; "if it is impossible for God to make himself contingent on the decisions of creatures, then God is limited." In fact, in creation, as in the incarnation, God has made himself a servant (Richard 1997:139); God has to act in the world for it to survive, and therefore is subject to it.

In favour of the idea of creation as *kenōsis*, Coakley (2001:200) cites human freedom, science, theodicy and love. The question that I also want to address is whether there is any Biblical justification for the idea, which naturally locates a focus for the discussion in the Old Testament. As McGrath (1997:267) points out,

> The doctrine of God as creator has its foundations firmly laid in the Old Testament (e.g. Genesis 1,2). In the history of theology, the doctrine of God the creator has often been linked with the authority of the Old Testament.

Significantly, the Philippian passage itself, while focussing on salvation, is firmly rooted in the Old Testament, with its conclusion echoing Isaiah 45:23, a passage which concentrates on creation. Indeed, it may also be observed that the creation of Israel as a nation was by means of their salvation (Dyrness 1979:65); Paul treats salvation as a "new creation" (2 Cor 5:17). Anderson (1967:94) notes that the interest of the "creation psalms, such as Psalm 104, is soteriological. This links creation with *kenōsis*.

It should then just be noted that Moltmann's affirmation finds its context in human suffering, and would be seen against the background of the intense experiences of the second World War. Human suffering, as creation, is due to God's self-limitation; it must then be noted that God was satisfied with what he had done; Genesis 1 repeatedly uses the phrase "God saw that it was good". *Kenōsis* has also found sympathetic reception in other contexts, as in Latin American liberation theology, and by no means least, in the experiences associated with *apartheid*. Moltmann is then not alone in finding it difficult to conceive of a God who is totally detached from the human experiences of suffering, but rather participates in them. This contrasts with the traditional Christian idea of an "apathetic" God, one who cannot, by very nature, suffer (or be limited), an idea which does come from human speculation, and which is increasingly questioned (Macleod 1998:263). At the same time, an understanding of the "pathos" of God has found an Old Testament home, notably in the teachings of Heschel, who Fretheim (1984:32) observes is one of the most often cited Old Testament scholars. He does however exclude suffering from the innermost being of God (Fiddes 1988:111). More recently the idea is stressed in Fretheim himself and Brueggemann. The latter indeed refers to the Philippians 2 passage (Brueggemann 1982:82). All portray God as actively sharing in the sufferings of Israel. So often in the Old Testament comes the expression of God's desire or longing for something, but without actually enacting it; his desire remained unfulfilled (cf Fretheim 1984:46).

The nature of creation

It is the act of origination that can particularly be seen as a *kenōsis*, as producing matter distinct, or separate, from God; this means a real beginning for the universe. More than this, the specific acts of creation can also be seen in similar terms, so of separation.

The concept of *kenōsis* in creation follows from the traditional understanding of *creatio ex nihilo*, that the created universe did have a beginning, and that the cause of that beginning was God. *Creatio ex nihilo* is an origination, not the forming of already existing material. Blocher (1984:61) notes the suggestion of Young who observes the similarity between the first two words of Genesis 1, which share the same Hebrew letters. For Eichrodt (1967:104), *b*ᵉ*rēsiyt* is an absolute beginning (also Anderson 1967:111); *bārā'* then carries the connotation of actively originating, so means primary, *ex nihilo* creation (von Rad 1963:47). Cochrane (1984:18) insists that there is no Biblical warrant for the existence of anything prior to creation, or it would not be a "beginning".

Biblical defence of *creatio ex nihilo* is usually from the New Testament, mainly Hebrews 11:3 (eg Grudem 1994:263). Romans 4:17 is also adduced. Genesis does not demand it (Sanders 1998:41), and the doctrine was not formalised until 2 Maccabees 7:28 (Scheffczyk 1970:7). König (1988:102) can assert that it is not necessarily Biblical. The idea has also been queried dogmatically; in the post Old Testament world view, matter came to be seen as inherently evil, so it was felt that it could not be the result of creation by a good God (McGrath 1997:286). Fergusson (1998:24) also notes that there is no obvious reason why it should have happened at a particular point in time if God eternally willed it. On the other hand, Grudem (1994:264) says that without *creatio ex nihilo* the ideas of God's independence and sovereignty are compromised; this of course relates to the very point at issue. He also says otherwise the uniqueness of worship would be denied. This latter is a strong argument in Isaiah 40f; the prophet ridicules worship of anything, so an idol, that is blatantly manufactured.

Biblically, it is only God who creates; people cannot create in the full sense. This is because of the power necessary; traditionally it has been felt to be an act of omnipotence, hence process theology rejects *creatio ex nihilo* (Moltmann 1985:78). The latter also puts God very much into the world, not so distinct from it (Boyd 2001:277). In fact, as a created thing, even the universe is finite, so creating requires only a finite, albeit large, amount of power; nevertheless, of course, creating, at least anything of significance, is not possible for people at present. People can form already existing matter, but creating *ex nihilo* is only possible for God. Eichrodt (1967:103) notes that the verb *bārā'* never has an accusative; there is no material already present which is being formed. Macquarrie (1978:3) suggests that creation implies a more personal relationship than the idea of making, which can be a very impersonal act. He suggests a parallel in artistic "creation", including the idea of caring. If this point is valid, which cannot really find definite Biblical support, then *bārā'* particularly implies a self-limitation, as a relation must do. Perhaps the idea of making, in contrast, rather involves dominion over what is made; in this regard it may be noted that *bārā'* is used in Genesis 1:1, but then also of the human couple (Gen 1:27), who are themselves given dominion. The same word is used in subsequent references (Gen 2:3, 5:1,2, 6:7). Nevertheless, although the rest of the creation is "made", *bārā'* is also used of the sea animals (Gen 1:21); perhaps this reflects a feeling that they are outside of human dominion, but that they rule over that sphere of creation. Certainly that was true in the time of the Old Testament and indeed still basically pertains. König (1988:18) notes the very common feeling of insecurity, even fear, when confronted with the darkness and the sea. Alternatively, if von Rad (1963:54) and Cochrane (1984:17) are correct in seeing Genesis 1:1 as a title or summary rather than a separate event, then *bārā'* is really used only of the origin of entities with which it is possible to have a relationship (von Rad 1963:54), those which have a measure of real freedom from God. Risk is then inherent in creation, hence the "lamb slain from the foundation of the world" (Peacocke 2001:41). Once again, the term carries the implication of his *kenōsis*.

Here it must be immediately said that modern science does in general support the concept of a distinct beginning, giving it a date of some 13,5 billion years ago. The universe would appear to be expanding from an origin, and, moreover, the speed of its expansion is greater than the escape velocity; Barbour (2001:16) gives some of the evidence. The latter point means that even if the speed of expansion is decreasing due to gravity, it will never decrease to zero. There will be no "big crunch" initiating a further "big bang" (Barbour 2001:16). The origin was a unique event, and so a real origination, not one of an infinite series of new beginnings experienced by eternal matter. Moreover, the concept of entropy indicates the reality of time; the devolving into increasing chaos indicates a real start. Brunner (1952:32) comments that the Greek philosophy of a world with no beginning is "clearly in conflict with modern scientific knowledge".

This also means that the universe is not infinite. Moltmann (1985:158) says it would then be divine; he speaks of it as "indefinite". Indeed, limitation is a characteristic of the world that God made. The universe is not infinite spatially, and certainly not temporally. Then the animate creation is restricted, manifesting in limited quantities in a limited number of species. Nature is inherently limited (Boyd 2001:278). In this case, it would be expected that limitation is a characteristic also of humanity as specifically in *imago Dei*.

Perhaps it may be added here that modern science also supports the notion of inherent freedom in creation. Murphy and Ellis (1996:36) suggest that "a basic element of free will enters through the openness of quantum uncertainty in microscopic systems."

The implication of *creatio ex nihilo*, which is taken up by such as Moltmann, is of a fundamental distinction of the creation from God. The world is then emphatically secular, with no divinity present in the material; there are no sacred cows (König 1988:20f). "For creation to take place, God must be free and distinct from the world, and that is the case only with the God of Genesis" (Blocher 1984:61). This stands in contrast to the accounts of creation common to the Ancient Near East, whereby the material is made from pre-existent material, usually the divine, either by emanation or from the bodies of dead deities, and people are descended from the gods (König 1988:122). The Babylonian myth, *Enuma Elish*, the "only extensive creation epic", relates the conflict of Marduk with the forces of Chaos and their defeat; the corpse of the monster Tiamat is the material for construction of the world (Eichrodt 1967:113-4). It is often felt that the Genesis account reflects these ideas, and describes an arrangement of already existing material. If this model is true, then matter is then essentially eternal (Eichrodt 1967:99).

It may be observed that *bārā'* is sometimes used of activities, which although creative in a wider sense, are both later and do not necessarily bear the sense of *creatio ex nihilo*; König (1988:121) cites its use in Psalm 104:30 and Isaiah 48:7. Some other passages may be taken to reflect a belief in a primordial battle; Brunner (1952:10) sees hints of this in Psalms 104:7 and 74:13. Scheffczyk (1970:14) adds others (Ps 77:17, 89:10, Is 51:9f). Nevertheless, Scheffczyk (1970:14) asserts that the Old Testament reveals no mythological concept of creation. Blocher (1984:60) says that it is only the Biblical account which made such a radical separation from the current mythologies. Citing Isaiah 34:11, 40:17 and Jeremiah 4:23, Eichrodt (1967:105) says that the emphasis in Genesis 1:1 is on the absence of any real prior existence. Eichrodt (1967:114) also notes the poetic nature of the Babylonian epic and the Psalms; he characterises reference in the latter as "isolated poetic ornament". Isaiah 45:7 affirms that God is the creator of all, not the bringer of good from an evil chaos (Brunner 1952:10). In the same way, Blocher (1984:160) points out that the Biblical view, in contrast to the myths, is that evil is not inherent to humanity, but a result of choice. Von Rad (1963:48,63) insists that there no suggestion of conflict ideas in Genesis 1; Westermann (1974:40) concurs, although hints at a pale reflection of Tiamat in *t^ehōm*, the "deep" (Gen 1:2). Hyers (1984:65) observes that this is not specifically said to have been created; Eichrodt (1967:102) however notes that Proverbs 8:22f includes the "depths", $t^e h\bar{o}m\bar{o}t$, in the things which were not yet in existence, and that this is implied also in Psalm 148:3-5. Barth's comment is then appropriate, "hostile non-being exists not before but by virtue of God's denial and exclusion of it" (Blocher 1984:64). In this regard, König (1988:120) suggests that an Old Testament perspective is then of creation "against", rather than "out of", nothing; God's activity affirms and promotes life and existence against the forces that destroy. Here the false deities are described as "nothing" (eg 1 Sam 12:21).

However, even if the Old Testament view of creation excludes a mythical conflict and pre-existent material, it does not exclude a suggestion that Genesis 1:1 refers to the original creation of matter in an unformed, chaotic state, and that the rest of the narrative after Genesis 1:2 describes an arrangement of this. The first two verses are then distinct, but more than just a title or summary (von Rad 1963:54), describe "creation proper". This was held by some of the early Christian Fathers, such as Justin (Brunner 1952:36). A "created chaos" would be the same as creation *ex nihilo*; for Eichrodt (1967:101), even where a watery chaos seems to precede the actual creation, the implication is the same. It may be noted that 2 Peter 3:5 talks of the creation being from water, so from an original material. Water, as in the flood narrative, can be seen as de-creative, destructive, an apt picture of chaos. This is then an affirmation, common to the Old Testament, that God is the ultimate source of all, including the forces that destroy, hence also he created (*bārā'*) the sea monsters (Gen 1:21).

Nevertheless, von Rad (1963:46) comments that "the notion of a created chaos is a contradiction"; he believes that an absolute chaos, without any form, cannot really be said to have existence. However, such a statement must be questionable, simply because it rules out the existence of God himself! The same is true for Hyers (1984:64), who cites Childs, "It is rather generally acknowledged that the suggestion of God's first creating a chaos is a logical contradiction and must be rejected. Also unsatisfactory is the ancient attempt to picture the chaos as the first stage in the creation since the obvious scheme of the seven-day creation is thereby destroyed."

A variant of this theory is the belief that an original creation suffered a disaster, associated with the fall of the devil, which could then have produced a chaos; in this case the rest of Genesis 1 describes a reconstruction rather than an ongoing process. Often this has taken the form of a "gap theory", which has been an attempt to suggest a timescale more compatible with Genesis; the geological ages then belong to the original creation. Blocher (1984:43) concurs with von Rad (1963:48) and dismisses this idea as "quite impossible"! Hyers (1984:40) derides it as relying on an argument from silence. However, this objection need not apply to the basic idea of a created chaos.

If the creation in the absolute sense is confined to the first verse of Genesis, it is possible to see the six days of the rest of the chapter in two groups of three. Vriezen (1960:186) draws attention to the repeated occurrence of threeness in the narrative, as in the number of types of animals, or of heavenly objects. The enigmatic reference to the earth being "without form and void" *tohu wabohu*, (Gen 1:1) can be seen in this light, especially as the first word is used of idols. Hyers (1984:69) then identifies a primordial three in the darkness, the watery deep and the formless earth of Genesis 1:2. He (1984:67) stresses that they are not evil as such, but ambiguous, the source of both life and death, but emphatically amorphous and empty. These are then not so much created, but overcome. God's work in the first three days is of giving form, so counteracting *tohu*, formlessness, ineffectiveness, (cf Is 40:23), in the latter three respectively filling them with life, so counteracting *bohu*, emptiness (Houston 1980:60). Interestingly Cassuto (1961:21) translates the latter as "without life". In this case, despite Blocher (1984:65), the second, *bohu*, is not just there to reinforce the first. Dyrness (1979:66) comments that the Genesis contrast is not between existence and non-existence, which is how the modern West tends to think, but between power and impotence.

It might just be observed here that it is the heavenly bodies that then "rule" the light; seen in the context of the denial of their divinity by Genesis (Hyers 1984:44), there is an acknowledgement of their "life", well before an appreciation of nuclear fusion, even that they "rule"! Their role is thus very consistent with a theme of God's *kenōsis* in order to give dominion. This would also explain a feature of Genesis 1 that has elicited repeated comment, in that light was made first, while the sun and stars were only made later (eg Cochrane 1984:20). It has been felt that this is unscientific. However, it is more likely that what was made in 1:3 was energy as a principle, while the specific luminaries were made later. In the process of *kenōsis*, the first act of God was to make energy independent of himself, and later make independent substance. This would be consistent with the normal scientific view, as in the "big bang" theory. The view that light here means understanding is unlikely (Houston 1980:51), despite the understandable metaphor; such allegory is unnecessary, and could even open the door to a form of Arianism. Incidentally, the same principle is true of time, which was made before the heavenly bodies by which its passing is observed (Anderson 1967:112); they then do not have inherent control over time, and are servants of God who made them.

The idea of overcoming chaos has some affinity to the most widely accepted modern view of origins, that of evolution. The latter has contributed to doubts over the Biblical account of creation; Fergusson (1998:1) comments that the idea of creation was never a matter for great controversy or heresy until the debates over evolution. Christian reaction has been mixed, but it may be suggested that evolution, especially viewed as God-guided, is not incompatible with the Biblical account, especially as a mechanism after an initial creation. Hyers (1984:33) goes so far as to suggest that the freedom of the created means that religious and scientific language are different; as is often pointed out, the Bible is not a scientific text. Moltmann (1985:100) sees the Spirit as the creator of possibilities, so the principle of evolution. As such it is not inconsistent with *kenōsis*, especially as God has given a measure of freedom to the world (cf Peacocke 2001:21), although it must be noted that the mechanism of evolution depends on an attitude contrary to it; biology is self-seeking (Rolston 2001:44), although de Waal notes that aiding others at a cost is common among animals (Jeeves 2001:66). Richard (1997:148) also notes that in evolution, progress is made by means of suffering and death; although as this is involuntary, it is not really *kenōsis*.

Of course, as Westermann (1974:7) insists, the idea of creation is rich, and can be presented by means of many pictures. Possibly the idea of a conflict with chaos, which was the Babylonian belief, became meaningful in the exilic situation, especially as it was significant in terms of Israel's liberation (Westermann 1984:37), so became reflected in its poetry. Israel reinterpreted the mythical symbolism, understanding creation historically (Anderson 1967:172). In this case conflict need not be seen as the fundamental concept of creation, and then in no way negates the implication of *kenōsis*. The emphasis in Genesis falls on creation by God's word; von Rad (1962:142) sees this as an interpretation of *bārā'*, and notes that this was also the method used by Marduk. As well as stressing God's power, this method implies that it was a specific act of will, or choice (Eichrodt 1967:100); this is consistent with an act of self-limitation.

In fact, any creation does imply some form of conflict, although not in a mythical sense. In the removal of chaos, the imposition of order, comes a limitation. Psalm 104:5 speaks of establishing the creation, so its limiting, again an aspect of *kenōsis*. Creation by conflict with chaos is quite compatible with *kenōsis*. In fact, even *creatio ex nihilo* implies the rejection, the "killing off" of other possibilities, itself a *kenōsis*, including that of continued nothingness. Any creation means change. What however tends to be enhanced by reference to conflict is rather divine power, and it can be easily forgotten that power may well be expressed in *kenōsis*. There are many Old Testament occasions where this is true, as in Gideon's victory over Midian (Jdg 7). Another common idea was that of creation by birth, which although equally poetic, tends to lose the idea of difference between God and the creation, although it better bears the sense that the process necessarily means a self-limitation, as any parent is well aware.

Whether or not there was pre-existent material, possibly existing in chaos, it is clear that repeatedly in Genesis 1 come God's actions in separating one thing from another. Creation by *kenōsis* involves the separation of matter from the divine; this rests on the divine nature itself, the distinction of the Persons from each other (cf Pinnock 1996:59). The concept of creation as separation is also found elsewhere, as in Psalm 33:6,7, and in Psalm 104:8,9,19; this emphasis is not surprising if the passage had a priestly origin, for priests are very conscious of the distinction between sacred and profane. Blocher (1984:71) stresses the importance of this concept of separation to the faith of Israel, manifesting in a variety of ways such as the distinction between clean and unclean and even today in "kosher" practices. The synagogue prayer to close each Sabbath is called *Abdala*, separation, and highlights this theme (Blocher 1984:72, citing Goldstain). Bernhardt (1977:245) suggests that separation is probably the original meaning of *bārā'*. This process involves defining, so of establishing boundaries, delimiting, indeed the removal of chaos. This is very consistent with creation by the *logos*, "word" or "order", which Hyers (1984:65) sees as the emphasis in the Genesis account. Words define, delimit, and also overcome chaos; König (1988:140) draws attention to the overcoming of chaos by the word in the Psalms. Here Psalm 89, which refers to the mythical victory over chaos, links it with the establishment of the Davidic throne, also as a means of giving order (cf Fergusson 1998:5). Blocher (1984:72) then contrasts this understanding of creation with the essential approach of paganism which is rather to merge, confuse, and eliminate distinctions, with obvious implications of little difference between moral and immoral behaviour. He notes that *Liber* was the Roman god of chaos! Ellis (2001:114) then points out that orderliness is an essential prerequisite for any real freedom.

It may be pointed out that the other account of creation in Genesis 2 does describe the origin of the first human as a secondary creation, again a rearrangement, this time of already existing dust, which is then enlivened. This difference is of course commonly viewed as originating in a different theology from that of Genesis 1, but also emphasises the making of a distinction between humanity and the rest of the creation. The stress in this account falls on the giving of life; it is here that the role of the Spirit becomes prominent (Gen 2:7), as the one who provides the inter-relationship that is the essence of life (Williams 2004:198). Blocher (1984:75) here cites Bonhoeffer that a key aspect of life is the ability to itself create life. This means the ability to give an existence independent of the one giving it, an idea very much in keeping with Moltmann. One must be reminded that the Bible repeatedly affirms that God is the "living God". Bonhoeffer also points out that life is dead unless it has freedom (Blocher 1984:75); this is only possible if God enables it by curtailing himself.

Original ordering is also demanded by entropy; order must exist for it to be able to devolve. What is important here is that any ordering of material itself requires a *kenōsis*, as any order is a limitation to one possible arrangement only. It is an emptying from beyond the defined limits. If this is taken together with an original creation, *ex nihilo*, this would then mean that creation is then a progressive series of events. As each of these is itself a *kenōsis*, the whole creation then has a nature very similar to the progressive self-limitation predicated of Christ in Philippians 2.

The earlier reference to morals also draws attention to the point that *kenōsis* is the result of an act of will. God's limitation is not inherent to him, as suggested by process theology. This is seen in the belief that creation was an act of choice, that God was not compelled to do it. This stands in contrast with the views of such as Tillich, and, to an extent, Barth and some other thinkers (König 1988:130). Likewise it was a specific event, an act of choice, God was not always creator but chose to be, a contrast with the views of such as Origen (König 1988:166).

The understanding of *kenōsis* in creation may also be supported by one noteworthy and much discussed feature of the creation account, the presence of the *rūah* "moving over the face of the waters" (Gen 1:2). It has often been suggested that this just means a wind or storm (eg von Rad 1963:47), but Blocher (1984:68) feels this to be most unlikely, both on the grounds of the descriptor "of God", but also of the verb, which pertains to the action of a bird fluttering or brooding, and not that of a blowing wind. This identification is particularly significant as the role of the Spirit is primarily to give relationships (Williams 2004:8). Blocher (1984:69) cites Kline, who describes the *rūah* as "neither in heaven nor on earth, but between one and the other". The significance of this assertion is that the relationship produced by the Spirit is necessary because of the differentiation produced in creation. For Beaucamp, the Spirit "'balances the principle of separation by being placed at the opposite pole'; if the Word brings about diversity, the Spirit unifies" (Blocher 1984:70). The action of the Spirit is especially significant in the light of God's *kenōsis*; as this means an independence of the creation from God, there was a need to give a specific relationship between the two.

It is therefore clear that the idea of *kenōsis* is completely compatible, even demanded by the idea of creation. This is particularly the case in the traditional view of *creatio ex nihilo*, but also true for other understandings of the process of creation reflected in the Old Testament description. This conclusion is then supported by other features associated with creation.

Human dominion

As part of the creation story, Genesis recounts the creation of the primal human being. Interestingly in that it is the second account which concentrates on humanity, it is the first that indicates that people were created *imago Dei*, a term which has occasioned a great deal of discussion as to its meaning. This feature of the story would support the notion that God's creation involved *kenōsis*.

Here Blocher (1984:82) draws attention to the fact that any image does reflect the prototype, so is dependent on it. This dependence therefore implies the limitation of the image. However, the existence of the image also means that the prototype cannot alter without changing the image. In effect, by making an image, God limited himself. This means that, as limited, people image this aspect of God's nature; the obvious difference is that while God is willing to limit himself, people are less happy to do so. This could well be seen as one way in which people fall short of being in the image, that it was to an extent lost, or at least marred, at the "Fall". Many in fact have distinguished "image" from "likeness"; a recent example is the view of Pinnock (1996:174), who refers the first to creation, but the second as acquired in sanctification.

111

The image also reflects limitation as it refers only to humanity, not even being predicated of the angels, and certainly not of other animals (Blocher 1984:83). This means that God limited his own creative options in this regard; there could, at least theoretically, have been other species created which although different, could have been made in such a way as could be designated as in the image of God.

A common view has been that the image refers to the spiritual nature of humanity, but other ideas have been suggested, notably creativity (Dyrness 1979:83). The human experience is that while creative activity does enhance a person, it is at the same time an act of self-limitation, at the very least in the neglect of other activities. The same is then true of the prototype.

However, although creativity, or some other attribute, may well be a valid aspect of what is meant by the image, it is not the usual understanding of the idea. Here there are two main suggestions. Firstly, in the discussion of the meaning of the image, the suggestion of Barth (1958:195) stands out, especially as it is made in the context of Genesis 1:26, that humanity was made male and female. If the image is plural, then this may well be a feature of the prototype. Certainly the "let us make" (Gen 1:26) would seem to imply plurality.

Obviously it is not sexuality that comprises the image, even though God is frequently depicted in sexual metaphors; the stress falls on relationship. Thus Cochrane (1984:27) sees the meaning of the image not so much in a quality or attribute which it has, but what it is, so in personhood, the ability to stand in relation to God in "I-Thou" relationship. This demands the ability to respond, implying a measure of freedom, and which then demands also the *kenōsis* of the creator.

More than this, the possibility of relationship demands difference, which itself requires limitation, just as the sexual characteristics of individuals are in themselves a restriction. So just as the existence of the pair means that each individual is limited, so God is limited also. In any case, the phrase suggests deliberation, which itself implies *kenōsis*, especially in an acceptance of the other. Not only is humanity a differentiation from God, but it contains in itself a differentiation (Cochrane 1984:26). The relationship even enhances the distinctions; because of the other, each can and should restrict the characteristics of the other that they would otherwise have manifested if there were no sexual differences. Interestingly, Blocher (1984:97) can suggest that sexual duality enhances worship in an awareness of dependence. Perhaps another way of putting this, in the light of the "fall" narrative of Genesis 3, is that in the limitation of the image that strives for divinity comes the fuller appreciation of the divinity that accepts limitation.

The most accepted interpretation of the "image" today is in terms of dominion, of the authority which God gave humanity over the rest of the creation. This stands in contrast to the Babylonian *Atrahasis* myth, in which people were created specifically to serve the gods. Whereas this enhances the power of the gods, the Genesis account reflects God's deliberate self-limitation; the contrast in Genesis 2 falls on God's concern for people (Zimmerli 1978:33).

The giving of dominion is not merely a giving of power, but means that people are able to do things that God does not intend or even approve of. This is graphically seen in that soon after the story of creation comes the committing of the first sin. This is also seen elsewhere, as in the story of the establishing of kingship, which is described as contrary to what God wanted (1 Sam 8:7). Indeed it is described as a rejection of God's authority. God did not insist on his own way, but allowed action which was contrary to it. Nevertheless, in this measure of semi-autonomy came the affirmation that it was good, and the blessing of God; an approval of what was done, and so of God's own self-limitation (Blocher 1984:75).

It must be noted that the Genesis account portrays the restriction, or limitation of this dominion due to the "fall". People became subject to other powers, such as that of the plants (Gen 3:18); interestingly, Cassuto (1961:53) speaks of the dominion of plant life. Likewise came death, the limitation of life, and suffering (Blocher 1984:184); they were not inherent to humanity. It is this that prompted the further *kenōsis* of God in his participation in human experience; emphatically, unlike that of fallen humanity, this is never forced but always by choice.

Power-sharing is the other side of the granting of dominion to humanity. Indeed, it would seem that use of agency is the preferred method by which God acts. Taylor (1992:210) refers to the raising up of the judges, and of Moses. The work of the prophets is another example. Here God's reticence to appoint a king need not be from an insistence on direct rule, but from the observation that "power always corrupts" (Deut 17:17). Fretheim (1984:73f) speaks of dual agency even in creation. Psalm 33:6 indicates that this was enacted by the "word", and through the "breath (*rūah*) of his mouth". The former is consistent with the Genesis 1 account, and indeed Psalm 33 is often dated at a similar time. Then the "breath" reflects back on Genesis 2:7, even if the specific word *rūah* is not present there. The Spirit may be taken as the creator, not of any material substance, but of life.

This does not presume that the Old Testament demands a personification of word and spirit, which in contrast have generally been taken as synonyms for the power of God, but it may be noted that the Old Testament does not definitely exclude this. Nevertheless, even if this is not accepted, the fact of the agency of word and spirit still indicates a desire to safeguard the transcendence of God. (A

Christian comment here must be that the transcendence of one of the Persons is preserved, who acts through the others, who are nevertheless equally divine. Bernhardt (1977:246) notes that *bārā'* is used exclusively of divine action.) Scheffczyk (1970:8) adds that creation by agency then excludes any hint of either emanation or pantheism, so preserving the distinction from God himself. This distinction from the material creation is a measure of self-restriction.

Covenant

The granting of dominion in Genesis 1 can be seen as the first of a series of covenants established throughout the period of the Old Testament. Creation is the first covenant (Cronin 1992:257). More than in the specific case of Genesis 1:26, the very idea of covenant presumes limitation, and a limitation by choice. The nature of a covenant is that it was a real historical event. God involved himself in the historical process by initiating covenant, which means that he tied himself to particular events; this is a form of *kenōsis*. This strongly suggests that creation is also understood as a definite occurrence, whether single or as a series. Indeed, even if it is felt that language about creation is different from the scientific (Anderson 1967:81), which could imply that the historicity of creation must, in a sense be different from subsequent history, the creation faith of Israel points to a decisive historical event (Anderson 1967:106). As with other kenotic acts, he took this step for the sake of relationship (Sanders 1998:61). Oliphint (2004:43) interestingly links the establishing of covenant to the fact that God "came down"; he cites the Westminster Confession of Faith which speaks of God's condescension expressed in covenant.

Fundamentally, covenant presumes a limitation of the agreement to one person or group of people, which must imply that it is not made with others (Deut 7:7). In the Sinai covenant, Israel is separated from other peoples (Taylor 1992:190). It is not for nothing that the Hebrew idiom means "cutting" a covenant. On the other hand, by accepting the covenant, the parties to it agree to limit their actions to those specified in the agreement. Even in the garden, the primal couple had to limit themselves by not eating the forbidden fruit. Sin is then the breaking of covenant, the transgressing of its limitations; Blocher (1984:136) sees this aspect in Hosea 6:7. Most famously, the covenant at Sinai incorporated the demands of the Law, and transgressing that law deliberately excluded the perpetrator from the benefits of the covenant (Num 15:30). The covenant with Israel involved it becoming God's servant, which anticipates the servanthood of Jesus as *doulos*, but with the privilege of the relationship of sonship as *pais*. Fretheim (1984:114), referring particularly to Isaiah 1:2, insists that the key issue is not so much disobedience but the breaking of relationship. It was, and still is, in the obedience to the covenant that Israel found its distinctiveness and identity as a people. Then at the same time, God was also limiting himself. His actions were also prescribed by the existence of the covenant.

It is also pertinent here that one of the signs of covenant was the *shekinah* (Moltmann 2001b:142), which has been seen as the "concentration" of God in one place. This withdrawal parallels the action of God in giving existence to what is created.

But covenant is closely related to creation. Cochrane (1984:13) writes that "the sequel to the act of creation is the covenant." Rather it is a part of the creation; as he continues, "creation is the work of God's love, the covenant is the expression of it." Barth (1958:231) sees covenant as the purpose of creation, as does Jacob (Dyrness 1979:68). This follows if the *kenōsis* enabling creation was done for the purpose of covenant, and the ultimate goal its *theōsis* (Ellis 2001:109). Implicit in the reference to the image of God come the associated blessing and responsibility which is fundamental to covenant. It may also be observed that in the later covenant with Noah, and still later in Jeremiah 33:20f, covenant is strongly connected with features of the creation, the regularity of seasons and of day and night. In the story of Noah, the self-limitation of God is also seen in that the destruction of the flood was not total, so God limited himself in consistency with his creative intentions, effectively in covenant with creation. Westermann (1974:17,24) in fact believes that Genesis 1-11 must be viewed as a unity and therefore that the stories of creation and flood relate; the latter results in covenant. Thus even if the actual word "covenant" is not present, many see its essential features in the creative narratives (Blocher 1984:111). Taylor (1992:190) perceives that through the prophets, the Jews saw a similarity between God's long-suffering commitment to Israel, and his relationship to the whole creation. It is not surprising that the preferred name for God in the Genesis 2 account includes the covenant name "LORD" (König 1988:23).

Incidentally, part of Westermann's reasoning rests on the parallels between Genesis 1-3 and the succeeding eight chapters. A number of times (eg 1974:28) he notes the similarity between God's questions to the fallen Adam and to Cain, "where are you?", "where is your brother?". In the Babel narrative, he goes down to investigate the situation. Elsewhere in the Old Testament, God is also described as seeking information, as in Genesis 22:12 (cf Fretheim 1984:46f). Do these not reflect a deliberate and real actual limitation of knowledge, as believed by the "open theists"?

Other covenants also relate to creation. Perhaps in particular, the institution of marriage, implicit in creation, both as a covenant between a man and woman, and as a covenant of the pair with God, needs to be highlighted. There is limitation in the leaving of parents (Gen 2:24), and even if not applicable to a primal couple, but important in later reference, the forsaking of other possible sexual relations. König (1988:32) notes the similarities between creation and the Exodus; "parallels too striking to be ignored"; an example is Isaiah 51:10. Certainly the exodus may be seen as a "new creation"; God's victory at the exodus was seen in Isaiah 40f as over chaos (Anderson 1967:127). Interestingly, the separation from captivity in Egypt was through a process of conflict in the plagues (König 1988:52). Possibly the "new covenant" of Jeremiah 31 plays the same role in the events of the exile as the giving of the law in the Sinai covenant? Thus the second part of Isaiah uses creation imagery for redemption; the return is a new creation (König 1988:58,106). This must remind the New Testament reader of 2 Corinthians 5:17. Certainly the experience of Israel in Egypt was one of *kenōsis*. This would support the insight of H-J Kraus that creation can be seen as liberation (König 1988:123). This is in the context of a victory over the power of chaos, but in the parallels, the Exodus is also obviously liberative, as was the victory of Christ on the cross. But then this too demands a form of *kenōsis*, or liberation is not real.

In this case, might it not be suggested that the enactment of covenant was part of the process of *kenōsis* started in creation? Particularly in the light of the Christian concept of the personification of Israel in Christ, the Sinai covenant can be seen as at the depths of the humiliation of Israel in Egypt, on the way to the glorification in the promised land. Just as the cross, the depths of *kenōsis*, enables salvation and re-creation, so the covenant enables the new creation of Israel. This must mean that just as covenant implies limitation, so does the creation.

Sabbath

It is significant that the covenant people took the observance of the Sabbath as one of the major features that delimited them, distinguishing and thus separating them from other peoples. It is this self-limitation in its observance that characterises them, and so which reflects their understanding of the nature of God.

This feature also relates covenant to creation. One of the most striking features of the Genesis account of creation, even dominating it (Vriezen 1960:186), is the six day pattern, and especially its culmination in the Sabbath. Cassuto (1961:14) draws attention to the number of occurrences of seven in Genesis 1, hardly coincidental; it also reflects the ordering of creation itself. This feature is unique in ancient creation stories (Westermann 1974:41). There are parallels to the Sabbath in Mesopotamia, but these were not workless days; rather the Old Testament institution (as the entire creation account) was in opposition to these, and free from any astronomical linkage (Cassuto 1961:65).

The Sabbath also indicates the self-limitation of God in his creative activity. In his resting, God ceased to work, so limiting his activity to what had been done. In fact even the very existence of days is inherently a limitation, since time is then automatically divided into distinct periods. Presumably it would have been possible to create in such a way that this was not the case, and indeed the Revelation 21 account of the new creation, in which *kenōsis* has been reversed, does indicate a situation in which there is no alternation of light and darkness. The existence of days, periods of light in which work is normally done, and darkness, in which it is usually difficult to work, puts a natural boundary on human activity. And the Genesis account does indicate that the same is true of God's activity, divided into six periods.

Even the very nature of work is a kenotic activity, insofar as when a person is working, then he or she is not doing something else; there is a limitation to the specific activity. In this sense, the fact that God did create the world over a period of time and not by an instantaneous *fiat* then demonstrates this aspect.

Moltmann (1985:276) interestingly sees the Sabbath as the goal of creation. God moved from being creator to expressing his Lordship over it (Cochrane 1984:28); similarly the Philippian hymn sees the culmination of Christ's *kenōsis* in his Lordship. In observing Sabbath, God's sovereignty is confessed. The aim is rest, a feature taken up again in the New Testament book of Hebrews, one most related to the Old Testament. The existence of the Sabbath, like the alternation of day and night, puts a limitation on time, although this is something that must be definitely complied to by people. Day and night is a feature that we cannot escape, but if we keep Sabbath, it is by choice, a willing self-limitation on activity.

Implications

The open theism lobby has tended to major on the implications of their beliefs for Christian practice, as it impinges on such fundamentals as assurance and prayer. Even if the understanding of creation can seem detached from life, which is why it could be neglected in the early faith of Israel, it was quickly realised to be important for practice, especially in conditions of hardship. The Jews in exile could draw great strength from an affirmation of God's ability in creation, and so of the creation of a new situation for them.

They were painfully aware that God had limited himself, but could take courage from a realisation that God suffered with them (Fretheim 1984:127f), and then that this was ultimately done for the sake of their salvation. This is of course the affirmation of Philippians 2.

Chapter 6a

Evolution through *kenōsis*

If God's creation is compatible with, and even a result of, his kenotic nature, this suggests a further intriguing possibility. If God has limited himself to allow the possibility of the existence of entities outside of himself, then he could well also have limited himself in the way in which those entities came about. In this case, rather than God directly creating everything, it is a possibility that in his *kenōsis*, he allowed the process known as evolution, one of the most widely accepted ideas in the modern world. Indeed, with qualifications, evolution and *kenōsis* may well be compatible ideas.

It was inevitable that, in the stirrings known as the *Aufklärung*, or Enlightenment, the Biblical account of origins, understood in a literal way, would become increasingly questioned. Not only was there a growing unwillingness to accept the account of creation presented in the first chapter of Genesis simply on the basis of authority, but the expanding amount of scientific evidence pointed to a far earlier origin for the world and for life, and that rather than being created in forms at least similar to what exists today, life-forms had evolved from earlier primitive species. The new way of thinking, despite almost total acceptance in the scientific world and then in society in general, nevertheless engendered considerable opposition from those who accepted the literal truth of the Bible. Grudem (1994:275f) notes several theological objections, such as the lack of purposeness in naturalistic evolution (also Gitt 2006:15). Without a belief that God created, there is a danger of losing meaning and purpose in life (Spanner 1987:14); to this could be added security. "The spectre of a godless uncaring world haunts the fundamentalist" (Ford 1986:93). Controversy is still by no means stilled, perhaps especially in the classroom, where legal wrangles have enforced the continued teaching of creation as a scientific theory beside that of evolution in many places. Numbers (2006) documents the course of the controversy.

What must be stressed is that despite the evidence for evolution, this falls short of proof, and there remain weighty objections to the idea, and not just that evolution, on at least the macro scale involving speciation, has not been demonstrated. Evolution falls short of the verification that scientific rigour demands (Johnson 1995:11). It is at best a hypothesis, questioned by several experimental factors (Andrews 1980:89). Johnson (1993) outlines the major problems; for example, the fossil record just does not show the gradual changes that would be expected from the theory, but rather gaps and stability (Davis & Kenyon 1989:92, also Gould, in Johnson 1993:50). Denton (1986:185) refers to "the remarkable lack of any direct evidence for major evolutionary transformations in the fossil record". Darwin felt that this was the gravest objection to his theory (Davis & Kenyon 1989:94). Then it so far fails to explain several essential things, such as the emergence of cells or consciousness (1995:66,70), the existence of life (1995:108), and even matter itself. It is commonly observed that the origin of genes, essential for life, require proteins which themselves demand life (Davis & Kenyon 1989:51, Spanner 1987:104). Thus "there is serious difficulty with the idea that living cells evolved by natural means from a primitive organic soup" (Davis & Kenyon 1989:55). Likewise Denton (1986:323) details the incredible improbability of the self-generation of life, and Larmer (2006:56) comments that naturalism is inadequate due to the complexity of even simple life. Gitt (2006:13) cites Kahane, a French molecular biologist: "it is absurd and absolutely preposterous that a living cell could come into existence by itself"; however, he does continue: "but, notwithstanding, I do believe it, because I cannot imagine anything else"! More than this, as even Dawkins admits, living organisms give the appearance (or "illusion") of having been designed (Johnson 1995:90). As Jones and Tyler point out (2005:229), there is "accumulating evidence for design" in the universe; Thaxton (1989:157) significantly points out that the search for extra-terrestrial life is actually a search for evidence of design. Then the much-vaunted changes within species, due to environmental change, may be seen not so much as evidence for genetic change, but for genetic preservation (Johnson 1993:26); Morris (1982:83) remarks that the main characteristic of life is not change, but stability. This feature is readily explicable in terms of Mendelian genetics (Davis & Kenyon 1989:9). Darwin admitted that this view of heredity is incompatible with the theory of natural selection (Davis & Kenyon 1989:60). Micro-evolution may well be well-accepted (Harbin 1997:641), as in the well-known case of the peppered moth (Davis & Kenyon 1989:60), but this does not prove macro-evolution! Most mutations are also disadvantageous (Johnson 1993:38, Morris 1982:85). Moreover, while the chance of a successful mutant is very small, its continuance is even smaller (Davis & Kenyon 1989:68). Without external intervention, a change in a species, such as due to a mutation or selective breeding, naturally disappears (Johnson 1993:18). Interestingly, deliberate breeding produces greater diversity in a species than seems to occur naturally (Thaxton 1989:159). There is no evidence for change of species (Johnson 1993:19, Denton 1986:81). More importantly, even with the timescale for the earth currently proposed in science, it seems unlikely that there was enough time for the development of the current diversity of life that presently exists (Grudem 1994:284). Even more fundamentally, the process of evolution seems to be contrary to another basic principle of the universe, that of entropy (Morris 1982:22). Whereas the natural trend in all things is of deterioration, evolution is a process of improvement. In itself, evolution would then go against the normal run of things (cf Andrews 1980:74).

If it is then the case that there is hesitation about accepting naturalistic evolution alone as an explanation for the existence of things, the possibility of divine action is more reasonable. This could even be seen as suggested by the very nature of life. Fundamentally, Davis and Kenyon (1989:6) point out that the essence of life is on the basis of coded information, specifically in the DNA; "the organization in a living creature is an expression of the information carried in the genetic material of a cell" (1989:55). Here it is then significant that creation was by the agency of the *logos*, the "word" or "rationality" of God. It is not an exaggeration when the Bible indicates that the creation clearly demonstrates God's action in its origin, as in Psalm 19 and Romans 1 (Lamoureux 2007a:84-5).

Nevertheless, the evidence for evolution is so strong that there are few who are prepared to reject it totally. Lamoureux (2007b:104) uses the word "overwhelming" to describe the evidence for biological evolution. While acknowledging that a purely naturalistic explanation of origins is both highly unlikely, and not compatible with the Biblical account, many who are totally committed to the inerrancy of the Bible accept the essential idea of evolution (eg Erickson 1998:506), but usually in combination with a belief in some form of direct creation. The current world, and especially its diversity of life, would then be due to both divine action and an evolutionary process. The essential idea is not new; many in the ancient world also had a view that could accommodate evolution; for example, Augustine wrote that "in the beginning were created only germs or causes of the forms of life which were afterwards to be developed in gradual course" (Ford 1986:75).

An example of the combination of origins can be suggested for the case of Adam and Eve. While evolutionary theory must reject the Genesis account of the creation of humanity, a Biblical view demands the uniqueness of humanity. A special creation is also implied in the light of the origin of sin and the importance of Adam for the unity of humanity (cf Grudem 1994:276). Paul contrasts the figures of Adam and Christ in Romans 5. This can well be one point where God specifically involved himself; Erickson (1998:504) suggests that the material nature of Adam (the dust (Gen 2:7)) was a result of evolution, but God then created in it the spiritual aspect. Alternatively, Spanner (1987:76) argues that he was a representative human called out to fulfil God's purposes; he cites the parallel case of Abraham (1987:109).

Erickson (1998:502) indeed argues that the Christian view of God as theistic, so both transcendent and immanent, supports the idea of a combination of both special creation and a form of evolution, through which God continues to act. It must also be pointed out that the fundamental intervention of God into the world in the incarnation was through a cooperation of divine and human. There have been two main proposals for this (Larmer 2006:47), although each does have variations (Lamoureux 2007b:105). On the one hand, the suggestion is that when God created, he included laws such that evolution would proceed according to his will. On the other, God intervenes from time to time in a directly creative way in the process of evolution.

The former is sometimes presented as a way of accepting both a more literal understanding of the Biblical account and of evolution, so of "compatibilism" (Johnson 1993:128), "concordism", or of "complementarianism" (Larmer 2006:49); however, Grudem (1994:279), citing the support of L Berkhof and the geologist Davis A Young, feels that it is not consistently Christian (also Andrews

1980:51f). It is often called the theory of "theistic evolution", a bit sadly, as it rejects the specific interventions characteristic of theism. Indeed, it could well be felt that the former is not so much theistic, but deistic (cf Lamoureux 2007a:81). It would be more consistent if the term were used for the second, which is however usually called the theory of "intelligent design". Erickson (1998:506) then prefers the term "progressive creationism". Lamoureux (2007b:101) also expresses unhappiness with the term, preferring "evolutionary creationism".

The so-called theory of "theistic evolution" is often hailed as more in keeping with science, as this is felt to demand that God does not intervene in the world, or prediction is impossible (Hewlett & Peters 2006:177). Dembski (in Numbers 2006:384) comments, "when boiled down to its scientific content, theistic evolution is no different from atheistic evolution." This applies to everything, even life: "evolutionary creation claims that the Father, Son and Holy Spirit created the universe and life through an ordained and sustained evolutionary process" (Lamoureux 2007a:81). Van Till suggests that God gives the material ability to organize itself and to self-transform, that God acts naturally not supernaturally, persuades but does not coerce (Jones & Tyler 2005:227). However, this would be placing a feature into the material that is directly contrary to the process of increasing disorder that is in fact observed. In contrast, because it presumes outside intervention, "intelligent design" is often derided as inherently incompatible with the scientific method (Johnson 1995:90). By their very nature, God's actions are not amenable to scientific investigation! Pennock (2001:xi) can justly say that there have been no "intelligent design" articles in peer-reviewed scientific journals, and Sarkar (2007:xv) that "there is no credible alternative to evolutionary biology ... as science".

However, it is basic to Christianity that God does intervene, not only in miracles, but fundamentally in the incarnation. But if he has intervened in incidents recorded in the Bible, it would seem reasonable that he also did in the biological process (cf Lamoureux 2007a:89). Advocates of "intelligent design" stress the "gaps" in a scientific understanding. He does act creatively after the origin of the world (Is 43:19, Jer 31:22, and especially 2 Cor 5:17), and will at the end of this world (Rev 21:1).

The evidence is that there was not the gradual change that natural evolution would have produced; the fossil record indicates sudden jumps, the appearance of new forms (Grudem 1994:282, Lamoureux 2007b:106). Johnson (1995:87) particularly remarks on the otherwise inexplicable "Cambrian explosion", the sudden emergence of complex multicellular organisms "without apparent ancestors" from which they could have evolved. Denton (1986:163) adds that the first representatives of all major groups of plants appear already highly specialized. Then complex organs, such as wings, suddenly appear in the fossil record (Johnson 1993:35f). Indeed, complex organs cannot partially appear, or they would be dysfunctional or disadvantageous, and so would naturally disappear again; Goldschmidt has catalogued a list of structures which could not come from accumulated small variations (Johnson 1993:37). Denton (1986:213) particularly remarks that it is extremely unlikely that the avian lung or feathers could be the result of successive variations. Davis and Kenyon (1989:100) likewise say that no examples of a partial wing or partial eye have been discovered. Although Darwin believed that *natura non facit saltum*, nature does not make leaps, that is doubted by many neo-Darwinists (Ford 1986:100). Even Dawkins accepts that there have been "macro-mutations" (Johnson 1993:41). Gould postulates some sort of "fast-transition" rather than trying to explain the disappearance of a universe of transitional species, which simple evolution has demanded (Johnson 1995:88). He feels that they never existed; Spanner (1987:104) also observes that the fossil record does not indicate the great richness of extinct forms that would be demanded. Even if the fossil record does include "striking transitory forms" (Lamoureux 2007b:107), this does not prove continuous evolution, but only that these changes, however produced, did not survive.

Jones and Tyler (2005:231) point out that naturalistic evolution has a principle of continuity, but that this is an assumption, and one increasingly vulnerable in the light of the evidence of these sudden "jumps". Here it is often pointed out that Christians in the past often appealed to divine action to explain what they did not understand; Lamoureux (2007a:82) refers to Luther and even Isaac Newton. Nevertheless, seeing divine activity in these "jumps" does not have to be simply due to ignorance. Indeed Larmer (2007:6) points out that increasing knowledge has even emphasized the gaps; he cites Jesus' miracle of the loaves and fish. Davis and Kenyon (1989:96) remark that as more fossils are discovered, the gaps in the record do not lessen, but become more prominent. Larmer also states that other earlier thinkers, such as Augustine, did not posit God's intervention just on the grounds of ignorance (Larmer 2006:55). Nevertheless, the theory of intelligent design is also often criticized as "non-Biblical" (Lamoureux 2007b:113).

However, what is definitely excluded by the idea of "intelligent design" is God's continual action. He acted at specific times only; Lamoureux (2007b:102) says that the theory commonly invokes this only for the creation of the first cell, of Cambrian phyla, and of humanity, although others add the introduction of the various "kinds" of living beings (Lamoureux 2007b:111). This can then account for the evident gaps in the fossil record (Denton 1986:194). Here Eldredge and Gould argue that these are not due to inadequate observation, but from the relatively sudden appearance of new forms of life; a suggestion supported by the biochemical evidence (Davis & Kenyon 1989:39). As Denton (1986:194) points out, the suggestion that all "transitional species" were unsuccessful is incredible. At other times God allowed the ordinary processes to continue. It is then rather an exaggeration to deride intelligent design as anti-evolutionary (Lamoureux 2007b:103). This of course does not exclude the possibility that this process was in accordance with laws that he had set to govern evolution; indeed, creation must include law! In this case, "theistic evolution" and "intelligent design" can then be aspects of a total explanation. Nevertheless, unless there was total control, the creation would naturally deviate from what God wanted. He would then intervene; this is not a sign of ineptness, as the Enlightenment Deists suggested, but of God's self-limitation.

It is this limitation that is characteristic of the nature of God as kenotic. Whether creation is understood as proceeding by means of pre-set laws, as in "theistic evolution", or though a natural process and a limited number of specific interventions, as in "intelligent design", or, more satisfactorily, by a combination of those, God has limited himself. It may be suggested that the mechanism of evolution is fundamentally kenotic, a feature which might be expected if a kenotic God created it. Indeed, if life is defined in terms of coded information in DNA (Davis & Kenyon 1989:6), this must be limited, as information never can be complete. Gitt (2006:14) notes the key features of mutation, selection, isolation and mixing; the second and third are particularly kenotic. If speciation does occur, it demands limitation of relationship of changed individuals with the parent group, or any changes would be submerged (cf Johnson 1993:52). In any case, a species is something that is limited by definition, being unable to reproduce with other species (Denton 1986:51); the organization of life as God made it, "according to their kinds" (eg Gen 1:24) is inherently kenotic.

This means that God's self-limitation was not only necessary to give independent existence to what was created, as Moltmann suggested, but could well also apply to the process itself. In this case, rather than just create by divine *fiat*, God was limiting himself to allow the process of evolution to take place. Just as the creative process was kenotic in that God chose to establish laws, thereby excluding other possibilities (Andrews 1980:36), so he could well have chosen to create in such a way that evolutionary development was possible. Likewise, in his *kenōsis*, there could be real chance; although the appearance of chance can well mean that we do not fully appreciate the actual cause (Spanner 1987:156), modern science rather accepts a measure of real indeterminacy (Andrews 1980:60).

The major objection that led to the demise of the proposals of a kenotic Christology was that it was felt that any limitation was impossible in God and incompatible with his sovereignty. Action, especially the chance assumed in evolution, that was not directly controlled by God could be seen as an infringement of his Lordship. This is of course effectively the same objection that is set against the idea of evolution, for the Genesis account of creation ably reflects the power and controlling wisdom of God. If animals and plants developed by a natural process, it could be felt that God was no longer in control of his creation. However, there is no need for *kenōsis* to be understood in a way that is incompatible with his sovereignty. The limitation of God is emphatically a self-limitation. God, in his sovereignty, is able to do anything, which includes limiting himself. Putting it another way, God is free to restrict his freedom.

Moreover, the *kenōsis* of God need not be understood to mean that God is absent from the creation. Even if God's absence need not mean, as Moltmann (1985:102) fears, on the basis of Psalm 104:29, the non-existence of the world, his self-limitation is necessary to give it a measure of independent existence. Indeed, very life, even if it had to be initiated by God, can continue by self-perpetuation; it does not need God's continual involvement. Although MacKay presumes that if God is active in any part of the creation, he is active in all (Harbin 1997:643), that is not necessarily so.

But it must be emphasized that, as *kenōsis* is a voluntary self-restriction, God is able at any time to choose to involve himself directly. The Bible is full of accounts of where God chose to do just that, and, in particular, he chose to involve himself, for the sake of an errant creation, by means of the incarnation. This action was done, by his sovereign choice, in a way that continued to respect the freedom of choice that he had given by means of his *kenōsis*. Thus the involvement of God, in the incarnation of the second Person, was also an act of *kenōsis*. God was enabling the desired result, a humanity in relation with himself, but in respecting human freedom, he did not force that result, but encouraged it.

A further feature of the *kenōsis* of God was that when he did choose to act, he maintained his separation from the world by acting indirectly, by means of agents. In the case of the creation, it was done through the second Person (1 Cor 8:6), who again was sent to enable redemption. Then again, without controlling, he sought to guide those who chose to respond to him through the Holy Spirit. Irenaeus is thus able to glory in the realization of God's acting in the world by means of his "two hands" (*Adv Haer* 5.16.2-3) (cf Williams 2003). Indeed, this is what he did in the incarnation itself. Far from directly acting to remove sin, or even simply creating a body for the second Person, he chose to act through the agent that he chose, the humble and responsive maid from Nazareth. In both evolutionary models, God's action after the initial creation continued through agents, both the laws he had given and creative acts by Son and Spirit.

Thus God is not just absent from the world, although he has limited his involvement in order to give the essential freedom of choice that he desires for what he has made; rather he continues to involve himself in it so as to guarantee the final result that he desires. One of the objections to a suggestion of total free will is that it would remove ultimate security, but a kenotic God both gives freedom and guarantees the ultimate fulfilment of his desires.

This strongly suggests that it is the same principle that operated in the creative process. Progress is made in a natural way, because God has limited himself to allow the process. Thus the things that God made, in the process known as "natural selection", interact and so are developing, the process alone naturally favouring the best (Davis & Kenyon 1989:66). Progress could even be said to demand limitation. Richard (1997:148) notes that in evolution, progress is made by means of suffering and death, so by limitation; although, of course, as this is involuntary, it is not really *kenōsis*; Spanner (1987:138) argues that death was a feature of the original creation. Johnson (1993:52) adds that speciation is more likely in situations where the survival of the parent group is difficult. Then human progress in civilization does depend on cooperation, so a measure of individual self-limitation. In this case, God allows the functioning of evolution, even if the process is far from in accordance with his nature. Indeed, much evolution depends on an attitude contrary to it; biology is self-seeking (Rolston 2001:44). By his *kenōsis*, God allows a non-kenotic attitude in the creation; this is seen most clearly in human society. Nevertheless, it is going too far to suggest that suffering and death cannot be part of God's creative activity (Andrews 1980:74); it is commonly pointed out that they can be seen as morally good if the ultimate result is good. However, even if Harbin (1997:644) feels that death and violence are a necessary part of evolution, this is not so.

Thus far from God directly making everything, he limited himself to give freedom, but as in other acts of *kenōsis*, far from just ignoring the process, he continued to involve himself by guiding it. Development by mutations and natural selection do not exclude God's providence (Spanner 1987:98). There are many instances in the Bible of God acting through other people (cf Andrews 1980:62). Harbin (1997:645) notes the suggestions of Ratzsch that God induced mutations, and of Mills, that God introduced new genetic information into DNA. Mutations can well be providentially ordered

(Spanner 1987:96). Darwin himself believed that natural selection was only the main, but not the exclusive, means of modification of species (Johnson 1993:16). Despite Harbin (1997), it is special creation, not theistic evolution, that tends to deism; Ford (1986:75) comments that God is "Living Spirit not a retired Architect". But this intervention was done though the interaction of the animals and plants that already existed. In the process of evolution, in effect, God then continued to act in character, and used agents to achieve what he wanted.

At the same time, he did intervene directly, at least, most likely by the agency of the other Persons, to perform specific acts of creation, in particular facilitating the emergence of life, and at key points in the creative process. Andrews (1980:22) queries theistic evolution on the grounds that it is unnecessary to introduce the idea of God if evolution was an adequate explanation for the present reality; the point is that without God, it is not!

Evolution is then, in accordance with the evidence put forward by science, a feature of existence, but it is a guided process. It is then quite compatible with the evidence for the nature of God put forward by other means, mainly, of course, by revelation. The Bible contains many instances of apparent chance fulfilling God's purposes (Spanner 1987:48). In this case, far from undercutting the traditional teleological argument for the existence of God (Ford 1986:85), evolution, as long as it is guided, rather strengthens it. Ford (1986:87) discusses evolution using the illustration of a game; a good game is enjoyable as it contains an element of chance, which a good player can deal with to ensure the desired result. Jones and Tyler (2005:230) give the illustration of a plane equipped with an autopilot; it can fly alone, but it is appropriate for the pilot to take over where necessary. It is simply not right to insist, with Andrews (1980:93), that it is inconsistent to question full special creation but accept God's intervention in evolution.

This does of course demand that Genesis 1 is understood not as a literalistic description, and certainly not as a scientific account of origins. Some Biblical scholars find a problem with reconciling any evolutionary understanding with a literal hermeneutic of Scripture (Harbin 1997:640). It is however often remarked how compatible the Genesis account is with the understanding of science, such as in the order of appearance of the various elements of the world. Even supposed problems such as the appearance of light before the heavenly bodies are readily explicable; energy, which included light, in the "big bang" preceded the sun and stars. On the basis of the terms used in Hebrews 11:3, Spanner (1987:134) supports the old idea that the "days" of Genesis 1 were longer periods of time, "aeons", and cites Blocher's view that the passage should be seen as a literary composition. Then it is not necessary to understand that in the seventh day creation was finished (Andrews 1980:74). God did cease that part of his work, but the text cannot be taken to exclude later acts of God in a deistic fashion.

What may be suggested is that the passage, which has communicated to people of various backgrounds for millennia, is, as Calvin put it, an example of God's accommodating his revelation to the nature of humanity. Basically, the Genesis account itself is also an example of God's *kenōsis*. Nevertheless, it must be reiterated that evolution remains a theory, and certainly not a "scientifically demonstrated process" (Harbin 1997:641, Denton 1986:75); Andrews (1980:33) insists that science, which deals with what is, can not explain origins, but only speculate. Nevertheless, the compatibility of evolution with *kenōsis* does make it more likely.

Evolution can then well be an inherent feature of the world that God has made, because it reflects the *kenōsis* that is a part of the nature of God himself. Moltmann (1985:100) sees the Spirit as the creator of possibilities, so the principle of evolution. The Trinitarian

134

idea of *perichōrēsis* includes the concept of the self-emptying of each of the Persons, giving to the Others. An interesting implication of this is that if *kenōsis* is a part of the nature of God, then creativity is also likely part of his nature. Thus even if, as any act of *kenōsis*, it was an act of choice, Einstein had quite a point when he asked whether God did have any choice in creating (Johnson 1995:59). Certainly creativity, and the drive to procreation, do seem to be a fundamental feature of the world that God has made. This is then kenotic. Indeed, de Waal notes that aiding others at a cost is common among animals (Jeeves 2001:66), especially of course in the work that parents are prepared to do for the good of their young. They may even sacrifice themselves to preserve their offspring (Johnson 1993:29); this is of course what Jesus did in his *kenōsis*.

Among others, Nietzsche rejected Christianity because he felt that its kenotic attitude is contrary to the progress of humanity through evolution (Grudem 1994:286). He would be absolutely right if evolution was totally Godless; but that "progress" led to the horrors of Naziism. If on the contrary God in his *kenōsis* continued to act to ensure the fulfillment of his goals, it is quite consistent with this for humanity to also act in self-limitation. Indeed, by this self-limitation, a far better world would result, progressing towards the harmony and care for others that is so contrary to unguided evolution, but so much in keeping with the example that Jesus gave us in his own *kenōsis*.

Chapter 7

Love by limitation: the question of evil

There can be no other single issue that has caused so many people to turn their backs on the Christian faith as that of evil and suffering. Richard (1997:4) correctly observes that this is the human experience most in need of elucidation. How many people have been confronted with a real situation of pain, perhaps of incurable disease, or of suffering which they are sure that they did not deserve, and then found that Christian faith seemed to be unable to deal with it? Perhaps even worse, they have seen something of the horror that people can do to their fellow human beings, such as at Auschwitz, and particularly perpetrated by a so-called Christian people. They have then rejected that faith. Pinnock (2001:133) suggests that evil is perhaps really the only argument for atheism. Even suggesting that evil exists "for a higher purpose" causes a rejection of God (Boyd 2001:14). Even if it does not cause the loss of faith, it may still damage it (Boyd 2001:260). Actually, Berger (1969:79) comments that the events of recent years have meant that the problem is not so much theodicy, a justification of God's action, but more often an anthropodicy, how people can act in such a way.

Perhaps more to the point, they have rejected what was offered to them as the Christian solution, trusting a God who is called "love", despite all the evidence that appeared to scream the contrary. Has God indeed turned his back, is he a sadistic monster, was he ever there at all? And perhaps even more likely, they did not receive a solution that means the "problem" is rather only a "question".

However, I do prefer to call this issue the "question" of evil, rather than, as is often done, the "problem", because my belief is that although evil is never nice, it is not a problem as such, because God has dealt with it. Indeed it is probably safe to say that it never really was a problem, because surely God can be trusted not to allow a situation to develop that he was unable to deal with. Indeed it may be affirmed that essentially he has actually already dealt with the issue that lies at the root of what is a problem for so many.

However, most emphatically, it must remain a question. In this area, it is very possible to provide neat theological answers, but ultimately it is a matter of a particular person's pain, and it can never be fully answered as to why one individual, and not the next, who quite likely seemed more to deserve it, suffered. Why is it that the non-smoker died in agony from lung cancer, while other people who smoked constantly since their youth got away with it? And that scenario can be endlessly repeated. Why did the rich man of the parable lead a happy and contented life, while the beggar at his gate only knew unending pain (Lk 16:19f)? It was no accident that Jesus told that story; the seemingly undeserved pain of the righteous is so common, and cries out for a satisfactory answer. The question, "why do the righteous suffer?" resounds through the pages of the Bible, especially the Old Testament, which does not so clearly affirm an after-life. The world is simply not just (Barry 1987:63). It was such a consideration that led to an increasing stress on an afterlife in the period of the later Old Testament and beyond, even if there remained several, such as the Sadducees at the time of Jesus and Paul, who, taking the Pentateuch only as their authority, denied the resurrection

(Matt 22:23f, Acts 23:6f). Not that the affirmation of an afterlife really solves the problem, for even if it is seen as a way in which justice would be done, and equality enacted, it does not answer the question of why the problem was there in the first place.

Although evil is of course always a problem, what is generally referred to in theology as "the problem of evil" is not so much evil in itself, but becomes one in the context of a God who is believed to be at the same time both perfectly loving and fully omnipotent. If God is both of these, how is it possible for evil, and specifically the suffering that comes with it, to continue? If it is taught that God's very nature is that of love, so a deity who could not be presumed to countenance the suffering of his creation, let alone of its apex in humanity, the experience of many is an enigma. But if at the same time it is affirmed that God is omnipotent, that nothing is too hard for him, this sharpens the issue; how is suffering and evil tolerated when he is able to remove them? In fact it is not even necessary to believe that God is totally omnipotent, but just as even the act of creation does not in fact need infinite power, seeing that the world, even the universe, is not infinite, it merely needs to be understood that God has adequate power, and if to create, then he is surely also able to deal with a little suffering. Of course if only the latter, God's adequate power, is affirmed, then there is no real problem, for such a deity has no real reason to deal with the question. Equally if only the former is believed, as in "process theology", where God is felt to be inherently limited (Boyd 2001:270), then also evil is explained, for God may not be able to solve the problem. It is when both affirmations, of love and power, are held together that the problem comes, and there is a need to do what is known as "theodicy", a justification, or explanation as to why God behaves in the way that he does. Particularly when there is an emphasis upon the sovereignty of God as the direct cause of all that occurs, it is hard to avoid retreating behind the inscrutability of the divine (as Wright 1996:197). Without a satisfactory explanation, then so often the only solution that people find is a rejection of the Christian affirmation. This has been the situation of so many on a personal level, a rejection that has at times been widespread. Here part of the response can be that of such as Moltmann and Bonhoeffer, that God suffers with the human situation, sharing its pain, but this cannot really help too much. The German people were conditioned by the liberal preaching of a God whose total nature is that of love, but when they were confronted with the intense pain and suffering in the closing years of the second World War, many could see no other option than to reject such a belief. This is in a way an even sadder situation than the pain and suffering that caused such a step, for when this is done, people not only turn their backs on God, but also on an explanation for the situation and also the solution that is provided for pain. They reject God's help both now and in the future. Is it surprising that so many, when they think about this, and do not just push it out of their minds, can only despair or seek temporary relief in hedonism or various chemical solutions. As Francis Schaeffer pointed out, when the pain does strike, there is really no other answer if God is excluded; he advocated pushing a person to realise this as an essential preliminary for explaining the gospel.

The question is actually two-fold. On the one hand there must be an explanation as to how an omnipotent and loving God can tolerate human suffering, but on the other, what God has done in response to it. And certainly the Christian affirmation is that God has not just ignored the problem, but has indeed acted, even if the solution may well not be what people either want or expect. Like children who desire their parents always to just give them what they ask for, they complain when it does not happen, not appreciating that the negative response may actually not be from perverseness or inability, but actually from love.

Towards an explanation of evil

Again, it must be stressed that it is only ever possible to generalise, and so it is rarely possible to provide a complete explanation for any specific case of suffering. Yet an explanation may well be suggested that must be more satisfactory than the answers that are so often put forward, such as the inscrutability or sovereignty of God, one who refuses to give any explanation at all. It is commonly observed that the depths of suffering are bearable if they are seen to be for a reason. How many mothers are prepared to give up all for the sake of their children? Give a reason for their pain, and it is able to be withstood.

What must really be true is that if both affirmations are equally held without any qualification, that God is totally omnipotent and totally loving, then suffering is indeed inexplicable. How can it be that God is able to deal with the problem, and want to deal with it, yet it continue? This means that if suffering is a reality, then one or both of the affirmations is false, or rather, has to be qualified. Perhaps it must be pointed out that the last sentence does include the little word "if"; there have been many in the past who have solved the problem by denying that suffering is in fact a reality, that it is an illusion, with no actual reality outside the mind. But surely, it may be possible to believe that in a situation when all is going well, but how many can adhere to this when the nerves all shout for relief? It is indeed the nature of the problem that it must demand a satisfactory and helpful answer. This issue understandably lies close to the heart of every religious system.

How satisfactory is it to argue that evil as such does not exist, but that it is only an absence of good, a *privatio boni*, as Augustine believed? Hunger does not exist, but it is only an absence of food! Then why does God not meet that need, if he is able? After all, he created the world in the first place. A few minor extensions could hardly present a serious challenge to him. This explanation queries both the omnipotence and the love of God; it can hardly be a serious answer.

It is also possible to argue that evil does not exist, only seeming to be present because of an incomplete view of reality. Evil is really good. This is the solution offered by pantheism. After all, what seems to be a totally horrible experience of toothache is absolute heaven for the bacteria in the abscess, and there are more of them than of us.... As C S Lewis dryly observed, a hell for people can be readily combined with a heaven for mosquitoes. But is this not again hiding behind the inscrutability of God? And if God is really love, would he not explain?

Rather the only satisfactory answer lies in the understanding that God has deliberately limited himself in *kenōsis*, and does not act in the restraint of evil and the relief of suffering. Indeed, Hick sees the existence of evil as evidence for God's self-limitation (Barbour 2001:5). Not only the act of creation, but his dealings with the world are from limitation (Birch & Rasmussen 1978:44). This enables the continued affirmation of both poles, indeed that evil exists not despite the love and omnipotence of God, but rather because of them! Because God is omnipotent, he is able to limit his power in *kenōsis*, and because he is love, he desires to. Incidentally, the first part of that last sentence is correct, for deliberate self-limitation can well require enormous strength (Soelle 1975:17). Unless God has in fact limited himself, choosing not to control everything, which he of course could, it makes him the direct cause of evil, of rape, of murder (Pinnock 2001:16). This has effectively been a traditional answer; Augustine said that all is from God: "nothing happens unless the Omnipotent wills it to happen" (Boyd 2001:12). Calvin is forced to say that God causes sin (Sanders 1998:239). How can Christians accept such an explanation? Surely evil cannot be willed by God (Vanstone 1977:64)! And this is still the case if it happens for the greater good, a solution which Vanstone (1977:65) rejects, for it taints the good. Rather, God allows evil and sin, as part of his *kenōsis*. Indeed, just because of the sin that occurred, God withdrew and hid himself still more; Cullmann comments that God's hiddenness is a part of his holiness (Woolmer 1997:67). In the oft-repeated words of Romans 1:18f, "God gave them up", allowing the results of their actions.

It must be insisted that even if in the *kenōsis* of God the possibility arises of sin, this emphatically does not mean that God causes sin. As Irenaeus insisted, God is omnipotent, but does not control (Boyd 2001:43). He is responsible for the possibility of evil but not its actuality (Pinnock 2001:47). Jesus said as much when he emphasised that he did not cast out demons by the power of the devil (Matt 12:24f). God would never cause what is totally antithetical to himself.

The Biblical explanation of the existence of evil is that it started in the Garden of Eden, as a result of the Fall, the first sin. This occurred due to the action of the devil. Because of this, the ground was cursed, with all the unhappy results of that tragic event (Gen 3:14f). But wait a minute, this means that although suffering and pain were a result of human action, they were ultimately caused by God himself. Suffering may well not be intended by God, but it is a necessary part of the sort of world that God made (Ward 2001:159); it was a possibility, perhaps even a probability. This conclusion is commonly denied by people, thinking that it is incompatible with the love of God, and yet there is a consistent witness in the Old Testament to the fact that God is the creator of evil. For example:

> I form light and create darkness, I make weal and create woe,
> I am the LORD, who do all these things (Is 45:7),

and that disaster comes upon a city just because God decrees it (Am 3:6). This may well be deserved suffering, but it is pain and suffering nevertheless.

The fact that so often it is indeed deserved suffering is not irrelevant. So much of what we endure is quite simply a result of human stupidity, or worse, a blatant disregard for what we know is the best. What proportion of people who visit doctors are there for reasons that should have been avoided? How many motor accidents are directly attributable to the fact that one or all of the drivers involved had been drinking, or had partaken of other drugs? How much cancer is due to lifestyle choices such as the decision to smoke, to eat the wrong sort of food, or too much of it, or because exercise seemed to be just too much hard work? And even if a person's own suffering is not directly traced back to him or her personally, then it can quite often be traced back to the action of somebody else, to the other driver who had been drinking, or to the constant exposure to the smoking of others, or even to the pollution generated by the lifestyle of people half a world away. And yet even if human suffering can often be explained directly by this sort of reason, there is much that cannot. The disciples asked Jesus about the man who had been born blind, whether this was due to his sin, or that of his parents (Jn 9:2), thinking perhaps that a common cause of blindness in babies is due to the infection in the eyes caused by venereal disease in the mother. Jesus had to insist that there was another possible explanation, the manifestation of the works of God (Jn 9:3). This need not mean that the man was blind just so that Jesus could heal him, but that his blindness did reflect the glory of the sort of creation that God had made. And yes, he did mean "glory"!

Specifically, much suffering is a direct consequence of the fact that God limited himself, and chose to give a measure of real freedom, of real dominion over the creation to humanity, but dominion that would carry its own consequences. This is commonly called the "free-will defence" for the existence of evil; Polkinghorne (2001:95) also suggests a "free-process defence", suggesting that even non-moral evil can be traced back to God's gift of freedom to the created order. Thus, by his self-limitation, God enabled the freedom of human choice, so the possibility of sin. Foster (2000:223) comments that we cannot cause the flow of divine life, but we can stop it. He permits what he does not actually want (Sanders 1998:217). Even the devil acts as he does by his choice (Boyd 2001:39). God then causes evil as a response to this, usually as a punishment for it. God is then not responsible for what happened as a result of that freedom (Boyd 2001:44). Quite simply, evil is a result of free will (Pinnock 2001:176); it had to exist for a valid choice (Tatian, in Boyd 2001:44). This means that our freedom is more important to God than the evil that it enables; in the context of his imprisonment and suffering, Bonhoeffer (1967:96) commented that there is no punishment by loss of freedom in the Old Testament law. Effectively God allows action and consequences within specific boundaries, just as our freedom is limited within boundaries; we cannot fly! Such limitation within boundaries is of course compatible with the ideas of *kenōsis*.

The fact remains that even if it is often due to human choice, all suffering can ultimately be traced back to God, whether by his direct action, or because of the sort of world that he had made. Even attributing sin, and so suffering, to the devil may only serve to push the question back a little, for where did the source of evil, in the person of the Eden serpent, the devil, come from? It cannot be satisfactory to say anything else than that God, in his omnipotence, created it and him (cf Sanders 1998:253). This is indeed an act of amazing power, for it is inconceivable that God would have created such a being, and such a possibility, unless he knew that he was able to retrieve the situation. We in our limitation may do things unaware of the consequences, but we can hardly suggest that God was oblivious of the possibilities of what he did, and of the solution to them. Effectively, this means that rather than keeping a tight hold on everything that was created, God gave the possibility of rebellion, of going against him. He limited himself to give freedom, within bounds, both to the devil, and to the primeval couple. Then they took advantage of it and rebelled. Ironically, sin, as it so often still is, was a result of the desire to overcome limitation.

And such freedom is a direct result of the real love of God. Although God could have made a "safe" world, in which there was no possibility of sin and evil, he chose to give it freedom, just because that was a more loving thing to do. The nature of love is that it does not seek to control, and then accepts the risk of doing so (Vanstone 1977:45). It seems paradoxical, but it was because he loved that he gave us freedom, including the possibility of rejecting that love and then of generating the consequences. Real love must be free, and a creation which was not free to reject could not really love. C S Lewis points out that it is only freedom that makes goodness possible (Pinnock 2001:126). Vanstone (1977:77) writes, "In every moment and every fragment of the precarious endeavour of creation there exist the twin possibilities of the triumph and the tragedy of love."

In this case, the suffering of the world is directly traceable back to the love of God, for he chose to give us what we really wanted, freedom. When in the 1950's the era of colonialism was obviously coming to an end, the leader of the independence movement on the Gold Coast, later to become the independent state of Ghana, Kwame Nkrumah, was asked why he so desperately wanted independence, for it would mean the loss of so many of the benefits that came from Britain, the colonial power. His reply, which surely did reflect the mind of the people, was that freedom was so precious that it would outweigh the losses that would inevitably come. The same has proved true in the collapse of so many totalitarian regimes, notably those in the former communist eastern states of Europe. So many today actually hearken back to the days when they were totally provided for by the state, and when, despite the drabness of much existence, real suffering was largely unknown; yet how many would really choose to cast off their new freedom and return to those days? As the old saying goes, "no gain without pain"!

And indeed, even if God did gain by creating people with free will, then he also opened himself up to pain, as people abused it. By creating freedom, not only did people suffer as a result of it, but God himself also suffered. The old meaning of "suffer" is to allow something to happen. Peacocke (2001:31) suggests that in the increased consciousness of higher animals comes the increased possibility of suffering; this implies that God suffers even more! Calvin wrote that just as Jesus suffered once in his own person, he suffers daily in his members (Foster 2000:243). Indeed, Jesus wept, but did not act, at the iniquities of Bethsaida and Chorazin (Matt 11:21), and this must reflect the pathos of his Father also. Ultimately, his self-limitation also led to the ultimate suffering on the cross to deal with the results of that human freedom. Religion is then the participation in the sufferings of God (Bonhoeffer 1967:198). It may be commented at this point that a common reason why people do not want to limit themselves in any way is not only the positive one of furthering themselves and their pleasure, but also the negative one of preventing the possibility of suffering; this is done by laying up surpluses in case of future accidents.

Closely related to the fact that real love demands freedom and so the possibility of its rejection, and therefore suffering, is a further factor. This is the value that people place on ultimate justice. They accept suffering if they feel that it is justified, indeed they so often complain where they see that justice is not being done. Is not justice, like freedom, so precious that suffering due to it is worthwhile, and so seen as good? It is better to have justice than the absence of suffering. This immediately produced evil, which God indeed made; this was not because he is not loving, but because he is love. It is loving to maintain a standard of righteousness and to enforce justice. It is more loving that there is a God who is holy, and therefore sin had to be punished. Suffering is a vindication of God's righteousness; if God simply ignored sin, he could not be holy. Such evil is particularly then a direct consequence of sin.

Of course, the function of justice is not just to repay error, to generate equality, as in the parable of the rich man and Lazarus (Lk 16:19f), or even to deter from wrongdoing, but more positively, it is done to generate a lifestyle that is correct. Discipline does not simply have a negative side of punishment, but is intended to generate improvement. Irenaeus felt that evil builds a person's character (Boyd 2001:256). Prisons in South Africa are run by the department of "correctional services", where the goal is not just punishment, or keeping criminals from inflicting further damage on society, but on rehabilitation. Here it is noteworthy that when speaking of discipline, the Bible points out that a father disciplines his own children, not those of somebody else (Heb 12:8), and so that this discipline is then a sign of God's love, that he is a father, not a vindictive tyrant. In this sense it is good (Soelle 1975:25), so an act of love. It may be expected that God's adopted children, for whom he specifically cares, might then know more of suffering than those outside of that special relationship.

Not that God wants to punish as a means of showing what is right and wrong, but just as any father, desires to teach what is right first, and the benefits of following it, then hopefully never need to correct deviation from it. The carrot is always better than the stick, even if it is often not so effective. One of the ways in which we see God's love for the world is that he does lay out what is the ideal way to live. Thus as soon as he had entered into a covenant with Israel at Sinai, he gave them the law to show them how God's people ought to live. And this as well is not a collection of arbitrary commandments, but all given for a reason, given out of love; they are simply a function of the way in which we are made. They are not made to hurt, to restrict, to spoil the quality of life, but to enhance it. Sometimes, for example, people feel too busy to observe the rest of one day in seven, and ignore it, failing to understand the reason behind it. But we are made to function best in that way, and have found that even trying to take a day in ten, as in post-revolutionary France, seemingly more consistent for beings with ten fingers, just does not work as well.

Even better is when, in the new covenant as predicted by Jeremiah (31:34), the demands of the law are internalised, and the human will or "spirit" is conformed to obedience to God by his Spirit. In this, as Paul says, there is real freedom, and so the best of both worlds. As in the Trinity itself, which must be a paradigm for the best in human society, each Person is indeed free, but there is total oneness of will, enabled by interpenetration, or *perichōrēsis*.

God's solution to evil

It may well be true that creation with the possibility of sin and therefore evil, and even that its punishing, were acts of real love, but the act of truly real love comes in the fact that God also made a solution to evil without just denying that freedom that caused it or reversing the process. It is indeed in this that real love is seen, but also in this that God's real omnipotence is worked out. He may not cause sin and evil for the greater good, but he does allow them for that reason (Helm 1993:197). Again, seemingly paradoxically, just as the original problem came from God choosing to limit himself, so the solution also came from God's choosing to limit himself, but this time in the sending of his Son to die for sin, to atone for it, and so freeing people from its consequences. It was only in this way that the demands of his utter holiness could be reconciled with those of his love; both could be satisfied in what Jesus did, and only through that. Even if God does not cause evil, or willingly permit it, he does suffer its consequences (Vanstone 1977:65).

God retained the real freedom of people, so that he did not just remove the consequences of what they had freely chosen to do, but laid that on Jesus, who had humbled himself to make this possible. By choosing to limit himself, he was able to become incarnate, and then to die in our place, so that we could be saved. No wonder the Christian message is called the *euangelion*, "gospel", "good news"! It is this act of Christ that really reflects the love of God, even more than giving the freedom that made sin a possibility. Augustine can even then exclaim *O felix culpa*, "O blessed sin", because the redemption is far more glorious than the spoiling of sin (Sanders 1998:254, Helm 1993:213). Incidentally here, the atonement does depend on the fact that Jesus is both fully human and divine; only with this is the atonement a valid solution to the question of theodicy (Berger 1969:77).

Thus, God's frequent refusal to act for immediate relief of suffering must be seen in the context of his ultimate purpose, which may be seen to outweigh present pain. The final result of salvation will be so glorious that present suffering pales into insignificance; indeed it will be seen, from the perspective of eternity, to have been worthwhile, even good. John's gospel (16:21) puts this same thing in a way that is very meaningful to the majority of women, and even to many men, especially those, who like me, were privileged to witness the actual birth of children. It is deeply burned into my memory how much my wife suffered in the birth of my first child, who had a particularly big head, so produced the inevitable difficulties. What I particularly remember is when the ordeal was finally over, she took Paul in her arms (how could we ever have called him "small"?) and just said, "when can we start another?"

Such was the joy of the final result that it just swallowed up all of the pain and suffering, making it of no consequence. Putting this in the wider context, so wonderful will be the joy of ultimate salvation, that even all the suffering along the way will be swallowed up. As Paul says, "I complete what is lacking in Christ's afflictions for the sake of his body" (Col 1:24). Indeed it contributes to the final joy; salvation could never be appreciated so much unless it is understood what salvation has been from. Even the very pain had contributed to the bond between mother and baby. Would that not also be true between a person and God? I have constantly marvelled, as somebody who has owned dogs ever since being in Africa made this both feasible and necessary, that a bit of punishment always seems to enhance the devotion that is such a characteristic of the canine species.

It is so apt that the name for God which so clearly speaks of his love and his care, that of "Father", actually has its primary reference in the fact that his fatherhood does not consist of his creating us, but refers to his sending his Son Jesus, and that through what he did we can be adopted as children of God (Rom 8:15, Gal 4:5). That is real love; as Paul also exclaims,

> For God shows his love for us in that while we were yet sinners Christ died for us (Rom 5:8),

and also John, in that most well-known and loved verse

> God so loved the world, that he sent his only begotten Son (Jn 3:16)

And in the epistle,

> in this is love, not that we loved God, but that he loved us, and sent his Son (1 Jn 4:10).

Ultimately, if suffering and evil is due to God's *kenōsis*, then it will only be dealt with finally in the eschatological removal of that *kenōsis*. Moltmann (1985:91) comments that there is evil which cannot be seen to have any good side; for this the only cure is resurrection.

And this is sure: creation is safe, not as predetermined, but through the continuation of God's creativity (Vanstone 1977:63).

And more than this

The provision of salvation as the ultimate solution to evil and demonstration of love must be the heart of the Christian solution to evil, but even this is not the end of the story. The answer to suffering and pain is not just that God overcomes it in an eschatological sense, so making it bearable in the knowledge that it is overcome and temporary. Surely one of the worst features of the traditional idea of hell is just this, that it is endless. Anything can be tolerated if it is known to have an end. As Moltmann has so stressed, this means that hope is one of the fundamental features of Christianity, and one of the essential characteristics of God is that he is a God of promise. After all, we are saved because we trust that God will indeed do what he has promised, even if, like God's promise to Abraham, we might have to wait to see the promise enacted. It is this faith in the faithfulness of God that saves.

We would be short-changed if we thought that the only manifestation of the love of God, of salvation, was in the future, after death. We would be sadly wrong if we thought that one part of God's self-limitation was ignoring our problems now, only blessing us in the future. Sadly this is what a lot of people do think about Christianity; they satirise it as the promise of "pie in the sky when you die". Hardly attractive to the instant coffee generation that wants the benefit of everything now, if not sooner.

Rather, even if it is true that we will only see the full benefits of our faith in the future, we are nevertheless saved in the present. We have eternal life now. Likewise the gift of the Spirit to us is a present reality, a foretaste and guarantee of his fullness later (eg Eph

1:13). And part of his ministry is to help us deal with our pain and suffering. After all, did not Jesus refer to him as the *paraclete* (Jn 14-6), literally "one called alongside", which is what, or rather who, we need in such circumstances. Hardly surprisingly, that word has often been translated as "comforter", a word which does not just mean one who gives pleasant words to aid us psychologically in our distress, good though that is, but rather, as seen from its Latin original, means "strengthener". And this is indeed one thing that God does do in our need. He may sometimes take away the problem, but if he does not, then he does give strength to deal with it. Paul would have been grateful if God had taken away his particular experience of suffering, the "thorn in the flesh" (2 Cor 12:7), but rather the reply of God to his prayer for this was rather that "my grace is sufficient for you". This is a reality; the story is told of one of the Reformers who had been condemned to be burnt alive for his faith. On the night before he was due to be executed, he was in his cell waiting for the dawn, and wondering if he would be able to bear the pain and die in a way worthy of his faith in God. He had a candle by which he was able to read, but then he placed his finger in its flame to see what burning would be like, but was totally unable to hold it there, such was the agony of burning. Nevertheless, when it came to the actual execution, he experienced, as so many have found, that he was able to die triumphantly, that God had indeed enabled him to endure.

His experience also demonstrated a truth of great relevance to this whole issue, which is that God does not do unnecessary miracles. There was no need for him to relieve the pain of the candle, there was only need for him to do that in the execution. This means of course that God cannot be legitimately asked to heal when medical science that can solve the problem is present. So many have been persuaded to stop taking medication to prove their faith, but have then suffered accordingly, even died (Farah c1980:1f). Thus God cannot be asked just to stop suffering when in fact he has done so much to solve the problem. He will not respond on our terms.

What is perhaps tragic in these circumstances is that so many people think of God's action as stopping with comfort, and so pray only for endurance. One of the realisations of the modern world with the emergence of Pentecostalism and its successors, is that God often does act to remove the problems that we have, whether disease, poverty or whatever. As James so rightly says even of his day and age, "you do not have because you do not ask" (Jas 4:2). A tragedy indeed! Indeed, while God may well limit himself and not do what he could have done, yet his ability is never curtailed to the point where it fails to be adequate for human needs. Indeed, more often the problem lies not in the ability of God which is quite adequate for any need, but rather in the fact that people do not allow God to work. Ironically, as long as people are resting in their own ability, they do not limit themselves sufficiently to ask God to act for them (Jas 4:2). Our response to God in his *kenōsis* is our own *kenōsis,* so our humility. At the same time, of course, we must not go to the other extreme, as some have done, and think that God is always going to respond to what we ask, as long as we pray in the right way, or have enough faith, or even give enough. That reduces the glory of faith in an almighty God to the level of magic.

What is also sad in a view like that is that it sees pain in an entirely negative way, as something that is always necessarily wrong, and never God's will. Rather, it is something that God has made, and so can well be good. Soelle (1975:107) comments that Christianity affirms suffering more than other world-views, as it is a part of the love for life. I was deeply impressed when I visited a leprosy hospital in Zambia after I graduated and before I started my working life. There I found that it was common for lepers to have lost their fingers. What I found amazing was the reason, for this was not a direct result of the disease. What happens is that the leprosy affects the nerves, and destroys the feeling in the hands. Without the warnings of pain, there is frequent damage by touching hot things, and even by being eaten by rats. O blessed pain, when its lack has such results!

Nevertheless, like everything else in this sorry world, pain has been warped and can be abused, so much so that it seems to be essential for any progress to be made, whether in school, where the fear of punishment can prompt learning, or even more widely, in that the theory of evolution holds that a species can only develop by the extinction of the weaker. Hardly a Christian sentiment; after all it is God who gives the growth. More than this, the idea of entropy is that things naturally tend to disorder, completely the opposite to that of evolution; it is this point that influences me against a simple acceptance of the theory, at least on the macro level. It does seem that the idea of development within species is well substantiated, but although there is a lot of evidence on the wider level, it does fall short of proof. Nevertheless within the theory there is a principle that has wider application, and that is that pain and suffering does prompt action to change the situation, to escape it. This is obvious on the personal level, where even the smallest degree of unpleasantness is often enough to seek to escape from it.

The same is true at a wider level as well, such as in the political sphere, where it is the suffering that a regime causes that prompts action to replace it. Even more significantly, surely it was in response to the evil caused by sin, and the consequent suffering, that prompted God to act. In a sense, as Moltmann has suggested, he participated in it, an idea poles apart from that of the ancient Greeks, who believed that God was impassible, incapable of suffering. But then they also felt that because he is perfect, he also never changes, thinking that any change must be to a state that is less perfect.

Thus, in our suffering, we receive assurance that there is not a God who is unaffected, but that he suffers with us (Pinnock 2001:56). In fact this suffering is augmented because of his determination not to interfere, to respect our freedom, to embrace powerlessness. This adds new meaning to the observation of Soelle (1975:11) that a feeling of powerlessness is a fundamental element in suffering.

Certainly Jesus suffered, identifying with humanity to the uttermost, sharing in its woes. There is great pathos in the shortest verse of the Bible (in English), John 11:35, that "Jesus wept", when he was confronted with the death of his friend Lazarus. It was that identification with, but also that response to the suffering of humanity, that compelled him to the ultimate sacrifice on Calvary. And surely it is also in response to that pain that prompts so many to repent in gratitude, to change, *metanoia*, and so themselves to experience the change of new birth (Jn 3:3), or re-creation (2 Cor 5:17). It is not only done from a desire to change to a better life, or to avoid future condemnation, valid though they are.

The ancient Greeks did have a point, because it is only because of limitation that pain is possible. If we had total ability to deal with our situations, we would never need to suffer. If we could deal with all our diseases immediately and totally, who would spend a moment in pain? It is only because God chose to limit himself, to give freedom to the creation, and not just to over-ride it, that the pain in the heart of God, and ultimately the cross, resulted. It is then only in the *eschaton*, when what is imperfect passes away (1 Cor 13:10) that suffering finally becomes a thing of the past.

The positive impact of good

God also does two other things in respect of suffering. Firstly he does actively restrain it. It would certainly be a lot worse if it were not for this aspect of God's care for the world. Our freedom is constrained, both by our history and from the rules that God has laid down (Boyd 2001:203). There have even been stories of angels protecting God's people from attack, just as in the Old Testament story of Elisha (2 Ki 6:17). One way in which this is done is by the example and witness of God's people, showing by word and deed what the correct way to live is. People have been ashamed to do what they would otherwise have been about to do just by the mere presence of a Christian. In particular, ministers have commonly heard the tone and content of conversation change when they arrive at a place. This example is not just transient, but has an ongoing effect in the consciences of many who otherwise have no thought for God whatsoever. And who can say what God does without anybody present? However, he generally does prefer to work through his people, which should be a tremendous encouragement to his Church to at the very least make their allegiance known, and better, to speak out against what they see as wrong. Christians have a tendency to feel that it is pointless to stand against what seems to be a great tide of evil, far less to actively resist it. That could not be further from the truth! After all, "one with God is a majority", and the ministry, power and help of the Spirit is a most definite reality. Let us always remember the words of God to Ezekiel, that he made him a watchman, but if he fails to speak out, then he is guilty himself (Ez 3:16f).

And more than this, of course, he sends us, as the disciples (Mk 6:7), to positively deal with evil, to feed, to heal, to help wherever possible. There is a conscious shouldering of the sins and burdens of others (Foster 2000:238). Christians have always been concerned for the weak in society, even when they are very little use to anybody. This is an attitude that the philosopher Nietzsche despised as weakness, only leading to the decay of the race. In fact, Paul indicates that we are afflicted just so that we are able to help those who suffer (2 Cor 1:6); this is a real echo of the sufferings of Christ for us. "The Son of God suffered unto the death, not that men might not suffer, but that their sufferings might be like his" (George McDonald, in Forster 2000:238). Then in the Holy Spirit he provides the ability to do just that.

Then secondly, he does not only restrain in the negative sense, but he can even turn what would seem to be evil into a positive good. The well-known Romans 8:28, "in everything God works for good with those who love him" has been the experience of so many. This is not a shallow optimism, wishful thinking, or even a refusal to see the negative side in things, but an affirmation that God can indeed transform what may even seem to be hopeless. Of course, evil is not justified in that God sometimes brings a good result from it (Boyd 2001:183), but it is wonderful when he does! The story of Joni is well-known, that she broke her neck diving into a shallow pool. That could well have been the end of a useful life, but in fact God has ministered through her suffering and disability to countless thousands. Many have discovered that the experiences that they have had have helped them to understand the situations of many, enabling them to bring help and comfort. It is noteworthy that Romans 8:28 emphasises the word "with". It is perhaps too easy to sit and to write about pain and suffering. It is especially easy when they are not being experienced. But it is when they are, or they have been, that a person can be most of help to somebody in distress. It was only after I had had a bit of trouble with my heart, and had come face to face with mortality, that I was able to appreciate what this meant, and be able to help others.

The sufferer naturally turns to the book of Job, to one who seemed to suffer unfairly, even if at the end of the book it would seem that God was indeed justified in allowing his suffering. Job cried out in his distress, "man is born to trouble" (Jb 5:7), and certainly it seems that this is an inevitable part of being human, of very existence. Indeed, this is the Buddhist approach to the question, that life, indeed very existence, and suffering are two sides of the same reality, and that the only ultimate cure is then to stop existing. Hardly surprisingly, the hope that is held out is then a loss of existence in Nirvana. Such is a far cry from the Christian hope which insists that evil and pain are not natural, not what God intended, and that the hope is one not of a loss of being, but "life more abundant", when all the negatives are swallowed up in total fullness of life. We do not, or should not, look to losing what we have; so many just find life unbearable and long for its end. Christian hope must affirm the joy of the present, but also anticipate the transcendence of the limitation in us that makes suffering possible, in total and unending life.

The freedom that God has given to people is not absolute, but is circumscribed. We are not able to do exactly what we would like. I would love to fly, but that is not part of the freedom that God gives! Such a restraint on freedom is a blessing, for it does mean that much of the evil that could otherwise happen just does not. If looks could kill, there would certainly be a lot more murders, but circumstances are such that they are at least difficult. The same is true for so many other potential disasters. That must be a great comfort! At the same time, the restriction in God's omnipotence that enables our freedom is not such that we need ever lose hope. Perhaps the worst thing about pain is that it weakens, and renders even consistent thought difficult. It is then a tremendous comfort that we can come to a God who understands, for he has experienced the ultimate in himself, by means of the deliberate choice of weakness in his *kenōsis*, and it is by that that we can be helped. In the context of suffering, as in temptation, the promise of 1 Corinthians 10:13 has been a tremendous relief to many:

> God is faithful, and he will not let you be tempted beyond your strength, but with the temptation will also provide the way of escape, that you may be able to endure it.

1 Peter 1:6 is also a very pertinent verse which has been a help to many. It speaks of the testing of faith, and certainly it is the experience of suffering that has revealed the genuineness of faith for many. But at the same time, the verse is in the context

of the purification of precious metals such as gold, in which they suffer through fire (which must remind us of the Spirit), in which the dross is burnt up, leaving the metal purified. By means of the "suffering", the metal is improved. A similar thing is true in another metallurgical application as well, for if steel is tempered by heating and sudden cooling, it becomes hardened and much more suitable for many applications. The process is quite complicated, usually involving a number of heatings to get the desired result, and no Christian should ever be under the impression that one experience is the completion of the process! Perhaps it should also be added here that many metals are hardened by work, and indeed it is often in service that Christians find a great result in their own faith; it needs to be stretched! Perhaps also, it must be noted that the strongest of metals are not actually pure, but are alloys. Steel is not just iron, but alloyed with a particular amount of carbon; sophisticated steels, such as used for tools, have a carefully controlled composition. The best parallel to this is that a person alone is really quite weak, and under pressure is liable to bend and even to snap. But with the help and support of other Christians, the overall ability to endure is enhanced. Indeed, the total is greater than the sum of the parts. More especially, as with the heating process, it is the *synergy* with the Spirit that achieves the ultimate.

Chapter 8

The *kenōsis* of knowledge

The Church has traditionally held to the omniscience of God, that he has total knowledge of everything that is and that was, but also of what will be. In addition to this, it is usually held that God, unlike people, never learns anything, but knows everything inherently. His knowledge, again unlike that of people, is immediate; there is no embarrassing delay as there so often is with human beings, and even with computers, while they search out the information that is desired. His knowledge is simultaneous; I often say this is one of the feminine attributes of God, for while I, as a mere male, am totally incapable of thinking of more than one thing at once, my wife is able to hold several conversations at the same time as well as be busy with a number of other activities. With God there is no danger of his being unable to hear the prayers of as many people who want to communicate with him at one time. His knowledge is distinct, in that there is no confusion, again as there often is in human memory between two things or two events. And, of course, his knowledge is completely true.

Such omniscience has been a tremendous source of comfort to people insofar as it may be affirmed that God is aware of all aspects of our situation, even more than we are ourselves. He knows our problems, knowledge that can sometimes be communicated to people, as when a person becomes supernaturally aware of the existence and cause of a sickness (Wimber 1987:181). We can be assured that there is no situation, no experience that we may have, of which God is unaware. In fact, there is no need for us to tell God anything, an affirmation that has even discouraged some from approaching God in prayer; why do we need to tell him what he knows already? Of course, this is forgetting that all relationships are dynamic, and that for the sake of them we spend a lot of time telling other people things that they knew already. God delights when we ask him anything, just as a father delights in his children, and quite often only gives when we do ask, even when he was well aware of our need before we utter it.

Then omniscience may of course also be a threat, just as it was to the prophet Jonah, who found that it was impossible to flee from either the presence or the knowledge of God. It may even be disturbing, as when we are suffering, and yet God seems to do nothing. This seems inexplicable if he knows what we are going through. Pinnock (2001:103) finds it "frightening".

Grudem (1994:190) outlines the main Biblical passages that are adduced to demonstrate the traditional doctrine of omniscience. Particularly noteworthy are Isaiah 55:9 and I John 3:20. Of particular reference to prayer is Matthew 6:8 "your Father knows what you need before you ask him". The writer of Psalm 139 rejoiced that there was nowhere that was away from the presence of God, which would include his knowing (but cf Pinnock (2001:40), who sees this as poetic, and in any case only pertaining to the writer). This knowledge would include the thoughts of the human mind, which are not hidden from God. It is however possible that some texts, such as Hebrews 4:12 "discerning the thoughts and intentions of the heart" may rather be understood as God's ability, not that he has actual knowledge at all times. Carasik (2000:232) concludes that "contrary to popular beliefs, most Biblical texts suggest that God cannot [read minds], but several narrative texts insist that God can".

That omniscience includes knowledge of the future is felt to be demonstrated by, among others, texts such as Isaiah 42:9 "before they spring forth I tell you of them", contrasting God's knowledge with the impotence of idols. This text is significant, insofar as an affirmation of God's perfection was crucial against polytheism with its limited deities; for Isaiah, foreknowledge is an attribute of real deity (Ware 2002:199).

Erickson (2003:39f) also provides an historical survey; again most in the past have supported a view of God's full omniscience, including that of the future. He writes, "A large number of variations arose on the question of *how* God knows the future, but there was strong agreement that he does" (2003:109).

A situation of paradox

The omniscience of God becomes an issue if it is also believed that people have genuine free will. It is the simultaneous affirmation of both that has generated problems. If God is fully aware of the future by virtue of his omniscience, can a choice actually be free; if a choice is really free, can the result of it be known beforehand? If God does know everything, then he knows what choices people will make, and so they are not free. On the other hand, if people do have genuinely free will, then God does not know everything. The two are logically incompatible (Peacocke 1993:122). Real human freedom adds an element of chance if the future is not controlled by God. If future events are dependent upon the free action of people, they are by very nature unknowable.

Thus Luther, in a piece entitled *The bondage of the will*, emphatically excluded the possibility of any free will, even of the angels, on the basis of God's foreknowledge (Renick 2002:42). He sees this as essential for salvation in that he feels that trust in God is impossible unless God is aware of the future (Erickson 2003:102). Likewise, as Paul points out in Romans 3:25, God could forgive people in the time of the Old Testament with perfect justice, even though the atoning sacrifice of the cross had not yet occurred. If he knew the future, the cross was a certainty, and so God could forgive in anticipation of it.

Traditionally, Christianity has taught that God is perfect in all his attributes. This is felt to be essential for his total lordship. Many then feel that the sovereignty of God means that he directly controls everything that happens, that the future is then pre-determined; if free will exists, then God has yielded up a measure of his sovereignty. However even direct control does limit God, to one mode of exerting his rule (Pinnock 2001:53, 96, Sanders 1998:208)! Swinburne even points out that if God has exhaustive foreknowledge, then in fact he is not free himself (Erickson 2003:167).

Then traditional Christianity has often affirmed that God is atemporal. Is not God completely outside the material by virtue of his spiritual nature? Aristotle held that God is outside time, and does not affect it directly (Hill 1975:4); he of course influenced Christian thought through Aquinas, who believed that God knows all (1975:7). The eternity and omniscience of God go together (Yong 2002:261). He is fundamentally different, and so transcendent, a quality impossible for anything in the least material. And if he is infinite, cannot this also not apply to time? In this case he is eternal in the sense of transcending time completely. Moreover, if he is not eternal, it does raise the issue of what God was doing before time, a question to which Augustine is said to have replied, scathingly, that he was preparing Hell for those who ask stupid questions (Sanders

1998:148)! It must however be pointed out that the existence of such an extra-temporal situation is of course speculative in any case. In any case, if God were present to every time simultaneously, just as he is present in every space, would that mean that he could change the past? The implications are far-reaching!

Moreover, if God is indeed totally sovereign, directly causing everything, which has been commonly believed, such as by Calvin (Sanders 1998:155), then it seems inescapable that God is also the direct cause of sin, evil and suffering. Foreknowledge aggravates the problem. Bulgakov insists that God was ignorant of the Fall, or it would imply that he caused it (Gavrilyuk 2005:259). However, at least partly for this reason, some do try to make a distinction between determinism, whereby God positively causes the future, and foreknowledge, by which he merely knows about it. The latter of course necessitates some self-limitation in God (Fiddes 1988:33). Thus Justin believed that God knows how people will decide, but does not cause the decision; for Augustine, God knows the future, but does not cause it (Sanders 1998:142,148). This was also the issue in the sixteenth century between Calvin and Arminius. With the latter, many (eg Picirilli 2000:264) insist that foreknowledge is a revelation of what will be, not its cause; but it is really impossible to affirm that a person really has free will if the outcome of his or her choice is already known; this presumes that the future is fixed, so that there is no freedom. Thus, although it is alleged that "foreknowledge does not imply foreordination", in neither case is there real free will (Grudem 1994:348).

Human free will

More than the problems attached to foreknowledge and especially determinism, the Bible would seem to indicate clearly that people can really choose what they will do. Again several texts are commonly adduced to support the existence of free choice, such as the evangelical appeal "come unto me..." (Matt 11:28). Perhaps more fundamentally, if people are not free, they are not really persons, God then dealing with them as other things, in what Buber calls an I-it relationship (Sanders 1998:210). Significantly, God's *kenōsis* is the precondition for the emergence of free self-conscious persons (Richard 1997:144). Of more practical importance is that if Jesus was not free, and was forced to the cross, his action loses its moral significance (Ware 2002:207). Boyd (2001:148) also remarks that we like risk and surprises, and so God does not want to fix the future; he adds that a God who does not force is particularly attractive to feminists. Fiddes (1988:215) points out that the idea of creation as risky is a common theme in recent theology.

At the same time, there are several texts commonly used to indicate God's ignorance of the future. In the story of Abraham and Isaac, God saw the willingness of Abraham to sacrifice his son, and says, "now I know that you fear God" (Gen 22:12); but did he not know that already? Sanders (1998:39f) describes many occasions from both Testaments which indicate that God has less than total knowledge. Boyd (2001:100-5) notes occasions of God's disappointment, of his questioning, of his regrets, of his seeking to discover. Erickson (2003:17f) again surveys the main evidence. However, he also points out that the evidence for the traditional view of full knowledge is considerably more substantial (2003:81).

The existence of prophecy is often taken as an indication that God does indeed know the future (Grudem 1994:347). However, the nature of prophecy is usually not so much foretelling, but "forth-telling", presenting God's requirements to individuals or a people, and confronting them with not only the benefits of obedience, but also with the penalties for disobedience. There are very few absolute, non-conditional predictions (Sanders 2002:228). Thus far from prophecy indicating that the future is fixed, the very existence of this aspect of prophecy would indicate that God wants to affect what was going to happen, that coming events could well be different. It opens, not closes, the future (Sanders 1998:86). Totally reliable prophecy in fact limits God by putting him under obligation; he is forced to do what was predicted. Indeed, much prophecy of the foretelling variety is actually conditional, indicating what would happen under certain circumstances. Moreover, whereas the fulfillment of prophecy is a strong reason both for belief in God and for the validity of his communication with people, there are many examples of unfulfilled prophecies in the Bible.

It was the professed ignorance of Jesus on a couple of occasions that contributed to Arius' belief that he was subordinate to the Father. At one time, he said that he did not know the time of the second coming, the *parousia*, and that the time of this was set only by the Father (Mk 13:32). Macleod (1998:165) comments that the knowledge of Jesus did not need to be infinite; what he knew was received from the Father. As some of the Fathers indicated, as incarnate he had to be ignorant (Macleod 1998:167). Nevertheless, Jesus' knowledge was sometimes more than that of an ordinary human being; he did seem to be able to know the inner minds of people, so especially of Judas.

Few today suggest that these affirmations of ignorance are not genuine, and reject any hint of docetism. This contrasts with an early understanding of the issue of the incarnation; effectively, this was that Jesus could not have been really human, but only seemed to be (Greek *dokeō*) (Macleod 1998:157). This started from an affirmation of God's total sovereignty; it was felt that God is indeed perfect, and therefore, quite logically, could not be incarnate. In particular, he could not suffer, because that would affect his perfection. Exactly the same solution was often proposed as regards the issue of human free will. Omniscience is one aspect of divinity, so "if Jesus were omniscient he could not be 'perfectly' human" (Richard 1982:299).

Jesus' "ignorance" could not have been real. Thus Athanasius believed that Jesus feigned ignorance for us (Fiddes 1988:27). Likewise any indication of human free will is not real, but it only seems to be the case. Biblical indications of this are metaphors.

Now the docetic solution was quickly rejected by the Church in the case of the incarnation. It seems to make God into a liar, a hypocrite, portraying what is not really the case. The same objection can then be applied to the deterministic solution. Any suggestion that human free will is not real casts doubts upon the veracity of God, and especially on the Biblical record.

Pinnock (2001:154) is surely correct in his observation that practical Christianity almost invariably assumes the free will of people and an open future. These are assumed in the practice of intercessory prayer, the preaching of the gospel in evangelism and the commands to sanctification, among others. Otherwise these are a mockery; it is surely far from satisfactory to practise these if it is believed that human action is really irrelevant, and that they are done simply because God commands them. It is hardly surprising that in response to practical concerns, but also in obedience to what was seen as the scriptural view, a view of real free will has been advocated. Wesley, for example, emphatically rejected predestination out of fear that it would undercut the drive to personal holiness (Pinnock 2001:168); it may be remarked that this was also Pelagius' concern!

Does this mean that it is necessary to just cast out centuries of belief in the traditional attributes of God, such as his omnipotence and omniscience? Not a light matter! Is this to "sacrifice or to attenuate the classical and scriptural view of divine omniscience in the interests of a risky providence" (Helm 1993:44)?

Attempts at reconciliation

Except a few such as process theologians, most accept God's omniscience (Pinnock 2001:99), but often also wish to affirm real free will. Over the centuries, Christian thinkers have battled with the issue, and although they have generally felt that it is possible to affirm both poles, have appreciated that there is more than a measure of paradox and inconsistency in holding both in tension. They seem to be inconsistent. Hall (1986:51) cites Tillich's presentation of the alternatives, on the one hand of heteronomy, control from without, and on the other, of autonomy, self-determination; he proposes that the Biblical position is of theonomy, obedience to God. Packer (1961:18f) believes that as both can be supported from Scripture, both must be true, there can be no inherent contradiction between them. Yet he feels that we cannot understand how they can be reconciled; for him it is an antinomy, an apparent contradiction. Can they be reconciled, or do we retreat behind suggestions that statements about omniscience are hyperbolic, or that those concerning free will are accommodative (Helm 1993:52)? This latter, incidentally, is a form of God's *kenōsis* (cf Oliphint 2004:49).

It seems to be inescapable that if there is human free will, then God does not control the future. This does not mean that the future has to be completely open; even if God may well permit some things that he does not actually desire (Sanders 1998:217), it need not affect his overall purposes; Sanders (1998:231) uses the example of jazz, where improvisation takes place to supplement the main melody, which is fixed. In any case it is obvious that the freedom given is not absolute, but is only possible within the limits set by God. The extent of freedom is not total, but subject to God's permission (Grudem 1994:330). Moreover, a person is subject to sin, which limits freedom (Sanders 1998:238). Boyd (2001:152) feels that the laws of nature are permissive, indicating what cannot happen, not what will. Peacocke (1993:75) points out that, in fact, free will is only possible in an environment of law, which means that it is largely predictable. It may also be noted that law is an aspect of *kenōsis*, as it excludes other options. However, difficulties abound; how can it be decided which aspects belong to what is predicted, and which to what is free; in any case, is this not a division in Christ or God?

That solution, although it maintains God's sovereignty, effectively denies his omniscience. Other proposals seek to affirm God's omniscience but without full sovereignty; there are various possibilities as to what this means (Sanders 1998:194f). Thus it may be suggested that even if the actions of individuals are indeed free, the actions of groups are predictable (cf Boyd 2001:154). If a coin is tossed up into the air, a person might be able to predict on what side it would fall if there were total knowledge of the way in which it was tossed up, but for all practical purposes its fall would be unknown. The side on which a coin falls may be taken as random, yet if a large number of tosses are made, it may be confidently predicted that almost exactly half the tosses would come down on one particular side. That is of course the basis of the insurance industry. Whereas a particular accident may be taken as total chance, or as erroneously described, an "act of God", overall the number of accidents in a particular population in a particular period of time may be confidently foretold, and the premiums to be paid set accordingly. Possibly the decay of radioactive material is also predictable if all the circumstances were known, but this is also commonly taken as a random event. In both cases, the overall result over a period of time is predictable and so a prophecy can be made with a fair degree of certainty.

This solution has been applied to the related matter of predestination, also in respect of free will. Although it is very clear from a number of Biblical references that God does predestine (eg Eph 1:5), it is by no means clear that this refers to individuals. All the references may rather be taken to apply to a group, that is the Church (eg Pinnock 2001:165), while individuals remain free.

Sanders (1998:130) observes that in the Biblical record, the object of God's foreknowledge is either Christ, or his people, as a group. They only become individually predestined if they freely unite with the Church as a body. Karl Barth has effectively said the same thing, while providing a rather satisfactory explanation. He has suggested that it is not actually the Church as such that is predestined, but Christ, as the Son of God, who is predestined in his total obedience to his Father. In this case individuals again become predestined as they unite with Christ and so share in his predestination, just as they live forever just as they participate in the eternal life that is only his by right. This point is also applicable to the question of whether sin is possible in heaven (cf Erickson 2003:252); where there is full union with God, sin is eliminated.

This is a welcome departure from the individualism that has been dominant in Western theology, but nevertheless does not solve all the issues. Omniscience is still not absolute, and moreover there are events that are not due to human decision, but are still part of the future. Events such as earthquakes do present a problem for theodicy if God was responsible for them, and even if he was merely aware that they were coming.

A commonly proposed solution is that God's complete knowledge can enable compatibilism (Erickson 2003:12); according to Craig, "Since [God] knows what any free creature would do in any situation, he can, by creating the appropriate situations, bring it about that creatures will achieve his ends and purposes and that they will do so *freely* ...in his infinite intelligence, God is able to plan a world in which his designs are achieved by creatures acting freely" (Picirilli 2000:269). Sanders (1998:230) uses the illustration of a chess master, who is able to deal with all the moves of the opponent. God is so great that he can afford to take risks (Boyd 2001:147). Indeed, ultimately God has caused the desire by which a person acts (Sanders 1998:211). God allows freedom insofar as it is compatible with his will (Helm 1993:66). "We are free to do as we please, but not to please as we please" (quoted in Erickson 2003:13). Picirilli gives an example; God sends the rain, so that I freely choose to stay inside! Grudem (1994:349) comments that if both the person and the circumstances are created by God, in practice, once again the future is fixed; Picirilli (2000:266) refers to this as "soft determinism". It must be noted that Jesus condemned not only action but motives (Matt 5:21f); this is unjust if either actions or motives are actually caused by God.

Of course, even if there is real free will, this does not preclude God knowing a great deal about the future. At the very least, he can be absolutely certain that there are a lot of things that just will not happen, simply because they are inherently impossible or beyond the capability of people to do them. I can confidently say that pigs will not grow wings and fly, at least not in the near future! More than this, Sanders (1998:125ff) then adds a further possibility, that God can foretell on the basis of his wisdom (also Pinnock 2001:102). God has such a comprehensive knowledge of us and all circumstances that he can predict with high probability (Peacocke 1993:129); although if free will is involved, even he cannot know the future for certain. This comprehensive knowledge is sometimes suggested as the way some prophecy is possible, such as Peter's denial of Christ (Erickson 2003:51). In this regard, Schleiermacher pointed out that the amount of prediction of a person's actions is proportional to the degree of intimacy (2003:103). This obviously contrasts with the oft-expressed view that prophecy was only written down *post eventu*.

In practice, there are very few choices that we make which are utterly free in the sense that they are totally unpredictable. This means that even if God has not actually acted to predetermine the future, decisions are not really free, in that a person is subject to all the influences brought to bear on him or her from outside so that in effect there is only one real course of action. To take a simple example; if I am offered a meal of fish or meat, my wife is able to predict quite accurately that I will choose the former. My choice would indeed be totally free, but my preferences are known. The same is true as regards much human action, which may be said to be determined simply from the genes inherited from the parents. Such action may be free, but it is predictable. Then if I sometimes surprise my wife by opting for the unexpected choice, then there is very often a very good reason why I acted out of character on that occasion. Unbeknown to her, I had already eaten fish that day and so wanted a change. The belief is that the situation is similar for God, such that the omniscience of God is actually so complete that God is aware of all the influences that affect a particular decision, so that even though the decision appears free in that a person does what he or she wants (Yong 2002:259), God in practice knows what it will be.

However, Pinnock (2001:100) is not alone when he questions whether exhaustive foreknowledge is in fact scriptural or philosophically valid. While Moltmann (1985:200) cites the opinion of Leibnitz, that if there is exhaustive knowledge of the present, then the future is predictable, he does note that modern science denies that total knowledge is in fact possible; at the quantum level, there is indeterminacy (Boyd 2001:137). Peacocke (1993:128) also points out that modern science also precludes full foreknowledge, that there is a genuine unpredictability in nature. Although especially at the sub-atomic level, this applies also to some larger systems (1993:152); this gives an explanation of human free will (1993:153). Erickson (2003:186) however cautions that God's exhaustive knowledge may well be able to predict these phenomena; their apparent indeterminacy could well be due to human limitations. Modern science, generally supporting evolution, is then also sympathetic to the suggestions of process theology, which are that God is developing along with the world, is gaining in experience and knowledge, and so again inherently limited. However, such inherent limitation can hardly be acceptable to traditional theology.

Even if people do have real free will, it is still possible that some things are known, and are certain to occur; the future is partly settled (eg Pinnock 2002:217). These are those that depend on God's action only; God knows what he will do (Erickson 2003:219). Thus some events can well be certainly predicted; an example is the cross of Christ, as in Psalm 22 (but cf Sanders 1998:101), or Isaiah 53. Other predictions are not certain, as they are conditional. Sanders (1998:125ff) here distinguishes between prophecies and predictions. Although it is clear that there are a number of things that are clearly predicted, such as the fact that there will be a second coming, there is much about it that remains indeterminate, such as the time of that coming. The reason for this is that the timing depends on the action of people in the world, specifically on the Church. In Matthew 24:14, it is indicated that first the gospel must be made known to all nations, and certainly this has not happened until comparatively recently, if indeed it has yet been fulfilled. The Church may well have not acted as quickly as Jesus and the early Church might have hoped.

These solutions all suffer from the fact that they do not really accommodate both full free will and God's omniscience, and so are not faithful to the Biblical witness and the affirmations of Christian tradition. However, recently, two proposals have emerged which claim to do just that, those of "middle knowledge" and of "open theism".

Middle knowledge

A further possible understanding of omniscience, one that really accommodates genuine free will, is that God knows both everything that will come to pass and everything else that could or would come to pass in all other conceivable sets of circumstances, "all possible worlds". The future is really free, but God is aware of all that can happen, of all the implications of all possible choices; he "over-knows" the future (Boyd 2001:130). As he knows all the various possible futures, and has decided how he would react to each possibility in advance; he therefore never changes (Sanders 1998:196). God's omniscience is then of "middle knowledge", a belief often referred to as Molinism, after the sixteenth century Jesuit, Luis de Molina (cf Sanders 1998:197, Erickson 2003:103). Picirilli (2000:269) notes that its best-known modern spokesman is William L. Craig, who suggests that "middle knowledge" offers the possibility for rapprochement between Calvinists and Arminians. Plantinga suggests that this idea is supported in 1 Samuel 23:7-11 and Matthew 11:20-24 (Helm 1993:55). In this case, however, as the future contains almost an infinite number of possibilities, there is no real omniscience (Helm 1993:61, Erickson 2003:221). The future is still uncertain, and there is a lack of real security (Sanders 1998:197).

Open Theism

In recent years, the issue of foreknowledge has been sharpened with the emergence of a new controversy, although the issue that has come to the fore is really not at all new, but one that has surfaced quite regularly in the history of the Church. Picirilli (2000:268) notes the discussion of the basic idea even in 1850. Followers of the theological scene will be aware of the debate that has been raging for the last few years about the nature of God. Discussion has largely centred in the United States, but with a little impact on the other side of the Atlantic. It has occurred particularly in the evangelical wing of Christianity, where it has been most intense due to the implication of the issues involved for the idea of the inspiration and inerrancy of the scriptures (Wellum 2002:269), and also because of the tendency for evangelicalism to be Calvinistic rather than Arminian, respecting the idea of the sovereignty of God. In a nutshell, the question that is currently generating so much hot air and the spilling of so much ink is that of the "openness" of God to being affected by the world, and especially by human activity. This directly impinges on the question of the relationship between the knowledge of God and the free will of humanity. At its heart, the debate is about that most American of virtues, freedom, and about its relation to that most modern of assets in the computer age, that of knowledge. It is really not surprising that the questions have arisen at this point in history. Erickson (2003:255) comments that the open view appeals to Western culture.

The current suggestion that is being made is simply that human choices are indeed real, but that this then must mean that the future is not fixed, but "open". The future has not yet happened, and what will happen depends on the free actions of people. Here what open theism is putting forward is something believed to be inherent in the nature of reality. The future is open simply because it has to be; it is fundamentally unknowable. Even if God had made people into robots and so totally predictable, which would effectively fix the future, it is really still unknowable as it has not happened. God is indeed omniscient, so it is emphasized that there is no diminution of his power or knowledge, but because the future has not yet happened, it *cannot* be known. Emphatically, any suggestion that this idea compromises God's perfection is rejected. Although Oliphint (2004:50) sees the ideas of open theism as a form of Eutychianism, in which there is no way in which God can take on another nature without abandoning part of his own, open theism would insist that God is not in fact giving up anything, but is consistent to who he is. Indeed, it is felt that accepting an open future magnifies God, as potentiality is more than actuality (Moltmann 2001b:150).

Hill (1975:3) notes that it is an old view that only what exists can be infallibly known. He writes (1975:7) that contemporary serious thought is practically unanimous in denying to God an infallible knowledge of the future. Thus God knows all that can be known, but the future is inherently not knowable, a view known as "presentism" (Sanders 1998:129). This is similar to the old question of whether God can do anything. The answer is affirmative, but he cannot make a square circle, not because his power is limited, but because it is inherently impossible.

The "open theism" view has many current advocates, such as Clark Pinnock, John Sanders and Gregory Boyd. Interestingly, they are often associated with other ideas deemed radical by conservatives, such as annihilationalism, sometimes called "conditional immortality", the view that the unsaved will be annihilated, not go to a conscious punishment in hell. Erickson (2003:235) notes the relationship between these ideas. As with these, their views have unleashed howls of protest from those who feel that open theism is a departure from orthodox Christianity.

Open theism is obviously attractive if only for the fact that it removes what is most definitely a situation of paradox. It is very difficult to accept that a decision is really free if it is believed that God employs exhaustive control and that the results of the decision are known beforehand! The idea also provides a solution to the contentious issue of human suffering. Likewise the relationship of prayer is really meaningless unless God has limited himself to give human free will; a fixed future empties prayer of its reality (Pinnock 2002:218).

Advocates of open theism believe that their position is not contrary to the scriptures; they commonly make a strong appeal to Biblical theology (Master 2002:585), and point to references to God being ignorant of the future or changing his mind (eg Boyd 2001:100f). This would indicate that he does not use exhaustive knowledge, even if he has it. Indeed, Sanders uses just over a hundred pages in examining the Biblical material (Sanders 1998:38-139). They feel that traditional theology, especially of the Calvinistic persuasion, was influenced by Greek philosophy (Erickson 2003:134). While the presentation of the attributes of God in "traditional theology" has long been attractive, what is being asked is whether, as in much of theology, this resulted in an overemphasis, a view of God supported not by Christian experience or the Bible, but by the more philosophical world-view of Plato and Aristotle. While this contrasted dramatically with the fickleness of the polytheistic deities and the insecurity attached to their worship, it implied both a static unchanging deity and therefore a fixed future, denying human freedom. However, the traditional view is of course also well-known for its scriptural foundation, as in revered texts such as that of Berkhof's *Systematic Theology*. Defenses of this latter position are common; a noteworthy recent work, reflecting particularly on Pinnock's theology, is that of Wright (1996).

One of the natural criticisms of open theism is that it appears to take away security from people. If God does not know the future, how can we know that we are safe? This is a form of the heresy combated in Colossians, that Christ is inadequate (Hall 1986:77). This is indeed the case for process theology, but even if the future is open, there is no need to believe that it is out of God's control! He is absolutely able to intervene, and to do so from a full awareness of what is likely to happen. He will not allow events to defeat his ultimate purpose. Most open theists then depart from the full consistency of their position and say that although God does respect human free will, he may override this and intervene so that his purposes will be met; he does not leave the future entirely to chance and the whims of human choices. The future is partly settled (Pinnock 2002:217). Erickson (2003:191) refers to this as an "internal contradiction". Schumacher (1973:187) here comments that God made some things predictable, but others non-predictable; he feels that either extreme would demotivate people.

A particular concern with the open view is that by emphasizing God's interaction with people in the historical process, it must minimize his essential otherness, his transcendence. It puts God definitely in time, with everlasting and not eternal life (Pinnock 2001:75, 96 etc) (for the distinction in terms cf Erickson (2003:164n)). If, as has often traditionally been thought, God is outside time, in eternity, he is perhaps able to look down on the whole of time, just as a pilot on an aircraft has a more extensive view than that of the rest of the world which is restricted to the surface by gravity. In contrast, the view of open theism effectively puts God in the historical process; the difference from his creation is not that he is eternal, so outside time, but as everlasting, contrasts with impermanence; he always was, and always will be. The view that God is in time is common today, especially as it accommodates the idea that God experiences suffering (Fiddes 1988:103).

It is not for nothing that the suggestions of open theism have been likened to those of process theology, although Pinnock (2001:140-50) is careful to draw distinctions from it. An understanding of God in time need not mean that God is developing, as held by the process theologians, but does mean that he experiences and is affected by events. The open theists are insistent that although there is an obvious similarity between their view and that of process theology, they are not the same (but cf Erickson 1998:306). In particular, process theology usually believes that God's knowledge is constantly growing, that he is by very nature not omniscient. Hartshorne however believed that God knew all that could be known at any time; he distinguished between God's completeness and perfection, the former of which was only future (Fiddes 1988:93). Likewise, the open theists believe that God is omniscient, that he knows all that can be known at any time. As the future unfolds, of course, and the unknowable becomes known, God immediately knows it.

The proposal of open theism is an attempt to retain the ideas of omniscience in a full way. God does know everything that can be known. Nevertheless it has been felt that the idea is not acceptable to at least conservative Christianity. The American Evangelical Theological Society decided in November 2001 that "the Bible clearly teaches that God has complete, accurate and infallible knowledge of all events past, present and future, including all future decisions and actions of free moral agents" (Field 2003:2). Because the concern of this society is to uphold the authority of infallible scriptures, argumentation has centred on the interpretation of scripture. However, the key issue is really that the view questions the sovereignty and perfection of God; and with that condemnation must go the view that God's knowledge is also inherently limited.

The kenotic solution

Both the solutions of middle knowledge and open theism are still subject to the objection that God is really inherently limited, as he is in the situation of time. He is not able to see the whole of time from some external vantage point in eternity. Erickson (2003:159) remarks that in this case there would actually be no such thing as God's foreknowledge!

Nevertheless, the traditional view of God's atemporality, and the affirmation that he acts in time, need not be incompatible. It must remain a possibility, and would be consistent with the view of Christianity as theistic, to affirm that God is both immanent and transcendent. In this case, God is both in and outside of time. For example, Barth holds that "God has time, because and as He has eternity" (CD 2(1):611, cited in Fiddes 1988:99). Then just as he refrains from changing the past, he could well also refrain from doing what he also could well do, which is to look into the future. (Incidentally, is there perhaps a sense in which forgiveness is achieved by affecting the past?) In these cases, God limits himself.

The openness of the future presumed in the proposals of middle knowledge and open theism also means that Christians would ultimately be insecure because there is no guarantee that God will provide the future that he has promised (Ware 2002:208). The wholeness that is salvation is then not possible; it can only be complete in the context of the security of the future. Fiddes (1988:3) therefore attempts to bring together the ideas that God suffers yet fulfills his purposes. The significance of this objection is seen in that both systems are usually modified to deal with this, in the first case by incorporating elements of compatibilism, and in the second by insisting that God may well intervene to ensure the future that he wants. These imply that God chooses to ensure that a particular result follows, which includes the guarantee of security. In fact, for God to do anything, he must choose and thereby reject all other possibilities; this is a form of self-limitation. It is however not necessary to say that God chooses to act in every situation; in this case essential freedom in human beings is preserved.

God's choosing and his self-limitation are both aspects of a further solution, of God's *kenōsis*. When Jesus, although the second Person, "emptied" himself of the exercise of attributes that particularly pertained to deity, omniscience was naturally one of the attributes that was curtailed. This followed from the very idea of incarnation; a human being simply is not omniscient! Indeed it was the desire for this that Genesis 3 portrays as the root of the first sin. Jesus was then genuinely ignorant, such as of the time of the *parousia*. This was actually one of the features that was attractive in the nineteenth century, as Jesus could then share the beliefs of those of the day, so, for example have an unenlightened attitude to the Bible.

If this is then predicated of God, it then goes a long way to explain the dilemma of human free will, for this can be possible if God has limited his knowledge of the future. The future then can effectively be open, and humanity can have real free will. This means that in the present situation of *kenōsis*, human choices can be free; yet as this is not due to an inherent limitation in God, ultimately the future is securely under his control: van den Brink (1993:219) cites the case of the control that a competent rider has over a horse, expressing real power. In fact the *kenōsis* passage of Philippians 2 presumes human free will, for it is set in the context of an appeal to "have the mind of Christ", and such an appeal is really a mockery if there is in fact no free will. Thus Hill (1975:14) speaks of God opening himself to the world "kenotically", so knowing a free future. He does speak however of the fact of people being in God's image; this imparts real creativity to them but also affects their choice. He adds that God does have ultimate control over the future. Although most open theists believe that the future is fundamentally unknowable, even to God, some also note this solution; Pinnock (2002:223) refers to Willard's view of "dispositional omniscience".

This must also mean that Christ himself had a free will, or conformity to it would make no sense. Philippians 2 also presumes that Jesus accepted self-limitation by choice; "he emptied himself" (Phil 2:7). Likewise in his humanity he chose to be humble (Phil 2:8). As the controversies of the seventh century had clarified, even though in Christ there were two wills, the divine and the human, yet they are effectively one and they are always in total agreement, naturally by *perichōrēsis*. Jesus said that he was always fully obedient to the Father (Jn 6:38), an aspect also of the kenotic process (Phil 2:8). This of course immediately also indicates the nature of human free will, for although free, it should exercise its freedom in the context of the will of God.

The essence of a kenotic approach is that God is indeed as traditional theology advocated, being affirmed as omnipotent, eternal and so on, but that he limited himself so that he could relate to the world and its inhabitants. Polkinghorne (2001:104) comments that God inherently accepts a *kenōsis* just by acting in time. He could totally control all that occurs, he could exhaustively know the future, but chooses not to. Jesus' ignorance was freely chosen, even while omniscience was always within reach (Macleod 1998:169). Here Sontag (1991:68f) helpfully observes that God's omnipotence does not in fact necessitate his omniscience; thus he can know all, but chooses not to; omniscience in the traditional sense is usually taken to imply that God does automatically know everything. Thus a kenotic approach reconciles both the power to be omniscient and free will. It also does not necessarily limit the relationship of God to time; as traditional theology has often affirmed, God is both transcendent and immanent. In relation to time, this gives the possibility for God to be outside time, and also in it; neither is necessarily excluded.

Boyd remarks that the controversy over open theism is less about God than about creation (Erickson 2003:221). Naturally in respect of omniscience, the kenotic approach also relates strongly to creation. If God created out of his free choice, it should follow that the future is also free. As Sontag (1991:71) believes, "eschatology is simply the counterpart of creation theory". Both are then aspects of God's self-limitation; in order to achieve his purposes, he has modified his omnipotence and omniscience by the same open-endedness that he has bestowed upon creation (Peacocke, in Richard 1997:137). He remarks that the God who creates out of sheer possibility cannot fix the future in detail, lest divinity contradict its own nature and make God appear to be out of harmony with Nature (Sontag 1991:68f). He could have fixed nature and human nature irrevocably in detail; but to do that would be false to the divine Being itself. Such a divinity has no need to fix the operation and decisions of men and women in advance. It is weak gods (and people) that attempt rigid control. Those who are secure in their power can allow others freedom without feeling threatened in their being. This means that he opens himself not so much to change, to being affected, as taught by the open theists, but to relationships. Bartholomew has argued that God and chance are logically compatible, but more than that, an element of chance is beneficial in producing a richer environment than would otherwise have been possible (Peacocke 1993:120); he writes that "God chose to make a world of chance because it would have the properties necessary for producing beings fit for fellowship with himself" (1993:156). God therefore benefits from his self-limitation.

While the idea of *kenōsis* by its very nature allows an affirmation that God created people with free choice, it also affirms that God acted, in the incarnation and atonement, to help people in the need that was produced by their choice. God's action was for the benefit, and ultimate security of his people. There is no indication in the idea of *kenōsis* that God is not ultimately trustworthy, but on the contrary, the whole process was done just because of his reliability, because it is the means of salvation. In fact, far from denying providence, *kenōsis* is yielding to it (Foster 2000:172).

Future security

In its portrayal of choice and self-limitation, the Philippians passage concludes with the distinct action of God in compelling the response of humanity. At that point there will be no further choice; "every knee shall bow" (Phil 2:11). God then takes a further action to consummate the process, in this case complete the act of salvation. This is the same thing that is part of the Christian view of salvation, that God is ultimately reliable despite present appearances, and so faith can, and should, be placed in him, enabling salvation. The classic example is of course that of Abraham, who believed the promise of God despite the clear indication that a child was an impossibility (Rom 4). So even though what we observe of Christ might seem to be incapable of saving, just because of his *kenōsis*, his action contains the promise of a future consummation. After all, the hymn which celebrates *kenōsis* does close with a prediction.

For Abraham, the future was secure, but only secure because it rested on the fact that the future was not completely open, but that God would do what he had promised. Basically, the fulfillment of his life came from his faith, his relationship, to God. For Christians likewise. Such fullness of life depends on a complete relationship with God as his children, which is only possible through *kenōsis*, the incarnation, humility and ultimately the death of the second Person of the Trinity. Through this, Jesus left the intimacy of the total inter-Trinitarian relationships so that people can be incorporated into that life. By the opening of the Trinity in the sending of Christ, the future of people in relation to him becomes closed; they become ultimately secure. The openness of the future is overcome in the openness of God. As with Christ, this includes the anticipation of future glory.

Chapter 9

Secularization as *kenōsis*

At the turn of the century, along with all the other fuss about the change of millennia and possible impact of the date on computer systems, the so-called Y2k effect, there was a little light-hearted banter about what the first decade of the new century and new millennium would be called. It was easy to refer to the "nineties", and indeed all of the decades can be referred to similarly, except, due to the strangeness of the English language, the first two. One very nice suggestion, which, just like all the other ideas, has not caught on, was that it be called the "noughties", opening it up to the idea of the "naughty noughties"! This would certainly fit one of the characteristics of the age, although the decline in morals is not a new thing, but goes back particularly to the second World War. It is, nevertheless, still a sufficiently significant feature of society that many governments, not least those of the United States, and, particularly relevant to the author, South Africa, have programmes in place to try to reverse the erosion of moral standards.

It is more likely that the first decade of the twenty-first century will be remembered not for moral decline, perhaps more a characteristic of the "swinging sixties", but for the impact that Islam has had on the western world, and especially on the United States and its major allies. Prompted by the attack on the Twin Towers in New York on "9-11" in 2001, America in particular has identified the "naughty one" as Osama bin Laden, and the "naughties" are fundamentalist Moslems.

But actually this is not so different, for the underlying reason for the opposition of such groups to the West is its lack of religion, and therefore low moral standards. It was probably inevitable that the invasions of Afghanistan and then of Iraq would rekindle memories of the Crusades of centuries before, but even if there are some in the West who are motivated against Islam from religious motives, they must be a very small minority. Likewise, the opposition to the West is not fundamentally against Christianity; indeed from the early days of Islam, it was more prepared to tolerate the other monotheistic "religions of the Book" than those of other religions or of none. On the contrary, the issue with the West is not with its Christianity, but with its lack, its secularization.

Secularization is the process by which a society becomes centred on, or dominated by, secular as distinct from religious concerns. Secularism is then the world-view of such a society. This is of course a generalisation, as segments of society have different degrees of secularization (Lyon 1985:70). It also has several aspects: Dobbelaere (2002:24f) distinguishes individual secularization, the lack of individual practice, societal secularization, the loss of influence on society, and organisational secularization, the effect on religious organisations by changes in society. What is important is that this is not necessarily a lack of belief in God, although secularism flows very naturally into atheism, the positive denial of the existence of God. Rather, in a secularized socity, it is not that God is dead, but that the word "God" is meaningless (van Buren, in Richard 1967:77). Secularization in the developed West possibly reflects more disenchantment with the church than with the faith that it represents; Dekker, Luidens and Rice (1997:280) have found that individual faith has proved to be much more resilient. Nevertheless, this is also declining, and without the support of a vigorous community, it is not likely that the faith of most individuals would do well; this then also becomes secularized. At the same time, even without widespread personal faith and in the weakness of the churches, Christian values have also not decayed as rapidly; there is still a Christian ethos in Europe, such as the upholding of the ideal of honesty. Rather secularism is the marginalisation of religion in society, human self-assertion in distinction to what had been clerical rule (Pannenberg 1989:vii). Even if, as Blumenberg (1983:30) argues, the structure of western society was largely moulded by Christianity, and still shows it in many ways, without the underpinning of real faith it will lose the benefits of its past. Even traditional morals are presented not from God's authority, but from secular logic; an example is that divorce is argued not as against God's will, but as bad for society (Bruce 2002:21). Alternative practices may well replace religion (as in "civil religion"; cf Bellah (Dobbelaere 2002:54), where, for example, a public holiday is based on a non-religious reason, or reverence is paid to a flag not a religious symbol). The essential motive is human autonomy; really this is idolatry (Lyon 1985:98). Religion may well be accepted as a valid part of society, but at its periphery. Its main concern is with other things, such as economic matters. Religion has lost societal function; it no longer legitimates the structures of society (Martin 2005:126, also Blumenberg 1983:61). In particular, morals become detached, being controlled by technology rather than religion (Wilson, in Dobbelaere 2002:32).

Until comparatively recently, the existence of God would have been taken as obvious, and it would have naturally followed that society would then have been centred on him and his worship. In European society, throughout the Middle Ages, communities were built with a church at the centre, a powerful reminder that all of life revolved about, and related to, God. Such centring on the divine is still seen in many parts of the world. In such circumstances the message believed to be from the divine is treated as having absolute authority and is not really questioned. This world-view is sometimes characterised as "pre-modern". However, in Europe a shift in thinking occurred, resulting in a different attitude, that of "modernism", very much allied to a secular world-view. In such a secular society, the natural centre and focus of cities in not a church building, but shops, offices, and a business district.

For a religious person, secularism is hard. It is, or should be, heart-breaking to see society dominated by other matters, which fill the place that should be occupied by God. Essentially, these things have become idols; it is totally understandable that Islam, which originated in an intense rejection of polytheistic idolatry, finds the ethos of the secular West abhorrent. Religion has many benefits, not least moral upliftment; the fervent preaching of the American revivalist Billy Sunday was dominated by his perception of moral degeneration (Frank 1986:188). Even such notoriously irreligious people as Hume (Barry 1969:11) and Voltaire (Chadwick 1975:10) said that religious doubts must be kept from the common people for this reason. Voltaire said that for the sake of morals, "if God did not exist, it would be necessary to invent him" (Chadwick 1975:104). Even Durkheim has noted that all great social institutions had a religious origin (Dobbelaere 2002:30), while much of the progress against oppression in the industrial revolution came from evangelicals (Bruce 2002:97). And how can a person exalt an aspect of the creation rather than the creator, the one who made it? How can a person fill his or her life with concerns that will last for a short time, when there are eternal possibilities? And just as a person whose spirit leaves dies, is not religion essential for the life of society? And is not the success of the West, its scientific progress, attributable to a Christian world-view (Barry 1969:39)? Secularization thus tends to be viewed negatively, as a "spiritual anathema" against changes since the Middle Ages (Blumenberg 1983:5). Blamires (1978:80) therefore sees this as a bigger danger even than the treat of nuclear war. Such bewilderment is actually not new; nearly three millennia ago, the prophet Jeremiah reflected the divine mind:

> my people have committed two evils:
>> they have forsaken me,
> the fountain of living waters,
>> and hewed out cisterns for themselves,
> broken cisterns,
>> that can hold no water (Jer 2:13).

More than the attitude, the religious person finds secularism hard to understand. If there is indeed a God, the very nature of deity should mean that belief in him and obeying him should dominate every part of life. Even more than this, the religious person must be further perplexed, for if there is indeed a God, particularly the sort of God that Christians proclaim, how has he allowed this situation? If God is indeed all powerful, all-knowing, totally perfect, could he have not intervened to display his existence in a way that would compel the sort of response that he is worthy of? And if he is as loving as Christianity proclaims him to be, surely he would act, for following him must be the best for people. The similarity to the old dilemma concerning the existence of evil is of course obvious.

This bewilderment must however be qualified. Could it in fact be that God wants a secularized society? Is it not in fact better for the Church to concentrate on its core functions (Parsons, in Dobbelaere 2002:30)? Although the Old Testament does reflect a sacral society, a theocracy, this was superseded by a system in which entry is not automatic, by birth, but voluntarily, by faith. So is the anomaly not so much secularization, but rather a society that had been sacralized? Outside of the Church, the natural state of humanity is of secularism! Does this not naturally follow from an idea of "original sin"? Indeed, there are many Christian traditions which do make a definite distinction between the Church and the world. The Puritan Roger Williams of Massachusetts Bay felt that Church control over society was a fundamental aberration (Lyon 1985:21). Logically, a Christian way of life is only for those who are "born again"; Christians are not subject to the law but to the Spirit, an impossibility outside the Church. The Old Testament ethic does not directly apply either to society as a whole or to the majority of Christians, as it was only applicable to those in that covenant (Acts 15). However, most would also believe that God's will is that all should be saved (1 Tim 2:4), resulting in a sacral society. Most would also hold that even without a faith commitment to God in Christ, a Christian lifestyle is still the best for the world. Then there are groups such as the Amish, and even proponents of a rigid predestination. Neither of these logically seek to add to their groups, although both would believe that their lifestyle is the best for the rest of the world. Then there are the varieties of monastic groups, but these would be open to people joining them. Like the Amish, they would not necessarily deny that people outside could be real Christians, but that they are infected with other views.

Secularization may even have good effects, such as being a *preparatio evangelica* (Barry 1969:15, claiming the support of Bonhoeffer), but that does not make it good in itself; the realisation of the emptiness of life without a spiritual element can be devastating. In similar vein, Paul had to argue against those who believed that the existence of forgiveness by grace made sin a good thing (Rom 3:8). More directly, secularization can well benefit the Church; Häring (1973:2) even calls it providential, as it purifies its witness; Cox (1968:31) also regards it as positive, and Barry (1969:15) as an enrichment of Christianity.

A further possibility is that God has allowed society to be secularized because he is primarily concerned with the individual. Such individualism has been a feature of Western society, but it must be questioned whether this reflects Christianity. Even if the focus of the New Testament seems to be on the individual relationship with God, this does contrast with the Old, and it is perhaps a better understanding that this is actually also the situation with the New, where God primarily deals with the Church, the community. In any case, one of the major influences on the individual is the surrounding environment; people are more likely to come to individual commitment in an atmosphere of commitment.

Secularization a result of *kenōsis*

Just as with the problem of evil, perhaps a solution to the question rests in the nature of God. I want to suggest that just as Jesus in his incarnation acted in *kenōsis*, or self-limitation, that this is fundamental to what God is like. He is the *deus absconditus* (Cox 1968:267), although not in any Gnostic sense; indeed his limitation is done for quite the opposite reason, just for the sake of relating to the world. It must also be stressed again that God's *kenōsis* is fundamentally different from the understanding of God in process theology. Whereas the latter understands God as inherently limited, *kenōsis* is a deliberate self-restriction. In line with traditional Christian doctrine, God is totally perfect, so fully omnipotent, omniscient and so on, but has chosen to restrict the use of his abilities in dealing with the world.

However, in this *kenōsis*, human experience of God naturally tends to fade, especially when life becomes more secure. Religion tends to be weaker in the prosperity of economic centres, stronger in the peripheries (Martin 2005:59). Nevertheless, when there are situations of rapid change, and when what is needed for living becomes scarce, people are drawn to remember God; thus religion temporarily revived in eastern Europe with the loss of the security that socialism had given (Norris & Inglehart, 2004:114).

It is then it is no surprise that in his hiddenness, a process of secularization becomes almost inevitable. Indeed the word *kenōsis* means "empty of significance" (Fee 1995:95), and this is exactly what secularization is; God loses significance for society. This is to make a direct link between *kenōsis* and secularization. Even the original meaning of the word, where a monk or priest was secularized from a monastic environment to one with involvement with the world (Cox 1968:33) has a hint of this; in a sense God gives them up, empties himself of them to a degree. God no longer controls property or people (Berger 1969:106). It may then be suggested that secularization has occurred as a natural consequence of the sort of world that God has made, which in turn reflects something of the nature of the creator. Thus, for example, in God's *kenōsis*, there is a self-imposed limitation of his knowledge, so that human free-will is a real possibility. Pannenberg (1989:vii) feels that the central idea of modernity is human freedom, and that, very significantly, this is Christian in origin. This freedom incidentally means that secularization is not inevitable (Bruce 2002:37)! But because of God's *kenōsis*, his very existence becomes less apparent to people, who then naturally espouse agnosticism, their own lack of knowledge, a natural companion to secularism. Ironically, as God limits his manifestation in the world, people reflect this *kenōsis* in restricting their perception of him (Richard 1982:19). People choose to limit their relationship with God such as to a part of their lives (Mackay, in Japinga 1997:29), resulting in secularization. Then significantly, the attitude of Christians should also be kenotic, in particular rejecting the attitude of domination that has often characterized the Church; Blumenberg (1983:7) specifically refers to "the biblical figure of the kenosis". It is therefore not surprising that secularization has been a feature of previously Christian societies (Martin 1978:1), even a result of Biblical faith (Gogarten, cited in Cox 1968:31, Richard 1967:139). Christians are now "heretics", literally "choosers", of what is contrary to what is commonly accepted (Berger, in Bruce 2002:233). Secularization can well be defined as a dependence on human ability rather than on God (Lyon 1985:1). Cox (1968:31) sees secularization as positive in that it is liberative, so a good thing for Christianity; this is indeed correct insofar as it is from ecclesiastical, so human authority, but sinful when this freedom goes against God. Christianity is indeed liberative (Jn 8:36), but this must be qualified. When liberation becomes rebellion, the result is, as often repeated in Romans 1:18f, that "God gave them up". Even if the Kingdom of God, so Christianity, is like secularization, in that they are inherently kenotic because both renounce (Cox 1968:125), they do not renounce the same thing, the former renouncing the world for God's sake, the latter inverting the emphasis.

Even if his desire is that all are committed to him, that all are "saved" and that society is sacralized, God has deemed it better that people are free. As part of their humanity comes freedom, and so the possibility of secularity (Richard 1982:263). He rejects the claim to absolute authority made by a sacral society (Cox 1968:35) or by any totalitarianism. Christians pray for, but do not sacrifice to, the emperor (Cox 1968:41)! This means that there is a possibility of rejecting him; moreover, this implies that the chance of a secularized society is acceptable to God. The first "secularization" was a direct result of the choice to disobey God, in the expulsion from Eden! The alternative would only be achievable by force, a removal of human free will, which then would be worse.

Compartmentalism

For secularization to be even a possibility, there must be a distinction between the secular, things of the world (Latin *saeculum*) and the sacred (Pannenberg 1989:3). If everything is treated as essentially united, aspects of one reality, then the sacred naturally constantly affects the secular. Modern Western life, in contrast to this, is highly compartmentalised, where one aspect of life is distinct from others, and not inherently related to them. In one way, this is part of the reason for its success, because this attitude favours organised thought and so the development of science. The success of the modern world is deeply rooted in Christianity (Barry 1969:39). At the same time, the application of science in technology is facilitated by division of labour and the mass production process, which depends on the separation of aspects of production, one person concentrating on one aspect, and doing it efficiently.

But this compartmentalisation is fertile ground for the growth of secularization, for the things related to the divine are naturally separated off from other aspects of life, which are then unaffected by them (Dobbelaere 2002:166). The modern person lives in a plurality of worlds each with different values and structures (Berger 1970:61). Marty has described secularism as the "chopping up of reality" (Japinga 1997:39). It is even the case that two religions can be held concurrently, not being perceived as incompatible. This is often seen in African society, where traditional beliefs and customs are practised together with an often devoted Christian belief. In practice, of course, most Europeans can be equally syncretistic, but the second religion is materialism. When this becomes dominant, the society becomes secularized. A "post-modern" world-view in fact sees no problem in holding contradictory views simultaneously.

But again, such compartmentalisation is fundamental to Christianity. Not only does it follow from monotheism (Bruce 2002:6), but the initial expression of Christianity was of a definite distinction from the *saeculum*. Christians were "saints", *hagioi* (eg Rom 1:7, Phil 1:1), a word which referred not only to the ethical holiness of the Christian life, but also to a separation from the rest of humanity. This was of course taken over from the particularism of the Jews, who indeed only survived the experiences of the exile by their rigid separation from the people and cultures with whom they were dwelling. It was the same thing that preserved them throughout the persecutions of the Middle Ages. This does follow from their absolute monotheism; if God is one, other gods are empty idols (Is 40f) and other religions are simply false. A worshipper of God must avoid anything which would spoil the purity of worship. In any case, God is a "jealous" God, allowing no rivals (Ex 20:1f).

Berger (1969:113f) contrasts the Old Testament worldview with that of both Egypt and Mesopotamia, where society is thoroughly sacral, so that there is "continuity between the world of men and the world of the gods" (1969:113). Israel experienced a "double exodus" from both these cultures (1969:115). "The Old Testament posits a God who stands *outside* the cosmos, which is his creation but which he confronts and does not permeate (1969:115, his emphasis). God therefore does not act cosmically, but historically, and so was a mobile God who could not be restricted to a specific place or people. He (1969:117) comments that the Old Testament clearly separates the divine and the world, contrasting strongly with the worldview of the ancient near East; this secularization did however give a sense of insecurity, and so the surrounding beliefs were always attractive to Israel (1969:114). Israelite religion is a celebration of God's acts in history, reflected in the nature of its festivals, but these acts "are performed by a God standing entirely outside the world" (1969:118). In his distinction from the world, God then acts by means of agents. In contrast, process theology puts God very much into the world, not so distinct from it (Boyd 2001:277).

Berger (1969:121) then feels that the secularizing tendency of the Old Testament is to some extent reversed in the incarnation, where God is again integral with the creation. In a sense, the world is resacralised (Berger 1969:121). Nevertheless, it is significant that the nature of this involvement was not so much a manifestation as divine, but in *kenōsis*, in the likeness of a man (Phil 2:7). This is then not a reversal of the essential kenotic separation of God from the world. However, the Church in the Middle Ages saw itself more in terms of God's presence in the world, resulting in a sacral society, a view reversed in the Reformation, which then prompted the development of modern secularization.

An attitude of compartmentalism is naturally encouraged by the fact that any new movement must initially be a small minority. Very survival depends on a rigid separation to preserve the distinctiveness which gives meaning to the specific existence of the group. At the same time, however, this does give the movement a vitality and attractiveness which would encourage its rapid growth. The irony is that with that growth, these features are liable to disappear.

In the early Church, this separation led to persecution by the Roman authorities, which from time to time was very severe. Part of the reason for this was that the Romans viewed a common religion, especially veneration of the emperor, as a powerful unifying factor. But "Caesar is Lord" could not be held by those for whom "Christ is Lord" (1 Cor 12:3). When, later, Christianity became so big that suppression became impracticable, it was replaced by toleration and then by adoption.

The acceptance of Christianity by the emperor Constantine and its adoption as the state religion meant that it became the norm for people to claim to be Christian, and the ideal of separation diminished. Christians, and especially the clergy, enjoyed special privileges in the state, such as reduction or exemption from taxation. The Church as an institution adopted secular structures such as a governmental hierarchy, and became involved in politics. In practice, this process was itself a secularization of faith (Martin 1969:23). The natural result is a dilution of the faith when it is adopted for secular benefit. However, at this point dissent from Christianity by other religions, and within it by heretics was persecuted; an attitude of separation was still present! These groups naturally distinguished themselves from the rest of Christendom; an example from when Church and state were basically one was the emergence of various Anabaptist groups, the "Radical Reformation". For their modern-day successors, separation is still a significant part of their ethos. For Mennonites, and especially the Amish, the desire is to have as few dealings as possible with the rest of society. Baptists and Pentecostals practise separation to varying extents.

At the same time, right through the period of the identification of Church and State, there was a consistent dissatisfaction with the sort of commitment that naturally resulted from this, and so a desire for separation. This evidenced in the hermits and then in the monastic communities throughout the Middle Ages. Not only was there a desire to spend more time in religious activity, but a rejection of the values of the world in the adoption of asceticism. Of course part of the motivation for this was the belief in the compartmentalism of human nature. Inherited from the Greek world-view, the belief was that human nature comprised a duality of an immortal soul and a mortal body. The latter was subject to temptation and sin, which could harm what mattered, the soul, and should then be suppressed by asceticism.

Compartmentalism is also what Jesus did in *kenōsis*. In creation, God effectively established a category in distinction from himself. There was a difference between secular and sacred. The second Person then entered the category of the secular by becoming incarnate. Christianity is in essence a "secular" religion (Martin 1969:25). More than this, human society, especially in those days, was compartmentalised, and Jesus chose the specific categories of the humbler in society, even being reckoned as a slave. The distinction between slave and free was a major division at the time (cf Gal 3:28).

While observing that the incarnation was an acceptance of humanity, making a distinction from deity, three observations may be made in this regard. Firstly the incarnation did retain a distinction between the human nature of Jesus and that of the rest of humanity. The Philippian hymn speaks of the "likeness of men" (Phil 2:7); if nothing else, he was sinless, a severe contrast to everybody else. Secondly, it is also clear that even if Jesus wanted to identify with humanity, most of humanity did not reciprocate, which is why he was finally crucified. Indeed, rather than integrate, the coming of Jesus rather divided (Matt 10:34). Nevertheless, the uniting of Jesus with humanity indicates his desire to bless that humanity; Christianity is not only a means of life after death, but is a benefit to individuals and society as a whole in the present.

The extent of secularization

Secularism is dominant in western Europe, where religious practice is increasingly rare. Belief involving deity is more common, but still held only by a minority (Bruce 2002:71). The process has accelerated since the second World War; Stephen Neill (1984:248) notes that in the Church of England, the number of baptisms and confirmations, which were the norm for the British population, halved in the decade of the 1960's. Numbers of members and adherents of most major denominations continue to decline. Interestingly the emergence of alternative beliefs such as New Age, and new Christian emphases, such as in the Charismatic movement, while popular, are insignificant against the overall trend of decline (Bruce 2002:75,175). In any case, and most significantly, the ethos of both is very compatible with that of modern society in that they aim for individual benefit (Bruce 2002:178). The situation is less marked in the USA, where Neill says that 80% claim allegiance to some church. At the same time, however, he alleges that 70% are effectively unchurched, which would bring the situation more in line with western Europe. Possibly the USA is a case of arrested development (Martin 1969:10)? Bainton (1960:198) however notes that the USA was originally peopled by dissenters, and at the same time less affected by the Enlightenment. Bruce (2002:206) in any case alleges that American church attendance is over-reported and is actually much less; it is also declining. Perhaps a good estimate is that in Europe, 10% are religiously active compared to 50% in the USA, although this may not reflect levels of commitment. A secularized person can well retain an area of life for religion. However, the very fact of claiming attendance does indicate that religion does maintain a status that it does not enjoy in Europe. More significantly, Barry (1969:19) accuses the vast American churches as really secular and cultural, reflecting societal, not religious concerns (also Berger 1969:108). The USA only appears religious, in fact the motives of many are secular (Martin 1969:10). Johnson (1995) indicates the pervasiveness of a naturalistic world-view in American society. Church-going and belief do not necessarily correspond (Barry 1969:23). Attendance remains high as the churches are "organisationally secularized" (Dobbelaere 2002:22).

Luckmann has described the American situation as "internal secularization" as distinct from the "external" found in Europe (Berger 1970:17). Nevertheless, there are several other factors which may well mean that religion in America has been able to survive better than in Europe. For one thing the constitutional separation of church and state has meant that a person belonging to the church has made a deliberate choice to do so; the situation is a little similar to that in the pre-Constantinian church, where persecution dissuaded all but the most committed from open expression of faith, but where after acceptance by the Roman Empire it was both fashionable and expedient to belong to a church, and so nominalism flourished. Secondly the American ethos of competition means that churches openly compete, and deliberately provide attractive programmes; here again this may well produce adherents but not those who are really concerned to worship; however, while noting this, Norris & Inglehart (2004:96,100) feel that the evidence suggests that pluralism has not increased participation. Thirdly, it is probably still relevant that many of the original settlers arrived in America for religious reasons (Norris & Inglehart 2004:225).

In South Africa, a frequently cited figure, emanating from census returns, is that 78% claim to belong to some Christian church (92% of "whites", 74% of "blacks"). A further very significant factor is the growth of the African Independent (or "Initiated", or "Indigenous") churches, which now account for about 50% of black church adherents. These are often said to be syncretistic, which indeed is often the case, but it is probably the case that a reason for the combination of beliefs is a dissatisfaction with the manifestation of Christianity in "white" churches, in short with white secularization. It must be noted here that many commentators (eg Dobbelaere 2002:158) feel that sectarianism enhances the privatisation of religion, and so secularization. What is important is that particularly in the black segment of society, religion still remains influential; secularization is proceeding, but has not gone very far, certainly compared to whites in South Africa, who reflect the European situation.

It may just be noted that other cultures manifest other types of secularization; Martin (1978:5f) provides a helpful summary.

The growth of secularization

If the *kenōsis* of God is to be accepted as an explanation of the phenomenon of secularization, it must then be asked how it was that society was even sacralized. One possibility is that it in fact never was, that there never was an overall commitment of the people to God. There is no necessary connection between belief and church-going (Barry 1969:23). Stott (1984:3) comments on the brutality of the eighteenth century, and the same could be said of much of the Middle Ages; this was before major secularization. One suggestion is that the adoption of Christian practice was imposed by the rulers, whether for political reasons or as a result of their own convictions. Lyon (1985:18), specifically citing France, suggests a generalisation that in medieval society, Christianity was only ever the faith of the rulers; Mehl says that the common people were essentially pagan in ideas (Lyon 1985:21); Chadwick (1975:3) simply asserts that a pre-nineteenth century religious society never existed. Agreeing with this, Martin (1969:5) notes Heer's observation that even a superficial conversion of society could take centuries. The same could well be the case for the Old Testament. When political and intellectual currents shifted, the natural result was a move to what was really the case all along. Nevertheless, even if the religion of the pre-secularized world may not have really been total or widespread, society was definitely centred upon it. Bruce (2002:45f) insists that basic Christian beliefs were held, even if not really understood; however lack of understanding must encourage their abandoning. It was this basic acceptance that changed, a change that can be linked to a number of key trends in thought.

In this case, the attribution to *kenōsis* suggests that there can well be a connection between these shifts in thought with that *kenōsis*, that these trends are a working through of it.

Impetuses towards secularization

The mainstream of Medieval society was almost the total opposite to a secularized society. Although not everyone was fervently Catholic, everyone did share a world-view based on Christian premises (Hamilton 1986:87). It was totally pervasive, even if this does not necessitate a idealistic view that there was widespread real devotion on the personal level (Dobbelaere 2002:45). The Middle Ages saw religion as integral to the whole of life, its nature as God-given and therefore basically unchangeable. All were believed to have been born with a specific role in society, and because God had given it, seeking to change it would be wrong. In particular, rulers felt that they owed their position to a divine mandate to rule; even if church and state were technically separate (the "two swords" (Hamilton 1986:16)), the temporal power was given by God. Rebellion against the civil ruler was also then against God and so sinful. In order to maintain this God-given order, even prices and wages were fixed in relation to social needs (Lyon 1985:33); a person earned only enough to maintain social standing, so that even economically it was difficult to change. Obviously part of the inspiration for this state of affairs was the integration of society with its faith in the Old Testament polity; it is notable that in that structure, deliberate sin was punished by exclusion from society (Num 15:30).

Nevertheless, in contrast to the Old Testament, of course, the New Testament makes a radical distinction between matters of civil society and religion; even if it does advocate obedience to government as obedience to God (Rom 13), this is only until its demands contradict the desire of God (Acts 5:29).

As well as critiquing the medieval ideal of an integrated society, Christianity must question its ideal of stability. Indeed it was the loss of this, the discovery of a sense of history, that itself contributes to the secularization process (Barry 1969:41). Blumenberg (1983:44) believes that it was the non-appearance of the expected end that moved the Church towards involvement in the world for the sake of being relevant, and so contributed to its secularization. Perhaps the Church needs to take 2 Peter 3 to heart and remain distinctive by its patience. The idea of creation need not be seen as giving stability, because it is itself a change; in any case, the very fact of creation actually implies the value of the secular (Barry 1969:54). This is even more the case with the incarnation, which is God's act into the world, with the definite intention of changing it. Both of these can be seen in terms of *kenōsis*, which is a process of emptying, followed by its reversal in glorification. Secularization can then be seen as an aspect of the developing changes in society, which is how Durkheim saw it (Lyon 1985:26); in a situation of rapid social change, all organisations suffer (Martin 1969:16); this is also due to a desire for anonymity in modern society. Just as evolution is generally viewed as good, so secularization is often viewed affirmatively as beneficial to society (Pannenberg 1989:ix); it could then be accepted as desirable to God. However, Durkheim believed that religion in society would naturally atrophy (Lyon 1985:30). *Kenōsis*, on the other hand is God's specific intervention, without which the changes just would not occur. It is indeed the case that the stability of the Middle Ages was broken by a number of movements, effecting the development of secularization.

First came the Renaissance. Because of the almost total integration of religion into society in the Middle Ages, there had been a general ignorance of anything outside of the Church in that period. The collapse of the Roman Empire had left Europe in the "Dark Ages". However, particularly due to the Crusades and the contact with the eastern Mediterranean where part of the old Roman Empire had survived, centred on Byzantium, came an appreciation of a different way of life. Contact with pre-Christian Greek and Roman culture stimulated thought in the West with awareness of long-forgotten riches. Not only was there development of science and culture, but there arose an appreciation that life before the coming of Christianity had also been good. It could be worth living without a Christian framework, and life could be more than just a preparation for heaven, which it could well tend to be seen as in the difficult and chaotic days after the collapse of the Roman Empire. A secular lifestyle was then perceived to be a possibility. At the same time, the influence of Greek thought and culture injected a humanism into the theocratic view of the Middle Ages. It put people, rather than God, at the centre (Lyon 1985:36).

Such opening to other influences was also part of the *kenōsis* of the incarnation itself. Before that event, the pre-incarnate *logos*, the second Person, was distinct from humanity, but when the incarnation occurred, he limited himself so that he could be opened up not just to a human nature, but also to all the thoughts, emotions, and culture of a person in that particular situation. It is a commonplace to point to the fact of Jesus' thirst and tiredness as indicative of a real and full humanity, but humanity is far more than just the physical. There were mundane thoughts, feelings and emotions, even temptations. There is more than just a sense that in the very incarnation, God himself experienced something of secularization.

Barry (1969:41) then identifies a recovered sense of history as a major feature of the Renaissance. This was contrary to the belief in essential stability of the Middle Ages. Such opened minds to the possibility of change. Here the incarnation, and other aspects of *kenōsis*, are most definitely acts in history; indeed one of the things that distinguishes Christianity from many other religions is its link to, and, it must be said, its verification by, the process of history.

The Renaissance stimulated natural theology, epitomised in the thought of Aquinas. This is in a sense a secularization, as Christian truth is understood as dependent on the world as well as on revelation. It has always been a struggle to balance these two aspects without overemphasising one at the expense of the other, but such a balance is characteristically Christian, reflecting the nature of Jesus as both fully human and fully divine. The two aspects, as in the formula of Chalcedon (Barry 1969:143), are both essential, neither should be neglected, and neither should they be mixed. Likewise the Christian view of God is that he is both transcendent and immanent.

Perhaps it should not be surprising that the view of salvation in that period also then became "secularized", with stress being laid on worldly action. A reaction naturally occurred in the Reformation, which may well be seen as stressing the divine to the neglect of the human, so stressing grace that human action is neglected (cf Jas 2:14). The reaction to this occurred later again in the Enlightenment, which then overemphasised the human; balance is hard to achieve!

Thus resting to some extent on the Renaissance came the Reformation, but despite a re-emphasis on the divine, it was a movement which Lyon (1985:19) believes also accelerated secularization; religion was "digging its own grave". Pannenberg (1989:11) asserts that it did not in itself cause secularization, but its consequences promoted it; in particular the result of the religious wars which followed the Reformation was an indication that a state did not have to rely on a specific religion. The Reformation therefore prompted a process which led ultimately to religious toleration, and so the emancipation of the political order from the Church (Pannenberg 1989:24). Berger (1969:123) notes that the Lutheran idea of the "two kingdoms" gives theological legitimation to the autonomy of the secular. Certainly it enhanced both compartmentalism in the division into denominations, and also the loss of a single authority, thereby encouraging doubt and so disbelief, the privatisation of religion (Dobbelaere 2002:89). Although some have suggested otherwise, religious diversity weakens overall commitment (Bruce 2002:22). The resultant competition has not increased religious participation (Norris & Inglehart 2004:100).

Part of this was the increased dignity given to the secular. The Reformation removed a stress on miracle, mystery, and a quasi-magical interpretation of the sacraments (Dobbelaere 2002:37). The magic and miracle which had characterised the Middle Ages were denied (Berger 1969:111). However, secularization can then even be seen as good, an enrichment of Christianity by regarding all of the creation as God's (Barry 1969:15). In his *kenōsis*, Jesus sanctified the world. Luther saw that a secular occupation, as much as the clerical, can well be a valid vocation from God. It was not a second class occupation, so naturally became more attractive. It is notable that Jesus himself was not born into a priestly family, but embraced the secular occupation of carpentry, even if he did desert it later for "full-time" ministry, and, as the epistle to the Hebrews indicates, he did become a priest "after the order of Melchizedek" (Heb 6:20). Paul also had a secular occupation, and was proud that he did not have to be supported by gifts but could earn his living (1 Cor 9:6).

In initiating the Reformation, Martin Luther in particular reacted to what he saw as abuses and corruption in the Church, notably in the sale of indulgences, which purported to free the purchaser from a period in purgatory. What is important here is that the Church claimed authority to do this. Luther however said that authority did not primarily reside in the church but is vested in the Bible. Then whereas the Catholic church of the day claimed that it alone had the power to interpret the Bible, the Reformers insisted that any Christian, aided by the Holy Spirit, could validly do so. The Church, as a body, then loses significance, so experiences *kenōsis*, as authority resides in other people.

This was a situation that was certainly paralleled in the ministry of Jesus, who rejected the authorities of his day, and the interpretation that they put on the law, for them the scriptures. He effectively claimed freedom from unquestioning obedience to such authority; it was his understanding of what it meant to be obedient to the law and to the Sabbath that ultimately led him to the cross. He was accused of undermining faith and morals (Barry 1969:30). It was the same basic idea that came out in Paul; in obedience to the Spirit we do not need to be obedient to the letter of the law. The locus of authority is not in an institution, but in the mind. Of course, this should be a more direct obedience to God, which it was in the case of Jesus, but the germ of rejection of religious authority was decidedly present which could readily blossom into the autonomy of the human mind.

This was a part of Jesus' *kenōsis*. Each step was a shedding of reliance, a leaving of a comfort zone. Certainly Luther would have felt that his action was an abandoning of the security that he had enjoyed, a step into insecurity; this is the same for any revolutionary, not least Jesus. In the incarnation Jesus left the security of heaven, and so the temptation to accept a place in the religious establishment would be great. That was given up, as it is given up by any who claim God's leading in a way outside of normal human channels. Even physically, from the events in Gethsemane to the horror of the cross, Jesus was yielding himself to the authority of others.

At the same time, the understanding of the Reformers was that a person was saved not primarily by the action of the Church but through individual faith. Whereas the understanding of the Catholic Church of the day was that it was only possible to receive forgiveness of sins and eternal life through having been baptised, confirmed, having participated in the Mass and other sacramental acts of the Church, Luther and the other Reformers appreciated that salvation was a gift of grace received only through faith, and so was in no way dependent upon what a person, or the Church, had done. The Church then lost significance as salvation did not depend on its action; in fact the Church became the result of salvation, rather than its enabler. Thus the essence of the Protestant view of salvation was of a yielding to God, a passive acceptance. This is effectively a *kenōsis*, so hardly surprisingly reflects the action of Christ, who in his own *kenōsis*, yielded himself to the will and action of God for our salvation.

Neither could the Church guarantee salvation. Before the Reformation it was compliance with the requirements of the Church in baptism and other sacraments that did this, but if salvation is simply by grace, there is no external indication that salvation has been received. A solution to this arose from the belief that God would particularly bless the saved, those who belonged to him. Prosperity was not only good in itself, but was an indication of God's favour to those who had been saved. Weber has noted the result of this sort of thinking in the emergence of the so-called "Protestant Work Ethic", whereby a person became industrious and frugal. Naturally emphasis then moved to business practice from participation in the activities of the Church, and secularization proceeded further. At the same time, the prosperity produced also encouraged the process (Bruce 2002:13).

At the same time, receiving salvation directly from God and not through the Church was bound to reinforce the individuality of people. The Reformation had been vastly helped by the introduction of printing, and its ideas then produced a desire for literacy, and ultimately independent thought (Bruce 2002:15). An effect of this was the subsequent division into a multiplicity of denominations that has characterised Protestantism. The initial expression of this was into state churches, a continued strong relation between the state institutions and the Church, the difference being that this could now be Anglican, Lutheran, or Reformed, rather than Catholic. It was only on the fringe that the Reformation was carried to its logical result in the Anabaptists, the "radical Reformation", which severed Church and state completely, a more complete secularization. The horrors of the religious wars of the seventeenth century, followed; religion was still important enough to go to war over, an attitude unthinkable in a really secularized society. Nevertheless, there was an inevitable growth of appreciation for the differing views of others. Each person's thought was valid in itself without reference to the authority of the Church. The movements both of growing individuality and freedom from the Church strengthened.

These came to blossom in a further major movement, the Enlightenment, the *Aufklärung*. This even prompted the seizure of church property, its "secularization" at the time of the French Revolution (Blumenberg 1983:20). Originating in eighteenth century Germany, this way of thinking spread to the rest of Europe, and then became world-wide, although there are still peoples who have not really been affected by it. Secularization grew rapidly when Enlightenment ideas extended to the masses (Chadwick 1975:9).

The major feature of this trend in thought was the belief in human autonomy. The belief was that people had "come of age" and could make rational decisions for themselves. Feuerbach and Nietzsche saw God as the supreme enemy of this (Mascall 1965:175). People had "grown up", and like children, no longer needed to relate all to their Father. There was no need to just believe and accept on authority, but people had the ability to assess for themselves. They were able to choose freely. Berger (1969:78) here comments that increased knowledge at the time led to increased awareness of evil, sharpening the problem of theodicy, and encouraging secularization. It is in this that secularization has become highly significant in modern society. Blamires (in Lyon 1985:18, Mascall 1965:43) speaks of the demise of the Christian mind; this is a relevant comment in view of the fact that the passage in Philippians 2:5f urges a conformity of the Christian mind to that of Christ, which manifested in *kenōsis*. Secularization is indeed essentially a mental matter, which has societal effects when its attitudes are adopted corporately.

In this regard, it is often suggested that religion is more influential among the less educated (Martin 1978:236), although, most interestingly, Bruce (2002:110) notes that natural scientists, especially medical doctors, tend to be more religious than some other segments of society. It may then be noted that the Bible does equate Jesus with the wisdom of God, and identifies him as the *logos*, but also that his incarnation included the *kenōsis* of his omniscience.

In contrast to the attitude of the Catholic Church, which had declared assurance to be a Protestant heresy, the Reformation attitude was that a person could know salvation. The Enlightenment attitude then reversed this, seeing doubt as a virtue; in a modern situation it is assurance which is the sin (Trueman 2005:1). The question can well be whether sin causes doubt, or vice versa (Chadwick 1975:12), but it is certainly a feature of modern secularism. It may be noted that one of the characteristics of the Old Testament prophets was their absolute certainty, a feature epitomised in the authority with which Jesus spoke (Mk 1:22). There is a sense in which this is a *kenōsis*, a refusal to countenance other ideas.

Certainly the loss of assurance opens the door to a toleration of other ideas which is a characteristic of modern society. It is inevitable that this means that faith becomes one option among many, and therefore not dominant, which is essentially what secularization involves. At the same time, as certainty is impossible, it becomes hypocritical to advocate religion for the sake of society.

The belief in rational ability was associated with a belief in the inherent goodness of people. Without this, decisions would naturally be biassed by self-interest, and could not be reliable. In distinction from this idea, the church had taught the people are inherently sinful due to inherited ("original") sin, which affects rationality. But if there is no inherent sin, religion becomes unnecessary, and secularization can proceed; the idea of human goodness then provides the "key that secularizes the world" (Morley, in Chadwick 1975:152). Significantly, the idea of the incarnation, so of *kenōsis*, does assume that although humanity fell into sin, it is essentially good; the humanity of Christ was normal, except insofar as he was without sin (Heb 4:15, 1 Pet 2:22).

Even with a belief in the goodness of people, mistakes can still be made due to ignorance. An Enlightenment view thus tends to be empiricist, only accepting as true what can be verified, at least in principle. This has meant that there has been a scepticism about many aspects which Christianity had affirmed, such as the miracle stories in the Bible, which were immediately doubted as unverifiable. This attitude naturally even affected belief in God, whose existence could not be proved. Here, even if, at least initially, belief in God was not rejected, he was usually understood in deistic terms, as the one responsible for creation, but not involving himself further in it in a direct way. The world is inherently secular, distinct from the divine. This is of course a self-limitation by God; many, such as Moltmann, do see creation in terms of his *kenōsis*. The Christian doctrine of creation implies a real measure of autonomy, albeit derived; to some extent the world does run itself (Barry 1969:132f). It must immediately be observed that Christ's own *kenōsis*, in his incarnation, is contrary to the full sense of Deism, as it is God's direct involvement in the world.

At the same time, the immediate result of Enlightenment thought was a change in the attitude to the Bible, for it was no longer just regarded as the inspired Word of God, to be accepted and obeyed without question. Rather, its statements were felt to be subject to rational enquiry. They were doubted because they could be the result of the misconceptions of the author, or even deliberately intended to mislead. Unless Biblical statements could be substantiated, they should not simply be accepted. The idea of divine authority became secondary to human intellect and was questioned. Naturally, the practice of the religion based on that Bible itself became marginalised.

However, this empiricism is actually a deliberate decision to limit what is believed to what is definitely known. Reappraisal of religion is not in itself wrong, although it has often been felt to weaken faith and morals (Barry 1969:30, who points out that this was one of the charges against Jesus). The early advocates of "kenotic" Christology suggested that even Jesus could well have erred, just because limitation of knowledge is part of his *kenōsis*; even though the second Person of the Trinity is the *logos*, his omniscience would be one of the characteristics that was limited.

It was hardly surprising that the cold rationality of the Enlightenment produced a reaction in Pietism, where the emphasis fell on experience and subjectivity. This naturally produced a concentration on the individual. Both aspects are kenotic, a limitation of interest from the external, and away from others. Then at the same time, both, albeit paradoxically, encouraged the process of secularization in a severing of religion from society at large.

One effect of the Enlightenment stress on the rational was the development of science, and therefore technology. As Marcuse and Heidegger affirm, this is effectively the control of things (Richard 1982:22), so for people is the antithesis to *kenōsis*; this is enabled by God's granting of dominion in his *kenōsis*. Interestingly, although it often results in increased personal freedom, technology can even reduce it by its demands (Richard 1982:23), an observation that Pannenberg calls enslavement; the servant becomes the master (Galloway 1973:21). Schumacher (1973:25,30) comments that it is the prevalent greed that removes a sense of perspective and delivers people up to the power of the machine. Again both aspects are from trends in society that have contributed to secularization, the capitalist process and technology. A kenotic attitude immediately blunts the effects of these in lessening the urge to acquire and in willingness to live a little less frenetically. Schumacher (1973:124) is tempted to suggest that the amount of real leisure is in inverse proportion to the number of labour-saving devices; the back cover of his book speaks of slavery to capital. It is no accident that the Philippian "hymn" describes Jesus as coming in the form of a slave; it is this that can atone for our slavery. In union with him comes liberation and the fullness of what human life should be.

Rejection of religion is often attributed to a perception that it is contrary to science, although this is questionable (Barry 1969:30). Science does not cause atheism, but its underlying stress on rationality weakens the role of religion; an empirical attitude cannot accept talk of God (Richard 1967:100). Nevertheless they can happily coexist, and the wonders of the universe even stimulate worship (Bruce 2002:27). Lyon (1985:123) notes that one reason for the survival of conservative Protestantism in a modern scientific world is that it can claim rationality. Indeed, Biblical Christianity can emphasise this, because it portrays as Jesus is the *logos*, the rationality of God. It is not surprising that the Church contains a relatively high proportion of natural scientists, doctors and other professionals (Lyon 1985:123). There is no link between education or science and secularization (Norris & Inglehart 2004:27). Bruce (2002:117) asserts that no sociologist says that science fatally undermines Christianity. Indeed, Chadwick (1975:155) feels that a more powerful issue than a questioning of the Bible was doubt about the teachings of the Church. He suggests the issue was a sense of justice; particularly the doctrine of predestination, but even the teaching of atonement by grace, was viewed as unjust, so rejected. It need hardly be said that the accusation is true, that if impartial justice were imposed, nobody would be saved (Rom 3:23); the whole point of the atonement is that God can show mercy, that the sinner may be acquitted. But this required the experience of Christ in *kenōsis*, who epitomised injustice, for he, of all people, did not deserve to suffer and die. Incidentally this doubting includes the doctrine of eternal punishment, which was just not believed (Chadwick 1975:105); there was certainly no impetus to good morals there!

Nevertheless, even if the rise of science does not directly undermine religion, it does result in a pragmatism and a profanity (in a neutral sense of "this worldliness") (Cox 1968:73). This has touched the Church; Blumenberg (1983:44) notes that there had to be less emphasis on unverifiable eschatology, and therefore the Church had to be relevant by involvement in this world, in itself a secularization. As Cox (1968:76) says, pragmatism is actually a form of asceticism, a giving up of less tangible concerns; the same is of course true of profanity. Both are therefore kenotic. In this regard it is noteworthy that Christianity is a call to action ("follow me" (Matt 9:9)); the Reformation emphasis on salvation through faith alone is laudible, but can result in ignoring the positive action that

God desire from his servants (also a word of activity!). Stress in the modern world falls upon what a thing does, its value, and this includes religion, which is taken as worthless unless it is seen to help; mere belief is despised. Here Cox (1968:78) quite correctly observes the Old Testament stress on what God does. This is quite consistent with the New Testament, where emphasis falls on what Jesus did, as in his own *kenōsis*; what he is by nature is secondary. Likewise in the modern world, a person's identity is largely seen in his or her occupation.

Perhaps more than science itself, its application in technology enhances a process of secularization. In the western world, the prevalence of technology naturally stimulates a view of reality as simply mechanistic (Blamires 1978:163). At the same time, as technology is a means of controlling the environment, it encourages an attitude of domination, contrasting with that of the dependence upon God that is at the heart of religion. In the very modern world, the ease of dissemination of information by means of computer technology has enabled the rapid transfer of ideas in a way unprecedented in human history. Ideas of secularism are then readily transferred from Europe to parts of the world previously untouched by them.

As a result of the growth of technology, industrialisation naturally followed; this had a number of effects which encouraged the process of secularization. Lyon (1985:7) suggests that religion is one of the casualties of the adoption of industrialisation; for Berger, secularization was an inevitable concomitant of industrial society (Pannenberg 1989:28). Martin (1978:3) helpfully summarises the relevant factors. However, it must be emphasised that this is not an inevitable result: Frank (1986:11) documents great growth in the American church in the middle years of the nineteenth century, at exactly the same time as industrial expansion. More importantly, the increased production that industrialisation gave resulted ultimately in economic security for many. This resulted in less perceived need for God's provision, and so stimulated secularization. Interestingly, a result of this security was a reduced demand for children to provide in old age. In contrast, Norris & Inglehart (2004:53) note that in less developed societies there is increased religiosity and population. The combination of these in fact results in increasing religiosity worldwide.

The essential reason for industrialisation was for production, the creation of items in an efficient way. This demanded division of labour in the manufacturing process; one individual concentrated on only one element, a limitation contrasting with the following of very many activities in pre-industrial society. May it be suggested that this is what Jesus was doing in the incarnation, the creation of a Church by the re-creation of individuals (2 Cor 5:17); moreover this was enabled by the concentration of his action in *kenōsis*. This latter was appreciated when suggestions of kenotic Christology were revived and popularised in the nineteenth century, as it was quickly objected that the second Person could not empty himself as he could then not fulfil the function of upholding the universe. The objection however does not stand in the light of the activity of the other Persons, but the point is clear, there was a limitation, a concentration of activity into one purpose. The former feature of industrial production is also paralleled in Jesus' *kenōsis*, as it is the means for most efficient production. The issue of inclusivism in salvation is still hotly debated, whether it is necessary for a person to know and understand what Jesus did to be saved; however, it would seem obvious that salvation is more likely if its means is understood, and this is what Jesus was doing in his *kenōsis*, demonstrating how salvation is possible, just so that "production" is maximised, so that as many as possible do receive what God intends.

Industrialisation was accompanied by urbanisation, which Chadwick (1975:100) feels was more significant for secularization than industrialisation as such; Cox's major exposition is *The secular city*. Norris & Inglehart (2004:58) document the decline in religion as society moved from an agricultural through an industrial to a post-industrial society. Berger (1970:48) tells of LeBras' well-known statement that a certain railway station in Paris appeared to have a magical quality, for rural migrants seemed to change from practising to non-practising Catholics as soon as they set foot in it! The mushrooming of industry led to great growth in cities with large numbers of people being attracted there from the rural areas. In so doing, they lost the immediacy of contact with nature, and with it an appreciation of their total dependency upon God. When food comes from shops and the link with sun and rain is not apparent, it is easy to forget human frailty and the acts of God. He is readily moved to the periphery of life, if acknowledged at all. Ellul has suggested that the city provides an alternative to religious faith and trust (Frank 1986:26). The city dweller, although not characteristically atheistic, becomes indifferent (Chadwick 1975:95). Statistically, the bigger the city, the smaller the proportion who attend church (Chadwick 1975:94). In any case, the infrastructure of the churches just did not keep up with the growth in population (Chadwick 1975:97). This concentration in cities is also a feature of what could be called the second industrial revolution, that of electronic and information technology, which Martin (1978:86) feels has had even more effect than the first, especially where the first had produced secularization.

Often the work of the Church has been done ignoring the situation and needs of the people. One example of this is that much of its efforts have been in rural areas, which were constantly depleted by urbanisation. In contrast, as in the missionary journeys in Acts, or in the policy of Wesley (Lyon 1985:49), effective work naturally concentrated on the cities, a self-chosen, but effective, limitation of scope. Of course, in cities, due to secularization, response is less likely, so the work of the Church is harder. However, it is there where the people are present who are influential in guiding the course of society, so its attitude to religion, which affects its secularization. It may just be observed that the depths of Jesus' *kenōsis* were experienced in an urban environment; "it cannot be that a prophet should perish away from Jerusalem" (Lk 13:33).

It must just be noted in passing that industrialisation has had detrimental effects not only for the Church but also for the world as a whole. It has been the prime culprit for environmental degradation of various kinds. It can be said, therefore, that this process has contributed to the deterioration of a favourable situation both for humanity as a whole, and also for the Church.

Perhaps more fundamentally, Engels (in Lyon 1985:26) saw the city as exacerbating individualism, and the growth of selfish egotism; this is a world-view very different from the Christian ideal. The essence of secularization is that religion becomes simply a private matter (Lyon 1985:60). Such individualism is generally seen as one of the results of an Enlightenment view. Even if the city results in contact with many more people than in a rural environment, these contacts are usually less personal; Cox (1968:55) is probably correct in his belief that most people want this, but in any case, this is also due simply to the numbers in the city. As he says, anonymity is maintained for the sake of a few deeper relationships (Cox 1968:54), which are what is desired. Ironically, of course, this is what is provided in Christianity, both in the Church, and with God. In contrast with the Christianity of the Middle Ages and of the Reformation, much of its modern expression is restricted to the individual, not society (Martin 2005:135). This naturally follows from pluralism, the multiplicity of beliefs (Dobbelaere 2002:89). Richard (1967:58) suggests that in the complexity of modern life, especially in the urban setting, it is essential for a person to limit themselves in order to cope with the multitude of demands; some things just have to be eliminated, and one of these is most likely to be religion, if it is perceived as of little value. In fact this is seen, such as by Cox, as positively good, as it liberates people to fulfil what God intends, the fulfilling of the dominion mandate (Richard 1967:59). Nevertheless, although the limitation of relationships is a form of *kenōsis*, the desire to be anonymous may also be a refusal to yield to others, a form of self-assertion. Here it may be noted that part of Jesus' experience of *kenōsis*, perhaps even its ultimate, was an experience of forsakenness by his Father, and the cry of dereliction (Matt 27:46, quoting Ps 22:1). In fact one aspect of crucifixion was the sheer loneliness of it; the victim died totally alone. Of course after the experience of his *kenōsis* went to the extreme, Jesus then entered the process of glorification, and increasing relationships, finally being acknowledged as Lord (Phil 2:11).

A further factor here, due to industrialisation, was increased mobility. This can be understood in two senses, firstly the physical, in movement to the cities and increasing ability to move from home, and secondly movement from one social class to another (Martin 1978:83). The first naturally includes being absent from the place of worship as well (Richard 1967:144). At the same time, work and residence have been separated (Richard 1967:155), another example of *kenōsis*; interestingly modern technology has enabled more people to work at home. Both forms of mobility are destructive of a sense of immediate community, so exacerbated secularization. Religion has been more influential in small communities (Martin 1978:236). The breakdown in community naturally results in less religion (Barry 1969:25, Lyon 1985:47); where a person has a close relationship with a small community, its expectations are important, which includes religion. In "societalization" (Wilson, in Dobbelaere 2002:33), a person relates to the wider society, there is less answerability, less conformity to previously held customs; in being effectively autonomous, secularization grows. Interestingly, Cox (1968:67) observes that Christianity is fundamentally mobile; he cites features such as the Exodus, contrasting with the sedentary nature of Baalism. A major Christian command is to "go" (Richard

1967:146). It must be observed that Jesus' *kenōsis* involved both senses of mobility; he left heaven, and became a slave. But the result of this, the essence of Christianity, is a relationship with God in Christ, which then, of course, should result in improved interpersonal relationships, and so enhance community.

Despite its enhancement of individualism, industrial activity is dependent upon cooperative human effort, each making use of the material and the work of others. This aspect is also part of the process of *kenōsis*, for rather than God working directly in the world, he chose to limit his own action, working by means of agents. A major part of Jesus' ministry in the incarnation was the training of the small group of disciples, who would carry on his work, acting for him, after his departure in the ascension.

Not unconnected with the growth of industry was a move towards a capitalist ethos. This was naturally encouraged by the Enlightenment view of individual freedom. In this regard it is noteworthy that the United States did not adopt extreme capitalism, but its harshest effects were originally mitigated by a strong Christian ethos (Frank 1986:34). Without this, greed naturally takes over, an attitude which Gandhi said could only be combated by the awareness of the soul (Schumacher 1973:32). In general, however, in an increasing secularism, the result of umitigated greed in capitalism was an increasingly pronounced division in society between rich and poor (Chadwick 1975:46). This division eventually prompted a socialist reaction, spearheaded by the writings of Marx and Engels. Due to Marx' view of religion as oppressive, their socialism was however coupled with an atheistic materialism, a natural bedfellow to the secularization process. Marxism was then "the most powerful philosophy of secularization in the nineteenth century"; the idea of religion as the "opium of the people" appeared in 1843 (Chadwick 1975:66,49). It has been particularly significant for Christians who have adopted the economic understanding of Marx that Jesus identified with the poorer elements in society, to the chagrin of the affluent of his day. 2 Corinthians 8:9, "for your sake he became poor", in the context of the charitable relief of the Jerusalem poor by the Macedonian church, is often linked to the more famous *kenōsis* passage of Philippians 2. Even the idea of alienation, integral to a Marxist understanding (Chadwick 1975:63), bears more than a passing resemblance to *kenōsis*. Certainly any form of care for the poor, whether by individual charity, or socialism, involves a *kenōsis* for the good of others; there has to be restriction for the sake of morality and justice (Chadwick 1975:47).

Most societies then espouse a measure of socialist practice, the state taking over much of what was previously done through religion. When the state took more responsibility for social welfare (Martin 2005:123), not only did people no longer need the Church to provide for them, but the link to God's provision became attenuated. Not surprisingly, Norris & Inglehart (2004:10) document the decline of religion in states with a developed welfare system. As with God, the role of the Church was limited, resulting in secularization; the difference is that usually the latter was compelled. It is this that may provide an explanation for Karl Barth's "neo-orthodox" reaffirmation of more traditional Christianity. He trumpeted that the Christian message is to be accepted independently of human thought and human history, insisting on its externality and non-subjectivity (Berger 1969:163). Its popularity was however a temporary reversal of the overall trend of secularization, due to the situation of the time; Berger (1970:24) sees the influence of the shocks to Western cultural optimism centred on the first World War.

This is one reason why secularization is a particular issue in the modern West. In many other parts of the world belief remains strong and religious organizations are thriving. As a generalization, these are those which are usually referred to as the "third world", in a situation of poverty; religion has always thrived where people are insecure (Norris & Inglehart 2004:5). It is the prosperous West which has experienced a decline, where people do not feel a need for God. It must also be said that in contrast with other religions, it is Christianity that has been particularly affected by secularization, as it has largely been the traditionally Christian world which has developed; that is of course not an accident. However, in large areas of the world, such as Latin America, Christianity is thriving in a situation of poverty, and in sub-Saharan Africa, Christianity is growing rapidly. Indeed, overall, the world is becoming more religious (Norris & Inglehart 2004:124).

A capitalist view results from an affirmation of freedom of choice, which can manifest either, as with Jesus, as *kenōsis*, self-limitation, or in the opposite. Indeed, an original feature of early capitalism was self-limitation, under the influence of the Protestant Work ethic (Norris & Inglehart 2004:160). Capitalism originated in Protestantism, with its antipathy to luxury (Lyon 1985:39); even asceticism has been a strong feature of Christianity, especially in the early Church. Paradoxically, a connection of faith with self-deprivation could well naturally result in secularization, the marginalisation of God, but it is well known that poverty both encourages religion and is encouraged by it; the same is true of prosperity and disbelief (cf Bruce 2002:25, Dobbelaere 2002:138)! The ethos of capitalism is however of concern for the self, an attitude contrary to self-limitation; this latter is never popular, and effectively absent from the modern world-view. A modern person is never encouraged to subordinate needs and interests to those of others (Richard 1982:28). Likewise, it is now almost absent from modern Christianity as influenced by modern culture, so secularization (eg Bruce 2002:181). Indeed, Norris and Inglehart (2004:178) observe that compared to other societies, the work ethic is weakest in historically Protestant societies.

It should not be overlooked that the capitalist class, which was undoubtedly guilty of oppression and exploitation, also claimed to be Christian. Thus in the rejection of exploitation came also the rejection of Christianity. A parallel case to this was in the South African situation, where a popular rejection of *apartheid* was often associated with a rejection of the Christianity of the pre-1994 Nationalist government. In both cases there was a perception, as seen in the view of Marx, that religion was used by the rulers to subjugate the workers. The promise of heavenly bliss was believed to be held out to ameliorate the suffering of the present; it was an "opium of the people" removing discontent with the present. Holding out such eschatological hope is not so fashionable today with its concentration on the present, especially as it is not empirically provable, but it must be observed that the whole process of *kenōsis* was only done for future benefit. On the one hand this was the salvation of those who would put their faith in Christ, but on the other, Christ himself "for the joy that was set before him endured the cross, despising the shame" (Heb 12:2).

Most recently, the independent thought encouraged by the Enlightenment has developed into postmodernism. This may have helped religion to be acceptable as an individual belief, but is completely contrary to any consensus which could influence society. This worldview is that any belief cannot become accepted as truth, but only as an individual opinion; whereas in the Middle Ages, Christianity was accepted as unquestionably true, and therefore effective, the case is now that religion only has validity for an individual, and so is precluded from influencing society. The assessment of Bruce (2002:240) is that the denominations which saw their role in terms of society are doomed, while the emerging alternatives, while they could well survive, so stress the individual as to be societally impotent.

It may just be noted that urbanization was also made possible by other factors, even if they had considerably predated the modern era. Cox (1968:24) observes that the introduction of currency and the alphabet made less personal relationships possible in that economic life and the transfer of information did not need face to face contact. Incidentally, both enable increased choice, which is always kenotic, as it involves rejection of some possibilities. Nevertheless, both of these can become idols (1 Cor 2:5, 1 Tim 6:10), but are fulfilled in Christ as both true riches and the wisdom of God.

The state of the Church

It is natural for the Church, in the face of its declining influence, to try to place the blame for this elsewhere, and society itself is the obvious culprit. However, as well as trends in society, it must be suggested that the state of the Church itself can be seen as contributing to secularization. Norris and Inglehart (2004:223) note that while people have often stopped supporting the Church, decline in belief has been less. If the Church was effective in its core functions of worship and aiding the people, particularly if it did facilitate the meeting of the felt needs of people, they would surely not have deserted it, no matter what the external circumstances. Stott (1984:3) points out that the situation in Britain was dramatically changed as a result of the evangelical revival, such as through the agency of Wesley; and this was at the time when the effect of the Enlightenment was having such an influence on the Church in Europe. The same is true in other situations, where religious revival had dramatic effects on morals. Classic cases, notably in the context of industrialisation and its accompanying effects, were the Welsh revival in the early years of the twentieth century, when breweries closed and the police became idle, and the revivalist preaching of Billy Sunday, which resulted in harm to the liquor trade and closure of brothels (Frank 1986:178,187). But whereas the growth of the early Church, and in later contexts, was stimulated by the quality of life experienced by Christians, the opposite can well be so. If the Church is perceived as cold and uninspired in its worship, irrelevant to the problems of the people round about, why should they attend its meetings and support it? If the Church is seen to be full of people, especially its leaders, who manifestly do not live up to the message that they proclaim, their hypocrisy will repel. The philosopher Nietzsche was hardly an advocate of Christianity; he said, "who among us would be a freethinker, were it not for the Church?" (Chadwick 1975:250).

Whereas it is natural, indeed right, for the Church to influence society, it has proved to be too weak to do this effectively. In the first millennium, this produced on the one hand inadequate sacralization of society, and on the other, it did not avoid influence on itself, so it became secularized. The inevitable result was the process of the secularization of society. However, this process has led to a clear distinction between world and Church, and benefit to the latter, its own desecularization (Martin 1969:33). Then if the Church becomes what it should be, there can then be a renewed sacralization of society. The danger is then of a renewed secularization of the Church itself; this can only be avoided if the values of the *saeculum* do not again infect the Church. This last is a possibility if the Church imitates, as it should, a kenotic nature as demonstrated by its Lord.

It must also be suggested that part of the problem has been due to the message proclaimed. Under the influence of an intrusive dualism, Christianity has so often been presented as offering only benefits after death, but with minimal help in this, indeed rather an onerous demand. It is hardly surprising that when conditions in this life improved, interest in the next waned (Martin 1969:11). This is obviously exacerbated when the world-view becomes more material. Nevertheless, of course, as Richard (1967:169) observes, secularism has no answer to death.

At the same time, the Church itself has shared in the secularization of society and has tended to become simply a human organisation, with social and political aims. It has generally done this while paying lipservice to the transcendent, whereas for most this must have seemed to be a sham. More recently, there have arisen those who openly advocate a Christianity without the transcendent. Bonhoeffer (eg 1967:153), notably, called for a religionless Christianity, removing the other-worldly (Richard 1967:11); in a secular society, "honesty demands that we recognise that we must live in the world as if there were no God. And this is just what we do recognize - before God" (cited in Richard 1967:24). He did however see this as consistent with Christianity's distinction between the sacred and the secular (Berger 1969:106). Bultmann advocated demythologisation of elements in the Bible, such as the stories of miracle, which he felt were incredible to modern people (Mascall 1965:8), and on a more popular level, the bishop of Woolwich notoriously published *Honest to God*. Arguably, the motives of the latter were to preserve the "essence" of Christianity in a way acceptable to the modern worldview. Significantly, both Robinson and Cox still accepted the reality of the incarnation and the formula of Chalcedon (Richard 1967:33). For these the essence of Jesus is the "man for others" (Richard 1967:44), or his perfect response (van Buren, in Mascall 1965:51), which is close to the reason for *kenōsis*; a link that Bonhoeffer did make (Richard 1967:122). Van Buren went still further, seeking to eliminate all trace of the supernatural (Mascall 1965:7). The ultimate in *kenōsis* was then the death of God in the theology of such as Altizer (Fiddes 1988:243f). However, without the reality of the spiritual, the Church surely has no distinct role in society; it might as well cease to exist as what it does can be more adequately done by other bodies. Barth commented on Bultmann that he effectively evacuated the gospel in his attempt to make it acceptable (Mascall 1965:46). Likewise Mascall (1965:105) says that Robinson despaired of converting the world to Christianity, so attempts to convert Christianity to the world. In this case, secularization is complete. Berger has described three reactions of the Church to secularisation; he feels that two of these, accommodating to it, are effectively suicidal, while the third is to resist and reassert the authority of the faith (Dekker 1997:14). People will surely only support the Church if they can see the reality of a relationship with God that it embodies; but if they indeed see this, it must assuredly maintain a role, indeed a growing one. In his response to Robinson, Fielding Clarke says that the need of the Church is not new images, but "to deliver the goods" (Mascall 1965:179).

Then the Church has lost the vibrancy of an alternative community that was so evident in the early centuries before its acceptance by the state. Cox (1968:60) thinks that the Church is often wrong to promote its community aspect, believing people want to be free, especially in an urban environment; he advocates rather a theology of anonymity. In fact loneliness is a major feature of urban life for very many, which can be dispelled in involvement in a church. Relationship, both with God and with others is at the heart of authentic Christianity, and if it is not present, the Church will naturally be ignored. The overcoming of loneliness, as well as increased contacts between individuals, explains the growth of the early Church in towns; Cox (1968:25) adds the attraction of freedom from social roles in a society where all are essentially equal (Gal 3:28).

What has happened is that instead of the Church continuing to influence the world, the opposite has happened. This cannot be seen as inevitable, as for example most strikingly in the expansion of the early Church in the midst of a pagan society, or again, at the time of Wesley. Is this not the intention of Jesus (Matt 5:14f), or of Paul (Phil 2:15, a verse following quickly after the *kenōsis* passage)?

Of course, without other factors, a poor state in the Church may well not result simply in a rejection of religion, or even its marginalization, but adherence to a different set of beliefs. Arguably, this is what happened at the Reformation, where many of the factors for secularization were still absent. Even in the modern West, the move is often not to total disbelief, but to other beliefs, where the attraction is a perceived effectiveness and compatibility with the pervading worldview (Bruce 2002:85f, Martin 1969:107). Even Islam has an attraction, despite the cultural differences, because of its moral tone. In many parts of Africa, the traditional churches, as originated by missionary work, have experienced a tremendous loss, but the people may well not become secular, but change to churches which do meet their needs. This can be the case for those with a premodern worldview, as seen in the growth in African Independent Churches, but can also be found in those who are most definitely post-Enlightenment, who are more likely to find roots in Charismatic groups. Interestingly, in both of these, religion is often the dominant feature of life, affecting every other aspect of it. Such groups are microcosms of a sacralized society, often reflecting deep commitment.

Unless the Church contains people who are really committed, it cannot be effective. And, in fact, such commitment is more likely in a secularized society, where belonging to a church is not just a matter of culture (Häring 1973:12). Secularization may then have a good result, purifying the Church (Blumenberg 1983:7). An example of this, especially pertinent in southern Africa, is that mission and colonialism used to go together, to the particular detriment of the former; mission is now usually detached from economic and political goals (Martin 2005:27). Indeed, just as the result of *kenōsis* was the glorification of Christ and the expansion of God's kingdom, so the result of secularization is ultimately good; the two processes are linked. Without this purification, it cannot then produce a change in life that will be attractive, such as manifest peacefulness. In particular, it is the pursuing of a moral life that is a strong recommendation for religion. In the early Church it was the evident love expressed between followers of the "way" that attracted new disciples, and it is still the case. This love is an imitation of Jesus, and specifically of his willingness to act, even in sacrifice, for people. Essentially the response of the Church to secularization is its affirmation of the Lordship of Christ, which, significantly, Philippians 2 presents in the context of his *kenōsis*. An attractive Christian lifestyle therefore manifests in self-limitation, *kenōsis*. Without this being seen in the Church, how likely is it that people will put their trust in what they perceive to be ineffective?

Mere intellectual assent is never enough; Chadwick (1975:238) in any case points out that this does not change morals, that requires affection. The same is of course true for society at large. Indeed, the affirmation of Christianity is that morals are not so much taught, but come naturally as a result of a commitment to God (Jer 31:33). The issue is not ignorance but rebellion, a refusal to humble oneself under the will of God, a refusal to self-limit. They have to be chosen with the free will that is a result of the *kenōsis* of God.

What is then striking is that God's solution to the *kenōsis* of people that has produced secularization, into what can only be characterised as "sin", can itself be characterised as *kenōsis*. This is not surprising, insofar as God naturally acts in terms of his nature. *Kenōsis* is typical of God's action, not affecting a problem directly, but by providing a solution which then does. He deals with sin, not by destroying the sinners and their actions, which he could, but by providing the means of atonement. This involved *kenōsis*; in fact, to deal with the effect of human *kenōsis*, Christ himself accepted it and bore its effects.

Secularization may not be God's desire, but it is noteworthy that the period which witnessed the strongest Enlightenment thinking also birthed Christian revival, with associated societal effects, and a flowering of missionary activity. It is therefore by no means an impossibility that the effects of secularization can be reversed, and a sacral society re-established. Indeed it must be affirmed that this is ultimately God's intention! The process of Jesus' *kenōsis* did finish with the cross, but that this led to his glorification and will ultimately result in the re-creation of the world, and the establishment of a new society, totally sacral. Significantly the way to this was through his *kenōsis*.

PART 3

The *kenōsis* of the Spirit

"… and the fellowship of the Holy Spirit"

Chapter 10

The *kenōsis* of the Spirit

If it is accepted that *kenōsis* is part of the nature of the first and second Persons, it would follow immediately that it ought to be applicable also to the third, simply because of the Trinitarian affirmation of the equality of the Persons. And conversely, if it is seen that the nature of the Spirit is kenotic, then it strengthens the case for the *kenōsis* of the other two. Indeed, from a Trinitarian perspective, the self-giving that is of the essence of *kenōsis* may be readily understood. Part of the classical solution to the Trinitarian dilemma of the simultaneous affirmation of both the equality and the difference of the Persons lies in the idea of *perichōrēsis*, which is the giving of each Person, so the self-limitation of each, to the Others. By nature each Person self-limits, simply due to the Trinitarian relationship.

The relationship of *perichōrēsis* then also means that the specific limitations of each Person affect the others. Thus when God limited himself in order to establish the independence of creation, the second Person was directly affected. The roots of the incarnation lay in the creation, and even the depths of Christ's *kenōsis*, in that the lamb was "slain before the foundation of the world" (Rev 13:8 (KJV)).

235

Although the latter verse can be read to indicate that it was the writing in the book of life that was before the world, that translation is a little strained, and in any case, the essential inference is still that salvation was effectual from creation. The same principle is seen in Paul's belief that sins before the historical atonement were passed over (Rom 3:25); this suggests that the atonement affected its own past. Then if the second Person was affected in creation, so was the Spirit. Finally in the reversing of *kenōsis* after the atonement, when the Son was glorified, all the Persons experience increasing *plērōma*.

The fact that the third Person is "spirit" does not mean that he cannot limit himself. After all, referring to his Father, Jesus identified the nature of God as spirit (Jn 4:24), which need not in itself mitigate against attributing *kenōsis* to him. Although some forms of limitation cannot apply to immaterial spirit, the fact that human beings have spirits indicates that spirits are not by nature infinite. Perhaps a better idea of "spirit" is that it is understood in terms of motivation, or bonding (cf Williams 2004:8); in this case, its limitation is most decidedly possible. It is not so much the nature of God which is limited, but his activity, especially in relationship; this is quite consistent with the *kenōsis* of Christ, who while being in the form of God yet emptied himself (Phil 2:6-7). In fact, Wheeler Robinson (1928:87) suggests that for spirit to be expressed in "degrees of reality" lower than itself, there necessarily has to be self-emptying and humiliation.

In fact, the observations that lead to the attribution of *kenōsis* to the other Persons do also apply to some extent to the third Person. Thus although creation of the material is not attributed specifically to him as to the other two (1 Cor 8:6), all three Persons are involved in every external action of God. In any case, the Spirit is particularly associated with the giving of life, which more than the creation of the material involves God's self-limitation as it is an imparting of freedom of action to what is enlivened.

More than this, if the *kenōsis* of the Son is especially connected with his action in the world through the incarnation, as indicated in Philippians 2, the fact that the Spirit is also the agent of God in the world indicates that he too self-limits, that his *kenōsis* is, just as the Son, the means by which he works. Just as one aspect of the *kenōsis* of the second Person is that he accepted being sent, so also the Spirit accepted this (Jn 15:26). Then just as the second Person indwells humanity in Jesus, so Wheeler Robinson (1928:151) sees *kenōsis* in the indwelling of the Church by the Spirit, and that, like Christ, the Spirit is gracious and accepts the hindrance of his purposes due to human failings. Indeed, Paul's use of the kenotic "hymn" of Philippians 2:5f is introduced by a reference to the Spirit who makes his appeal to emulate the attitude of Christ feasible. "If there is … any participation (*koinōnia*) in the Spirit, complete my joy by being of the same mind…". A person self-limits by identifying with the self-limitation of the Spirit. Indeed, just as human *kenōsis* is possible by the Spirit, so was the *kenōsis* of Jesus himself; the very incarnation, a major step in this, was through the Spirit's coming upon Mary (Lk 1:35). It must be observed that this immediately resulted in her limitation, as she was overshadowed by the "power of the Most High", and this was just the start of the effects on her life. This was also, as any *kenōsis*, an act of choice, freely accepted. Then of course, the ministry of Jesus was empowered by the Spirit, and also the final act to enable atonement; it was "through the eternal Spirit that he offered himself" (Heb 9:14). It is often pointed out that both the character of Christ, such as his sinlessness, and his works, were enabled not by his Sonship, but by the Spirit (eg Macleod 1998:222). This immediately suggests the *kenōsis* of the Spirit, both as enabling the *kenōsis* of the Son, but also as acting primarily through him.

Although Moltmann understands the very existence of the world as made possible by God's self-limitation, he insists that its continued existence depends on God's continuing action though the Spirit. Without this, existence, especially of life, is not possible; he cites Psalm 104:29 in support of this (1985:102). The action of the Spirit is then guiding, so the power behind evolution (1985:100), and in generating unity. Both of these are affected by *kenōsis*, which then has a universal affect; Fiddes (1988:9) contrasts the universal action of the Spirit with that of the *logos* in the single person of the Christ. Thus as the action of the Spirit undergoes *kenōsis*, the result can be the aberrations in evolution, and disfunction in creation, such as crime (Moltmann 1985:102), and ecological deterioration. The existence of these then points to the *kenōsis* of the Spirit. Nevertheless, just as Jesus' *kenōsis* was not total, neither is that of the Spirit; the effects in the world are not total.

Nevertheless, despite these indications, little has been said of any *kenōsis* of the Spirit. Perhaps on the one hand this has been due to the obvious neglect of the Spirit at least until the last century; apart from occasional periods, such as the controversy over *filioque*, he has been largely ignored. In contrast, this neglect would seem to have been reversed in the prominence of the action of the Spirit during the last century, at first sight hardly kenotic. But despite renewed interest in the Spirit, those who might have been particularly concerned to look at his nature, those in the Pentecostal tradition, which includes later developments such as in the "Charismatic movement" or "Renewal", and the "Third Wave", have been far more interested in the experience that the Spirit gave than in the understanding of it, and even less in investigating the nature of the one who gave it. In those traditions, teaching then usually concentrates on experience rather than on the wider body of Christian truth (Porter 1995:116). Pawson (1995:26) bemoans the diminishing of preaching and sacraments in Pentecostalism. Theology is treated with scorn, as coldly intellectual, and commonly viewed as harmful (as it has often been!); it is seen as irrelevant and divisive. "Theology divides but tongues unites" (Gaffin 1996:334). Thus although there have been a number of recent theologies of the Spirit such as by Pinnock (1996), it is still a general trend to ignore or despise the intellectual side of belief. As recently as 1969, James (1969:16) could complain that there had been no great work on the Spirit since that of Owen in 1674. Of course, this very observation, and also the fact that interest in the Spirit has been very little for most of the life of the Church, immediately suggests something of the *kenōsis* of the Spirit.

Observation of the *kenōsis* of the Spirit

However, although not common, there have been those who have noted that the Spirit shares the state of *kenōsis* with the Father and the Son. Certainly the manifestation and experience of the Spirit has been limited; he has been referred to as the "self-effacing", or "shy" Person of the Trinity (Ferguson 1996:186). Moltmann (1985:97-102) also speaks of the *kenōsis* of the Spirit insofar as he can be grieved and suffers, such as in the face of ecological destruction; this is of course in the context of his view that the Spirit is active in all creation. Richard (1997:116) comments that the *kenōsis* of the Spirit is more radical than that of the Son. He does not glorify himself, but Christ (Jn 16:14); as enabling the mind and attitude of Christians, this is surely an example for them to emulate. This naturally affects Christian life; Budgen (1985:205) says that "we must recognise and respect the limits that the Holy Spirit has set upon himself".

As God, he has the attribute of omnipresence, so appropriate to his nature as Spirit. Yet when the second Person became incarnate, he limited his presence, restricting himself to a single body, and therefore to a single geographical location. In keeping with this, John 14:17 categorically states that the activity of the Spirit is limited to the Church, that he is not known in the world as a whole. Likewise, just as the Son limited his ability to relate to others in incarnation, so does the Spirit. Congar (1983:5) has suggested that a part of this *kenōsis* is that he has not revealed his name. He limits his personality to act as a bond (Gavrilyuk 2005:256). Personality can primarily be understood in relational terms, so is limited both in extent and depth.

Even if the primary limitation of the Spirit is in terms of his personality and so the extent of his relationships with the world and even with Christians, he is also limited in the attributes characteristic of the other Persons. He is limited in knowledge, seen in the Pauline observation that he searches the depths of God (1 Cor 2:10), indicating that he does not have exhaustive total knowledge in his own right. Then he is also limited in power; what he enables people and even Christ to do are not acts of omnipotence. Then even the gifting of his Church is limited in that he does not give all the gifts to everybody (Gavrilyuk 2005:251). Moreover, of course, since the power that he applies is limited, sanctification does not occur instantaneously, but is a gradual process.

The role of the Spirit as giving relationship naturally has profound effects in those that he bonds, but as Isaac Newton realised in other contexts, every action has a reaction. This means that the Spirit himself is affected simply by his action of bonding. For those that are bonded, this action is naturally, at least to some extent, a limitation on them, and therefore, in his act of bonding, the Spirit also experiences limitation. In the case of the Spirit, this is of course in no sense a restriction imposed from outside; as God, he is sovereign. However this restriction is accepted by his free choice; it can therefore be seen as an act of self-limitation, of *kenōsis*.

The path of *kenōsis*

These statements of the *kenōsis* of the Spirit must however be seen in the light of the fact that just as the emptying of the Son was a process, so also is that of the Spirit. Philippians 2 sees the expression of the *kenōsis* of the Son in terms of his incarnation and the progressive humiliation culminating in his death. Although Bulgakov feels that this process goes further into his resurrection and ascension, this being a unique feature of his kenotic theory (Gavrilyuk 2005:265), most see these as the start of the reversal, the beginning of the *plērōsis* that culminates with the glorification described at the end of the Philippian hymn (Phil 2:9-11). In fact Jesus even spoke of his death as a glorification (Jn 12:23), although Westcott (1958:124) comments that "in another aspect His glory followed after His withdrawal from earth". *Kenōsis* was needed in the physicality of the incarnation, but could be relaxed thereafter. What is indisputable is the fact that the degree of Christ's *kenōsis* changes with time. In this case it is reasonable that the degree of *kenōsis* of the Spirit also alters. Therefore there is a contrast between the types of activity of the Spirit in the two Testaments, and between the current state and what will be experienced in the future when Christ is indeed glorified, and when, by *perichōrēsis*, the self-limitation of the Spirit has also reversed.

The Bible opens with the story of creation and with it, the enigmatic reference to the Spirit "moving over the face of the waters" (Gen 1:2). Although there have been suggestions, occasioned by the common term, that what was meant was a great wind, the natural understanding is of the third Person (Blocher 1984:70). The presence of the Spirit was at that point evident, but this could well be so, for it was before the creation of any entity independent of God, and especially before the creation of any being with free will. *Kenōsis* had therefore not occurred. But as soon as creation was at all in place,

God necessarily experienced self-limitation, which included that of the Spirit. He was therefore no longer so clearly in evidence.

Also enigmatic is the next probable reference to the Spirit; in the creation of humanity, life was breathed into the clay figure, animating it (Gen 2:7). Again, the most likely explanation is that the reference is to the Spirit as the life-giver, who enlivens by giving inter-relativity to the elements of the figure. But at that point there is a further *kenōsis,* for the couple had the ability to procreate and to impart life themselves. The direct activity of the Spirit was no longer needed, and apart from isolated instances of his life-giving action, as in the valley of dry bones (Ez 37), and probably in events such as the raising of the widow's son (2 Ki 4:32f), the Spirit limited his involvement in the world.

Naturally, of course, his activity was not limited to giving life, but included such things as giving ability, as in the case of Joseph (Gen 41:38) or of the builders of the Tabernacle (Ex 31:3), and especially in prophetic activity. Nevertheless, in the Old Testament period, the activity of the Spirit was limited, both to a very few people, and as very occasional. There were just a few hints that the situation was not to remain like that, as in the promise of Joel (2:28), so wonderfully fulfilled at Pentecost, or in the promise through Jeremiah of the internalisation of the Law (Jer 31:33). This was also true in Jesus' designation as Son of God at his baptism, where there was also the manifestation of the Spirit in the form of a dove, and the voice of the Father.

The reversing of *kenōsis*

It was with the reversing of the *kenōsis* of Jesus after the cross that the *kenōsis* of the Spirit also started to reverse. It is then in his increasing *plērōsis* that the full extent of his *kenōsis* in the Old

Testament period became evident. Indeed it is often only when a lack is removed that it is appreciated for the first time; it may well be asked whether we are aware of how far God, and especially the third Person, are still in a situation of *kenōsis*.

Simply because of the equality of the Persons of the Trinity, whose Deity is fundamentally kenotic, and because of the perichoretic interplay between the Persons, it should be expected that the Spirit manifests *kenōsis* and therefore that the depth of his self-limitation coincides with the depths of the *kenōsis* of the Son, so during the crucifixion. This was, after all, when the Father withdrew his own presence most completely, even from the Son, who would appear to have lost even the sense of the presence of his Father, being reduced to cry not "Abba", but "Eloi" (Macleod 1998:176). Insofar as the Spirit acts as *vinculum amoris*, the bond of love between Father and Son, the diminished relationship reflects the limitation of the action of the Spirit. How appropriate that there was darkness, the loss of the light that often symbolises the presence of the Spirit. But then, as the Son commenced the move to his *plērōma*, reversing his *kenōsis* in his increasing glorification, the Spirit also moved towards increasing *plērōma*, and so could manifest his presence in the world in a way that had not been previously experienced. Thus, when Jesus gave the promise to his disciples of the coming fullness of the Spirit, he said that he had not yet been given, because Jesus had not been glorified (Jn 7:39). This links the giving of the Spirit with the glorification of Jesus (Murray 1963:39). Why otherwise was there this delay? Incidentally, as Westcott (1958:123) remarks, what was now given was not a Person, but his activity; in *kenōsis*, the person's attributes are not limited, but he restricts their operation. The delay was of course not that Jesus was the incarnation of the Spirit, who, if this were the case could only then come after the end of Jesus' bodily existence, but it was due to the *perichōrēsis* between Son and Spirit; in the reducing of the *kenōsis* of one came that of the other.

The increasing fullness of the Spirit was only then possible because of the increasing fullness of the Son.

Thus shortly after the ascension of Jesus into more of a state of glory came the impartation of the Spirit to the Church at Pentecost. Instead of his restricted and occasional activity came a more permanent indwelling. Just as Jesus, in heaven, is now not restricted to interact with those in physical proximity to him, and just as he no longer has no settled home, the Spirit could relate to more people, and there could be a more settled presence. Even the impersonality of the Spirit, an aspect of his *kenōsis,* can be seen to be in the process of reversal, in the manifestation in discrete elements of fire.

There is of course then an anticipation of further *plērōma* in the future. For none of the three Persons was their fullness manifested instantly, but for all three, there was an increasing move away from the previous *kenōsis* towards *plērōma.* It is clear that the working of the Spirit in the present, wonderful though that is, is a foretaste of what the future will bring. Paul speaks of the "first-fruits" of the Spirit (Rom 8:23), or of an "earnest" (2 Cor 1:22 etc). The new creation by the Spirit in the gift of eternal life (2 Cor 5:17) is obviously not to a final state, but there is an anticipation of life in fullness in the future.

The contrast between Old and New Testaments

It is this reduction of the *kenōsis* of the Spirit that can then explain a number of the differences between the Testaments. Of course the fundamental reason for the differences is that they are separated by the events of the incarnation, but when this is seen as the culmination, the end, and the start of the reversal of *kenōsis,* both of the Son and Spirit, the differences become more explicable.

That there was a significant contrast between the Old and New Testaments was a hard thing for the early Church to accept. The early chapters of Acts record the difficulty that Jews such as Peter had to accept that the situation had fundamentally changed. To convince him required a clear revelation of God's intention by the events at Joppa (Acts 10:9f), after which the Spirit told him what he must do (Acts 11:12), and then by the clear manifestations of the Spirit at the home of the Gentile Cornelius (Acts 10:44f). Such acts of the Spirit were of course now part of his reducing *kenōsis*. This intervention by the Spirit was vital, especially when he came under an understandable attack from the Church. If God had not made the new situation clear, Peter would almost certainly had reverted, as indeed he would seem to have done later, at least to an extent (Gal 2:12). But the new situation was so hard to accept that it took what has come to be called the first Council of the Church, held in Jerusalem, to resolve the matter (Acts 15:6f). Essentially, the Church realised that there were two new factors, firstly the inclusion of the Gentiles into the Church, and secondly that these Gentile Christians did not have to keep the Old Testament law. It was these two that can be linked to the reduction in *kenōsis* of the Spirit.

The situation had now changed, the Old Testament had ended. Not that this should be over-emphasized, as is such a common reaction in theology to anything novel. Marcion well understood the difference in situation, but over-reacted in trying to throw out the old completely. The new situation did not in the least mean that the Old Testament could be abandoned; how could it, when the Lord himself claimed not to abolish the law, but to fulfil it (Matt 5:17)? Rather, *kenōsis* is not something new and disruptive, but the continuation of the out-working of a process. The death of Jesus was not a disruption so much as the completion and fulfilling of the old, the process of *kenōsis* taking its natural course, continuing into *plērōsis*, passing the bottom point of what has been called the "great parabola" (Boice 1971:125).

The reversing of *kenōsis* which started with the resurrection of Jesus also of course applied, by *perichōrēsis,* to the Father. It is a striking contrast to the Old Testament that in the New, God was commonly referred to in this way. Although there was a sense in which Israel as a nation had an awareness of being in the special relationship of sonship to God (eg Is 1:2, Hos 11:1), this did not extend to understanding God in terms of paternity. The new situation was not just that the experience that Jesus had of God as his Father was appropriated by his disciples, but reflected a real change in situation. In the reduction of his *kenōsis,* God became more commonly experienced by people. There was a deeper relationship now possible, and so God was perceived more in relational, so personal categories, so as Father.

The increasing manifestation of the experience of the Fatherhood of God occurred as grace became available to all, not just to Israel, and the infant Church was expanded by the inclusion of Gentiles. The Spirit did not then relate just one people to God, but as many as choose to be included in the new Israel. The adoption as children of God that had been a prerogative of Israel, as the Spirit linked them to their Father, was now extended as the activity both of Father and Spirit expanded. Right through the Old Testament period there had been an increasing sharpening of focus, from humanity, to Israel, to Judah, to the remnant, and finally to the Messiah, as Cullmann observes (König 1988:28). This increasing *kenōsis* could then be reversed, the particularism of the Jews replaced by the relation of God to the Church of both Jew and Gentile. In the last days, the Spirit would be upon all flesh (Jl 2:28 = Acts 2:17).

Putting this another way, in the Old Testament the *kenōsis* of the Spirit, his self-limitation, reflected upon the limitation of his action to one people. It is often pointed out that the *kenōsis* of Christ was an act of his free choice, not surprisingly as God's *kenōsis* in general is in order to give choice to the creation, people in particular; then the limitation of God's particular relation to Israel had been by his choice (Deut 7:6f), just as creation itself had been by his choice. But with the reduction in the *kenōsis* of the Spirit, the inclusion of people in the kingdom of God is broader. This is not just because he widens the scope of his action, but because there is now an action of the Spirit, linking each person, individually, to God in Christ. Citing the opening of book 3 of Calvin's *Institutes*, Ferguson (1996:100) can therefore point out that the idea of union with Christ is at the heart of evangelical theology. The Heidelberg catechism states that the Spirit "is also given me, to make me, by a true faith, partaker of Christ and all his benefits" (in Lederle 1988:239). The expression "in Christ", or its variants, is so significant that it occurs over 160 times in the New Testament (Ferguson 1996:100).

In the Old Testament, in contrast, belonging to the covenant people was done without the direct participation of the Spirit, because it was a natural thing, based on race. Repudiation of the covenant then naturally resulted in exclusion from the covenant people (Num 15:30). While God continues to relate to the people of the ancient covenant, belonging to that people is now possible by the direct action of the Spirit. The true Israel continues as the Church (Gal 6:16); but the relationship to God is directly through the Spirit. This also means that in contrast to the Old, the New Testament sanction was spiritual, the delivery to satan (1 Cor 5:5).

Indeed, protecting that covenant also had a different basis. Insofar as the Old Testament covenant was effectively physical, it was protected by physical means, and warfare was constantly necessary, even directly commanded by God. To protect the covenant, the nation had to be protected. In contrast, in the new situation, there is no national identity for believers, so warfare is obsolete, and Christians have commonly repudiated any resort to force. "The weapons of our warfare are not worldly" (2 Cor 10:4). Indeed, Christian warfare is not so much against human aggression, but to the source of that

247

aggression, the "principalities and powers", for which only spiritual weapons can be effective (Eph 6:10f).

It then follows that the sign of belonging to God's people was different. The old system was physical, circumcision reflecting the basis of belonging simply by the process of procreation. Celebration of belonging was likewise physical, so that the Old Testament feasts were really that, and were occasions of eating, when the physical body benefited, and the bonding between individuals was strengthened in the fellowship of eating and drinking together. In contrast, belonging under the new covenant was on the basis of relating to Christ through the bonding of the Spirit, this now being possible through the relaxing of his *kenōsis*. We are baptised into that body by the Spirit (1 Cor 12:13), water effectively symbolising his action. Likewise the central act of worship in the Church reflects the union with Christ, eating and drinking the symbols of his body and blood; the relationship with each other is not so much a result of the common experience, although this is by no means absent, but in the common relating of each individual to Christ, and then to each other. It has therefore been important for most Christian traditions to understand that Christ is actually present in the celebration of the Lord's Supper. It was the Spirit that solved the problem of the presence of Christ in the Lord's supper for Calvin. He explained how the real presence of Christ could be present at its celebrations without resort to the Catholic idea of "transubstantiation", or the Lutheran variant of this in "consubstantiation". Calvin accepted that Jesus was indeed present, that the supper was not just a memorial of the event, simply done in obedience, without any value in itself, as Zwingli was teaching. For him, Christ's presence is not ubiquitous, as Luther believed (Wendel 1965:331), but is localised in heaven at the right hand of the Father (Wendel 1965:348). It is only through the Spirit, and through his bonding (Wendel 1965:351), that Christ can be present at the celebration of the Supper. The supper is really an "organ of encounter" (Berkhof 1979:367). This is an aspect seen in the early Church, reflecting their understanding that their covenant status depended on their relationship to him (Dunn 1975:185). Indeed, the supper can be aptly referred to as the "communion", seeing that it celebrates the linkage with Christ that is absolutely essential for human salvation. The physical act conveys, not just attests, forgiveness and acceptance (Tinker 2001:25). Thus even in the last supper, Jesus could validly refer to the bread as his body, seeing that the Holy Spirit, even then, could provide a bond between him and the elements. Thus neither baptism nor communion makes sense without the action of the Spirit; and therefore they did not occur under the old covenant. Even if, when the Jews did accept a proselyte into Israel, the sign of acceptance was not just circumcision, but baptism, Beasley-Murray (1972:42) denies that John's baptism is derived from this proselyte baptism.

Conformity to that covenant then has a different basis, that in the New Testament being enabled by the action of the Spirit. Under the Old Covenant, obedience to God was done simply by obedience to the written law. It was a laid-down requirement, a set of rules, which had to be adhered to. Naturally it was possible to fail in its requirements simply by ignorance, and in that case there was a method to remedy the matter, through the offering of sacrifice. However, with the presence of the Spirit, there is no longer a need for a written set of rules; as Jeremiah had foretold (31:31f), the requirement of God was internalised. Ezekiel 36:26f relates this to the Spirit. Thus a Christian is led by the Spirit, and is obedient to God in obeying the inner promptings of the Spirit. The law remains as a guide, but is not absolute. There is of course no contradiction, insofar as the Spirit had inspired the scriptures, but there could be a flexibility and immediacy in the directness of his leading. It follows of course that where the Spirit, in the reversing of his *kenōsis*, becomes more active, people become better, more sanctified. It has been a feature of revival that there has both been an increasing awareness of sin and moral improvement in society.

Naturally the content of ethics itself is also transformed. Jesus himself commented on the justice of an eye for an eye (Matt 5:38), frequently cited in the Old Testament. His attitude was as scandalous to the Jew, as often incomprehensible to us, one of refusing to claim rightful justice, of humility, in short of *kenōsis*. It is in the deliberate choice of self-limitation that many have seen the heart of Christian ethics. But if Jesus was acting according to the divine nature of *kenōsis*, a Christian lifestyle which reflects the image of God should then be kenotic. Humanly speaking this is foolishness and impracticable, and therefore demands the enabling of the Spirit to make possible what Jesus so clearly wanted from his followers.

It is here that comes that magnificent contrast between the seventh and eighth chapters of Romans. In the former comes the absolute impossibility, and so the frustration with trying to obey the law, but in the latter comes liberation. While the Spirit is not mentioned in Chapter 7, the following chapter is full of him. Perhaps ironically, with the empowering of the Spirit, obedience to the law becomes more of a possibility, but in his guidance giving the internalisation of the will of God, this form of obedience becomes obsolete. A Christian need not obey the written code, but rather follow the promptings of the Spirit. In practice of course, they usually coincide.

It then follows that the basis of salvation changes with the presence of the Spirit. In the Old Testament, salvation depended on obedience to the law, so, "by works". However, the basis of salvation in the New is the relationship with Christ enacted by the Spirit. This manifests as faith, a reliance on God as faithful, and resulting in faithfulness to him. As James insists (2:14), faith leads to works, as a result of it. The relationship with God in this sense of faith was rare in the Old Testament due to the *kenōsis* of both Father and Spirit. What then of Abraham, who Paul puts forward as a paradigm of the faith in God needed for salvation (Rom 4)? Was he not in fact in a position of privilege, insofar as God did speak to him, and he was obedient to that? It would seem that in his case, the normal situation of *kenōsis* was to an extent relaxed; he was in practice New Testament. This is indeed possible, as *kenōsis* is not an inherent limitation, or imposed from without, but freely chosen. Thus if there is a reason for its relaxation, it could be suspended. Indeed, the ministries of the prophets are examples of this relaxation; but they do not detract from the observation that in the Old Testament the ministry of the Spirit was limited, and at best intermittent. Indeed, the *kenōsis* of God was not absolute in the Old Testament, but on an occasional and intermittent basis God did relate to some individuals. The obvious group was the prophets. However, it is striking that they did not in general refer to the action of the Spirit, attributing their message to the "word" of God.

There is a further contrast here between the Testaments, which emerges, although not explicitly, in the "Jerusalem Council". Such a body could not really have met before the reduction in *kenōsis* of the Spirit occurred in the filling of the Spirit at Pentecost. In the Old Testament situation, there was no real possibility of any change in practice, as it had been given directly by God through Moses, with whom, just as Abraham, he had specifically decided to relate to in a way that was unique in that situation. No decision to change the worship, composition, or organisation of Israel was possible without God's direct intervention. In fact this did occur later, when the monarchy was established, but again this was done through one specific individual, Samuel, through whom God acted. Likewise the change that soon occurred, as the throne passed to David, through whom there were indeed some changes with the establishment of the Temple, even if these were only fully enacted under Solomon.

What would have been unthinkable would have been any change without such an intervention of God and his calling of a specific individual through whom his will would be made clear. But the unthinkable could now occur, just because God had now enabled all the members of the infant Church, and could act through each of them. There was no change insofar as it was still the will of God that was being expressed, but instead of this being manifested by the rare individual, it was through any and all of the Church, because God, through the reduction of *kenōsis* of the Spirit, and so his filling, related to each one. A council to change fundamental aspects of belief and practice was then a possibility.

Even if such a gathering was possible in the Old Testament situation, it could only have consisted of very specific people, only those who could claim some specific relationship with God. It would be limited to holders of the traditional three offices of prophet, priest and king, and certainly could not include any of the ordinary people. But the group of Acts 15 was probably wider; although Acts 15:6 speaks specifically of apostles and elders, it would seem that others were there. Acts 15:12 speaks of the *plēthos*, the "multitude" or "assembly" (RSV), and when it came to the communication of the decision, it was on behalf not just of the apostles and elders, but of the whole church (Acts 15:22). Significantly, the decision was also attributed to the Holy Spirit (Acts 15:28). Indeed, the offices of the Old Testament were now no longer restricted, but as Peter (significantly) wrote, the church is a "royal priesthood" (1 Pet 2:9); there is a "priesthood of all believers". There is also a sense in which all Christians also bear the prophetic office as well, as the text continues "that you may declare ..." Nevertheless, this does not mean that each Christian individually fulfils these roles, but that they are held by the community, which function together, as parts of the body (1 Cor 12:4f) (Williams 1997:197f).

Therefore, in contrast to the Old Testament, a set-apart ministry is not needed in the New, where "they shall all know me" (Jer 31:34). In the presence of the Spirit, each individual is led by God, and able to worship God without the mediation of any human office. Although there is still a ministry, set apart for particular service, it does not have the same function as in the offices of the Old Testament. In particular, one aspect of the priesthood falls away as there is no longer any need for sacrifice, although the other, that of a religious expert, is still valid. Even the ministry of the apostles was clearly unique, and as for a limited duration, is still almost as kenotic as the offices of the Old. As witnesses of the resurrection (1 Cor 9:1), that aspect of their role could not be passed on.

Therefore, despite the belief of some Christian groups, there is no indication that the power of the Spirit is limited to one group of people, who alone can minister to the rest. What is limited is the gifting of the Spirit, where in persisting *kenōsis,* any individual person receives a limited gifting. But the glory is that as in a human body, where the interaction, the communion, of the various parts overcomes the limitation of each, so the ability given to each Christian complements the lack in others. Charismatic churches have thus often practised "body ministry", where each member of Christ's body has a function in its life and worship, reflecting specific gifting. These groups commonly appeal to Ephesians 4, where the unity in the Spirit is indeed stressed (Eph 4:3). The role of the ministry is described a couple of verses further on as "for the equipment of the saints, for the work of ministry, for building up the body of Christ" (Eph 4:12). The first comma, which of course does not occur in the original, has been called the "devil's comma"; its omission clearly implies the reason for the equipment of the saints. Incidentally the choice of name for Christians here, *hagioi,* "holy ones", does reflect the role of the Holy Spirit in them. But this does give a role for a human ministry, of equipping the people; as the priests in the Old Testament, they are "religious experts" and teach the people. Although the presence of the Spirit in Christians does educate them, what he does is rather to apply the teaching of Christ (Westcott 1958:208). Then he also enables their recall of what they have learnt and experienced in other ways. Jesus spoke of the Spirit bringing to their remembrance what Jesus had said (Jn 14:26). In general the Spirit does not give supernatural revelation; Jesus had not just relied on the Spirit in this regard, but had taught his disciples. The same is true of the Old Testament prophets, who received revelation from the Word, and do not attribute it to the Spirit. Christianity has always seen a balance between Word and Spirit. There is then a role for ministers insofar as they have specifically studied, especially if they are gifted to communicate this to the rest of the people.

Of course, a "body ministry" is only possible by the unity that the Spirit gives, relating the individuals together as parts of the body. This can overcome otherwise intractable barriers, as between Jew and Gentile (Eph 2:18), or between racial groups in South Africa. Indeed the reality of this is manifested in many Christian organisations, where human differences seem irrelevant, perhaps especially in those that stress the work of the Spirit. Obviously this is not automatic, and it is a tragedy when Christians are divided, as Jesus himself indicated, where his prayer indicated that he expected division (Jn 17:11). The reason for this is that unity does depend to a degree on individual sanctification, which is a process; love and tolerance of others develops over time! But secondly, unity is never enforced by the Spirit, who only encourages and persuades, and never compels. He does not force a person (Williams 1971:14), but as in seduction, rather entices. He does not overcome human free will, which is after all the reason for the *kenōsis* of God in the first place.

Increasing *plērōsis* of the Spirit

The reduction of the *kenōsis* of the Spirit in the ascension of Jesus was not absolute, simply because the glorification of Jesus was not yet absolute. Speaking of Jesus, the Philippian hymn looks forward to the time when "every knee shall bow" (Phil 2:10), and even that will not be the ultimate. Rather there will be increasing *plērōsis*, not just of the Son, but also of both the Father (eg 1 Cor 15:28), and the Spirit. This then results in an increasing closeness to God for his people as the fullness of the Spirit increases.

Worship can then become even richer. The Charismatic renewals made possible through the increased fullness of the Spirit have been steps along this path, but these *charismata* are in themselves kenotic, and even if wonderful in themselves, are an anticipation of much more in the future. The promise of the cessation of the gifts (1 Cor 13:8) is not of the present, due to the close of the apostolic age or of the completion of the scriptures, both of which are in any case manifestations of *kenōsis*, but when the increased presence of the Spirit simply supersedes them. Such limitation, as the ministries of the Old Testament, was transient.

Hardly surprisingly, human life then becomes more spiritual as well. Whereas before Christ life was simply the biological interrelation of the elements of the body, when the Spirit came there was the addition of "spiritual", or eternal life to this, which would survive the trauma of the death of the body. But this is by no means the final state; Paul speaks of being "unclothed" in the loss of the physical body (2 Cor 5:4), but then of being "further clothed". The current presence of the Spirit, giving eternal life even in the present, as in which John thrills (Jn 3:36, 5:24, 6:47) is naturally a guarantee of this (2 Cor 5:5). Incidentally, what a contrast between the modern western church, which demands proof of the presence of the Spirit, and the New Testament Church, which could use the evident presence of the Spirit as a proof of new life (Gal 3:2)! This "further clothing" is the reception of the "spiritual body" (1 Cor 15:44), where the adjective does not refer to the substance of the body, but its motivation (Williams 2004:231). The very life of the body is Spirit, as it was in the first human body when it was breathed into by God (Gen 2:7).

Redeemed humanity will then come into its full inheritance, which had previously only been received as a taste, an earnest, as first-fruits. Healing likewise will be total, not occasional, partial and intermittent as in the present. In this regard, Kelsey (1973:33) points out the striking contrast between the Old Testament, where although some healing did occur, it was a rarity, and the sudden abundance in the New, where nearly one fifth of the Gospels relates to healing (1973:54). This is because the King has now arrived in his Kingdom, seen in the presence of the Spirit (Kelsey 1973:58).

There is a sense in which the picture given by the book of Revelation is the counterpart to the primeval state portrayed by Genesis. There is, for example, once again access to the tree of life lost in the Fall. Yet it is not simply a restoration but a fulfilment; the final state is a city not a garden. But the means was through *kenōsis*, and the final state was then better than the first would have been. Jesus gained glory through his *kenōsis*, God gained the multitudes relating freely to him that he would not have had (Pinnock 2002:216). Can the same be said of the Spirit? Perhaps just a hint of this can be seen in the contrast between the violent impersonal power of Genesis 1:2 and the delightful very personal invitation of Revelation 22:17. The purpose of *kenōsis*, for people as well as for God, was for the enabling and strengthening of relationship; it is this that the Spirit shares in. We can look forward, with him, to the enjoyment of all that this means in the fullness that resulted.

PART 4

The *kenōsis* of the Church

"... be with you all"

Chapter 11

Salvation by *kenōsis*

The heart of the Christian message is of salvation; the *evangel*, the good news, is that salvation is possible, and available through Christ. It flows out of the love of God. Then if the incarnation was by means of *kenōsis*, outlined in the Philippian hymn, the salvation that this was done for is also kenotic. So how Christ achieved salvation is most naturally understood in the framework of *kenōsis*, and the human response to this will also be that of *kenōsis*.

Thus the Philippian hymn is firmly in the context of atonement. It is evident there that *kenōsis* deepened as the drama of the atonement progressed, with the most complete emptying occurring in the actual crucifixion. This was no negation of his power and authority; Richard (1997:38) stresses that redemption occurred because Jesus positively accepted death; it was by his choice of love, not something forced on him. He laid down his life voluntarily (Jn 10:17).

Sin as producing *kenōsis*

Any understanding of salvation, what it is and how it is achieved,

259

must relate strongly to what salvation is from, so to the nature of sin. Many in the early Church, such as Irenaeus, connected sin with finitude, others, such as Tertullian, with an act of will (Bray 1979:89); these come together in Christ's choice of self-limitation for the sake of salvation. Just as the limitation of humanity is due to the free choice of sin, it is this which is behind the *kenōsis* of Christ. Thus, salvation is naturally by *kenōsis*, as the sin that it deals with is kenotic; it was because of sin that *kenōsis* was necessary at all.

Sin must be understood in relation to the one committing it. A very young person can hardly be held as guilty as one who is more mature. Paul makes a contrast between those who have an awareness of the details of God's will in the law and those who are ignorant (Rom 2:1f), even if he insists that all are guilty on the basis of the understanding that they do have. More than this, sin must surely be understood in relation to the nature of a person. It is here that we will naturally go back to the Genesis account for its description of what human beings are. Strikingly, people are described there as having been created in *imago Dei*, in the image of God. Much ink has been spilt in discussion of what this means; suggestions are legion! What has rarely been done is to understand it in terms of the fundamental Christian concept of God, that he is Trinity; the suggestion of (Barth 1958:181f) is perhaps the closest, in which he related the image of God to humanity as "male and female" (Gen 1:26). However he stopped with a recognition of plurality in God, not wanting to accept reference to the Trinity in an Old Testament context. As many today, he felt that the doctrine of the Trinity is a later development, really not even to be found in the New Testament, let alone the Old.

However, if God is indeed what later thinkers proposed, and after all they did not intend to do more than explain the Biblical data, then when the Genesis account speaks of humanity in *imago Dei*, this must be understood as in *imago Trinitatis*. To be even more specific, the nature of unfallen humanity reflects the immanent Trinity. This has several key features, those of three equal Persons, differentiated by relationship, and related by interpenetration, *perichōrēsis*. It must immediately be said that this does not mean that the first couple was actually a triplet, as the nature of the Person depends on the Person involved, and the third Person, the Holy Spirit, is often described more in impersonal terms as the bond of love between the other two Persons, the *vinculum amoris* (Williams 2004:1f). The parallel with the other two Persons is clearer, as a man and a woman are fundamentally equal (Gal 3:28), and differentiated by relationship. It is the last feature, that of *perichōrēsis*, that is most significant for the understanding of the nature of unfallen humanity, and then helps a realisation of what sin was.

The discovery of *perichōrēsis* was one of the keys that unlocked the Trinitarian secret. Throughout the period of the Arian controversy there was a constant battle over how the Persons could be totally equal, yet at the same time differentiated, for if they were different, they could not be equal, if equal, they could not be different. It is hardly surprising that it was hard to steer between the Scylla of Arianism and the Charybdis of Sabellianism. But if the Persons are different, yet fully interpenetrate, then they are indeed equal. The secret lies in the total relationship between the Persons. If that relationship were lost, limitation would result. After all, the very fact of there being three Persons demands that each alone is limited; the Father is not the Son, or *vice versa*. But that limitation is transcended by *perichōrēsis*; the Father is unlimited, just, and only because of, the full relationship to the other two Persons.

It is this that likewise characterises the primal couple. In *imago Trinitatis*, they enjoyed total harmony, reflecting the divine *perichōrēsis*. The fundamental characteristic of humanity is openness, so relational (Richard 1982:211). This is seen in Jesus, who was totally "the man for others", which is why he did what he did; in his total openness, he was reflecting what humanity was originally, and so should still be. But it was this that was damaged by sin, which damaged the relationship both between the man and the woman, and between them and God. The image of God was marred. It is this that then manifested as limitation, and, appropriately, they were expelled from the Garden, both a spatial limitation and a limitation from life. Such was the value of relationship that when it was damaged it was costly to restore (cf Placher 2001:138); this is reflected in the legislation of Numbers 5:7-8, where payment is made to an offended party. Because the loss due to sin was the limitation in relationship, the appropriate cost for salvation was then also limitation of relationship; this was borne by Christ in his *kenōsis*.

Salvation as kenotic

Thus the human being suffers inherent limitation in sin, and indeed this finally manifests in the totality of limitation which we call death, when there is total relationlessness (Richard 1982:219). And it is this that was experienced by the Son in his enabling salvation; the essential experience of Jesus in this process was therefore that of limitation, of *kenōsis*. If he was to bear our sin in its fullness, he had to undergo the fullness of *kenōsis* himself, and experience it fully. He therefore became incarnate, obviously *kenōsis*, he went through the entire process of slavery, again obviously that of *kenōsis*, especially as it is essentially dehumanising, even depersonalising, then to death. But even this is not the depths of *kenōsis*; Richard (1982:217f) therefore sees the absolute forsakenness of Jesus, his absolute *kenōsis*, as the key aspect of what he took for our sins. And in union with his resurrection and glorification, the reversing of *kenōsis*, comes the fullness of our salvation. "Solidarity with God in Jesus means salvation ultimately from death" (Richard 1982:230). The resurrection is not just a proof of God's accepting Jesus' sacrifice, but a vital aspect of salvation (Pinnock 1996:99).

Salvation is then intimately related to the kenotic action of God in creation, which is why it is described by Paul as a re-creation (2 Cor 5:17). Salvation is a restoration to what God originally intended (Vanstone 1977:70). Thus Moltmann (1985:89f) sees salvation as a continuation of God's creative activity, his continued action to overcome nothingness, although he remarks on the contrast in the travail involved in salvation compared with the original creation. Nevertheless the similarity indicates also that the same fundamental action effects them; both are actions through God's *kenōsis*. Tillich believes that it is non-being that generates fullness (Fiddes 1988:250), an interesting link to a common modern understanding that creation occurred naturally in reaction to nothingness. The Christian response would be to ask why that should be, but also to note that God's way is to generate *plērōma* by the path of *kenōsis*.

It naturally follows that just as creation was by God's choice, so at the same time, salvation must imply choice, as God chose to save, which is in itself a *kenōsis*, as any choice must be. He then limited himself so that our choice is possible. The result of this, however, is that if it is by choice, it naturally follows that some choose not to avail themselves of the opportunity, and therefore that salvation itself is limited; there is no universalism. At the same time, of course, if salvation is limited, it means that God's relationship is limited, itself a *kenōsis*; there is no *kenōsis* in the immanent Trinity, where *perichōrēsis* is absolute.

More than this, God's love in self-limitation can be seen in one of the beautiful pictures of salvation in the scriptures, that of the adoption of believers as children of God (Rom 8:15, Gal 4:5). God is not just creator, but is also Father. Here it is the essence of being a father that he stoops, self-limits for his children. What may be stressed is that the power and strength of a man are not inherently affected by being a father, but that he chooses, for the sake of the relationship with his children, to curtail them. And perhaps, it must be added that in a different situation, such curtailment will not be done, but his power and ability will be used to the full. Such may indeed be done just for the sake of those children, to protect and care for them.

That Galatians passage contrasts the adoption of the child with the previous state of slavery. God sent his Son to redeem those in slavery under the law (Gal 4:4). Here the *kenōsis* of Christ was into slavery, but he was freed from that through death, which naturally ends slavery. In our union with Christ, we then share in the end of our slavery (Rom 6:15), and are free from sin and the law. Salvation is a liberation to service to Christ. Our adoption as children is then possible by the Spirit uniting us to Christ, so it is by the Spirit that we can call God "Abba, Father" (Gal 4:6).

Insofar as salvation is a relationship with God, it must be by *kenōsis*, for any relationship involves giving up to some extent; in the human context it takes at the least some time (Barry 1987:17). God gives, and likewise the human response to salvation is also itself a *kenōsis*. This can hardly be surprising, as the essence of the Christian understanding of salvation is that it is *sola gratia*, entirely by grace, so that its acceptance must mean humility, or self-emptying. Appropriately it is accepted in the yielding that is baptism. At the same time as people accept that they are unable to save themselves, so empty themselves, they adopt the repentance to obedience that goes with this acceptance. The result of this is theologically very satisfying, as those who are saved then reflect the nature of the one who saves them, which is what salvation must essentially be.

Then if salvation was necessary because of sin damaging relationship and causing limitation, it follows that salvation reverses this and produces wholeness. Barry (1968:47) indicates that in Christ humanity attained its full realisation and completeness; it is then this humanity in wholeness which is communicated to Christians. Although the action of Christ is usually presented in the obvious terms of the contrast between life and death, sin and holiness, the same principle is applicable in a wider context of the humiliation of Christ. The very reason for his assumption of *kenōsis* was that people, through the effect of their sin, were already experiencing powerlessness and emptiness. It is this, equally an effect of sin as is death, that is experienced by Christ for believers. Certainly an aspect of salvation is the giving of wholeness, enabled by the voluntary yielding up by Christ of his own. A frequent theme in the Patristic understanding of salvation is that of the so-called "amazing exchange", that Jesus, as sinless and divine, died for sinful human people, experiencing the effect of their sin in his death and giving them his sinlessness so that they can be forgiven, and his life so that they can live eternally. The book of Hebrews in particular presents the action of Jesus as a sacrifice, fulfilling the Old Testament pattern; it is obvious that sacrifice is a form of *kenōsis*, of giving up, even of life. In the case of Jesus it was a voluntary act; he willingly sacrificed himself. Christian salvation is not just limited to the forgiveness of sins, not even the attainment of eternal life, but so that people could become whole, as fully human as God created them to be, open in their relationship to God, and so to each other. As personality is relational, the Christian becomes more fully personal (Richard 1997:167). As Irenaeus said, the glory of God is humanity fully alive (Hall 1986:200). And so more Christ-like; although after the glorification of Christ, his *kenōsis* would have ceased, Jesus would not have stopped being human, indeed he is only then what humans should be. At our resurrection, we become really human for the first time! Macquarrie comments (in Peacocke 1993:315) that our humanity is not just a natural endowment, as felinity to a cat, but needs to be discovered and realised; we are not so much "human beings", but "human becomings". This process is in the process of *kenōsis*. In the words of Irenaeus:

> Verbum Dei, Jesum Christum Dominum nostrum
> qui propter immensam suam dilectionem
> factum est quod sumus nos,

uti nos perficeret esse quod et ipse (Adv Haer 5:preaf).

(The word of God, our Lord Jesus Christ,
Who of his boundless love,
became what we are
to make us even what he himself is (in Peacocke
1993:189)).

Vanstone (1977:74) writes, "for the richness of the creation, God is made poor: and for its fullness God is made empty". And at the same time, sin is robbed of its strength, death of its sting, and the devil of dominion (McDonald 1994:39); effectively all suffer *kenōsis*!

Indeed, salvation is not only the negative, the release from sin, but the positive, "wholeness", in the identification with Christ in his glorification after the cross. There is a solution here to modern emptiness, the all too prevalent sense of alienation (McGrath 1992:113), and the receipt not only of life in abundance (Jn 10:10), but of a new reason for living, a new motivation, a new "spirit".

What happened at creation was the removal of the primeval formlessness, *tohu* (Gen 1:2), by making matter, and the overcoming of the void of *bohu* by the filling with life. It is then significant that at the cross, darkness covered the earth, a reversal of even the first act of creation, and perhaps even more so that the one who was dying is described in the Johannine prologue as the "light", the one who created it (1 Cor 8:6). The essence of sin is of a return to this original state; it is no accident that the makers of idols are derided as "emptiness" (Is 44:9). It is this that Jesus carried, so that we can receive the opposite, "fullness of life" (Jn 10:10). For this to happen, a person must then empty him- or herself from what leads to emptiness, to repent, and to reject false "idols", even the more sophisticated ones of wisdom and law (1 Cor 1:23), becoming as little children. Putting this another way, the receiving of grace for salvation and the filling with the Spirit demand a prior emptiness.

Because of what Christ has done, wholeness then became possible to his body, those in union with Christ through faith. Purification is enacted through suffering (eg 1 Pet 1:7), but we are purified through Christ's sufferings; then in our purification, the relationship with God can become closer (Placher 2001:135). Incidentally, this highlights the essential action of the Holy Spirit, who unites us to Christ, so giving us holiness, or "wholeness"; the English "holy" comes from the Anglo-Saxon *halis*, "whole" (Fitch 1974:111). Immediately there was a possibility of relationship with God, openness to him, and therefore the life of God could be received. A Christian, in relation with God, has eternal life (Jn 3:36 etc). The Spirit then conforms us to Christ in sanctification (Bray 1979:108). More than this, the gifts of the Spirit then reflect the empowerment of the believer, manifesting such as healing, knowledge and other aspects of the overcoming of limitation. There are even descriptions of the overcoming of spatial limitation, seen Biblically in the teleportation of Ezekiel, but occasionally reported today (Bennett & Bennett 1974:139, cf also Budgen 1985:210). Nevertheless, as Christ's glorification is progressive, so is this personal sanctification; it is this that prevents the exercise of full humanity.

Kenōsis and the means of salvation

I have elsewhere (Williams 1997:101f) outlined my understanding of the Christian doctrine of the means of salvation, that it comprises three essential and inter-relating components. In brief, these are as follows. Firstly, the death of Jesus on the cross is a sufficient sacrifice for the sins of the entire world. This enables the forgiveness of sins. Secondly, the union of the believer with Christ means that he or she receives the life of Christ and therefore eternal life. Then thirdly, the believer repents, forsaking sin and adopting a lifestyle and practices acceptable to God. Although there are as many as sixteen concepts of redemption (Schillebeeckx, in Peacocke 1993:322), they can be subsumed into three basic ideas.

There are those who accept each of these as a total theory of the atonement. Thus many, especially of an evangelical persuasion, accept the first, interpreting it in a form generally known as the "penal substitution" theory. Those more "liberal" tend to favour the third, believing that the example of Jesus influences a person to change his or her lifestyle, so that God is able to forgive them; this is often linked with the name of Abelard. Advocates of this understanding often point to the parable of the Prodigal Son, where the son humbled himself, and so the father forgave him. The second is sometimes called the "classic" theory. Christ overcame sin and death, and Christians share in his victory by their union with him. Aulén (1950), in his *Christus Victor*, argued that this was in fact the belief of the early church and of Luther, but that under the influence of Anselm and of Calvin who favoured the first, it was overshadowed by the first. Interestingly, seeing that Calvin tended to follow Augustine in the doctrine of salvation, the latter held to the "classic" view (Aulén 1950:75). A more modern variant on this is Barth's view that Christ is the predestined one, in whose election Christians share (Barth 1957:310). Barth also holds that the central aspect of the atonement is the cancelling of sin rather than the placating of wrath (Fiddes 1988:265); this is through union with God in Christ.

However, each of the theories, in itself, can be strongly criticised, and indeed has been by proponents of the other two. My belief is that the objections put to each are met by features of the others, which implies that a full theory of the atonement incorporates all three as aspects. This may be seen because it must be impossible for a person to unite with Christ unless sins are in fact forgiven, and there is a determination to obey. Then the forgiveness of sins is pointless unless it is accompanied by eternal life. Then following the example of Christ is not possible without God's power; Peacocke (1993:330) indicates that Abelard's view was that Christ was not just moving people to obey, but creating the necessary desire in us.

For example, the understanding of the atonement by Aulén, described in his *Christus Victor*, has been subject to criticism as it seems to make us the booty of warfare (McGrath 1992:88), but this criticism is blunted in the realisation that it is we who win the victory in our participation in Christ. Most especially, the example theory seems to ignore the power and reality of sin. It both implies that a change of life is within the power of people, and of itself has no means of dealing with sins of the past. They cannot just be ignored.

The penal substitutionary theory has come under especial criticism, a serious matter as many Christians feel that this is the main way that the New Testament presents the mechanism of atonement. It has been felt that it puts the love of the Son against the wrath of the Father, which would give a fundamental discord in the Trinity. In contrast, the classic view sees the work of all three persons together. One of Aulén's key points is that the atonement is a work of all the Persons, as indicated in 2 Corinthians 5:18. Richard (1982:218) points out that it was the Father who delivered up his Son, forsakenness and loneliness are key aspects of his *kenōsis*. Aulén also sees the atonement as primarily a work of the *logos*, while the penal theory is viewed as an action of the humanity of Christ (Aulén 1950:50). Here Wiersbe (1997:26) observes that Jesus imparted life through his word (Jn 5:24, 11:43, Lk 7:14, Heb 4:12 etc). Incidentally, in two of the cases cited, the word is spoken to dead people. It does not have to be understood to be effective, as the key aspect is the relational intention of a word; nevertheless it is responded to in obedience. This observation is pertinent to an inclusive interpretation of salvation.

It has also been argued that this theory reflects essential injustice; why should a person suffer for the sins of another? The Socinians, for example, reacting to the Reformation understanding of justification, felt that it was immoral to transfer the punishment which was due to the sinner onto a party who was innocent. Substitution in legal matters is felt to be illegal (Berkhof 1958:378). Thus although the theory was put forward in response to the justice of God, it was felt to be fundamentally unjust itself. It is also hard to see that universalism can be excluded without injustice. However, a view of salvation as brought about basically by relationship with Christ, which is the key affirmation of the "classic" theory, immediately solves this problem, for just as husband and wife are often treated in law as one unit, so by virtue of the closeness of the relationship between Christ and the Christian, they are also treated as one unit. Thus it is not so much a matter of the punishment being transferred from one person to another, the idea of substitution, or that one representative is punished instead of the rest, but that the unit as a whole bears the punishment due to the sin of the unit as a whole. Just as the Christian shares the life of Christ, so Christ shares the punishment of the Christian; both experiences are common. The union of the believer and Christ, *as a union*, is punished (cf Letham 1993:131), and the believer lives eternally in union with Christ. Because of the union with Christ, it is therefore possible for Paul to say that he makes up the sufferings of Christ, and that he rejoices in sufferings (Col 1:24); for him they are a common experience. We then suffer with Christ, and in that are purified, often seen as done by suffering (Placher 2001:135). Moreover, at the same time, a Christian in fact even keeps the law, but in Christ. He or she shares in the perfect life of Christ. In fact, while the Protestant affirmation is that salvation is granted through faith in Christ, Galatians 2:16 may even be translated as salvation by the faith of Jesus Christ! He is the source not only of saving grace but of the faith that expropriates it.

Then on the other hand, the relationship with Christ enables new life through sharing in the resurrection of Christ from the dead. For Paul, the atonement is almost always linked not just to the cross but also to the resurrection (Baillie 1956:199). Forsyth (1910:202) comments that God's action in salvation is not just removing punishment, but positively giving eternal life. Here, while the penal substitution theory has little place for the resurrection except as a proof that God had accepted the sacrifice of the cross, the classic theory unites them as two aspects of a process (Letham 1993:151). Stott (1986:238) may well be correct in his assertion that the New Testament does not locate forgiveness in the resurrection but in the cross, but the atonement is more than just forgiveness; without the receipt of eternal life through participation in the resurrection, forgiveness is of little value. More than that, the death is only meaningful in the context of the preceding life (Richard 1982:215); if for no other reason, it shows Christ's sinlessness, and therefore the adequacy of the sacrifice. Nevertheless of course, what he did in life, teaching and healing, was also of value; he came to die, but not only to die. Immediately this understanding of the atonement supplies two aspects in which Western theology is generally defective, firstly by giving importance to the life of Christ as well as to his death, and secondly, even if the immediate application is to the individual, the idea is readily applicable to the Christian community in society as a whole.

Thus the problems in the penal substitution theory are met by combining it with the others, especially the "classic", as aspects of a more comprehensive understanding. It is significant that the reference to eating flesh and drinking blood in John 6, which pictures union with Christ, is parallel to the synoptic references to taking up the cross (Driver 1986:98). Moberley remarks that buying something at a price for a stranger is in fact a bit of an insult, but not for somebody who is related (Morris 1965:303). Indeed the penal substitution theory is probably better understood as penal representation (cf Richard 1982:224), which implies the intimate relationship with

Christ. Among others, Hooker and Dunn prefer to see Christ in this way (Peacocke 1993:323). Bockmuehl (1997:133) draws attention to Isaiah 63:9 "in all their affliction he was afflicted", a text richly developed by the Rabbis.

That the three basic ideas form a comprehensive theory may also be suggested in that the first aspect emphasises the work of God the Son, the second of God the Father, adopting the believer as child of God, the third of God the Holy Spirit, who enables the transformation of motives. Not that there can be a division in the Trinity, because all three Persons are involved in each action. Likewise, the action of Holy Spirit, as *vinculum amoris*, is essential as it links the work of Christ to the present, both in time and in place, and the Father to the believer. Then the first aspect, forgiveness, is related to the cross, the second, eternal life, to the resurrection, and the third, lifestyle, to Pentecost. Interestingly, the historical order here follows that of the benediction of 2 Corinthians 13:14, which can otherwise seem odd (cf Williams 2004:252).

What must then be observed is that each aspect implies a form of *kenōsis*. This should not be surprising as essentially salvation is a relationship with God, and any relationship involves the self-limitation of the parties involved. An example of this is in Ezekiel 3, where Ezekiel was overwhelmed by the vision of God, even though this was not complete; also in Revelation 1, John fell down at the feet of the risen Christ. In both cases, as is inevitable, God had to limit himself in order to relate. This is of course why the Son of God became incarnate as a man, for it was in that way that relationship with us was best achieved.

In the first aspect of the understanding of the means of salvation, the "penal substitution" theory, the stress falls on the cross, so the self-giving of Christ as a perfect and complete sacrifice. Jeremias has observed that the Aramaic word for "lamb" can also be translated "servant" (Bonhoeffer 1967:199). By the voluntary action of Jesus, the process of *kenōsis* came to its ultimate in death. It is this that is the "wages of sin" (Rom 6:23), and therefore is a sufficient payment for sin. The gospel of Mark is often seen in connection with *kenōsis*; here the evangelist records that "the Son of Man did not come to be served, but to serve, and to give up his life as a ransom for many" (Mk 10:45). It is important here that it was God who died, for the death of a single human being could hardly be adequate for the sins of the world. It is this point that is effectively made by the author to the Hebrews, when he insists that the blood of animals is ineffective for atonement. The theory has tended to confine the atonement to the death of Christ, although it is more reasonable to see it as by the whole life of Christ, not just by three hours of pain (Letham 1993:133). It is then appropriate to see the whole life of Jesus in terms of *kenōsis*, even if it was concentrated in his death. Forsyth (1910:111) points out that it was not the physical pain that paid for sin, but Christ's obedience.

The experience of *kenōsis* was in any case an appropriate part of the punishment of sin. The heart of sin is pride, portrayed in the Genesis story as the cause of the primal sin; the opposite to this is the humility of *kenōsis*. In any case, it is this humility which Paul sought to encourage in his readers.

More than just the aspect of punishment, sin itself leads to emptiness and loss, and was this which was being experienced, in a substitutionary manner, by Christ. 1 Corinthians 1:18, 25 link weakness to the cross. Right at the beginning, sin caused loss in access to the Garden and to life, then loss of ease in getting food. Examples could be multiplied, from the loss of health as a result of immorality to the loss of freedom in addiction, which includes to sin itself (Rom 7:15). Even if an understanding of atonement does not necessitate Christ experiencing every specific sin in detail, there is a significant principle here. It must then be added that in

Christ, so many have experienced their own *kenōsis*, so freedom from bondage. McGrath (1992:106) recounts a story of release from addiction to cocaine; other examples are legion.

The third aspect of salvation demands that a person empties him- or herself in the act of repentance. The idea of obedience to God, and so of humility, is prominent in the Philippians 2 passage. This is not just a repentance, but is also a *kenōsis*; "unless you turn and become like children, you will never enter the kingdom of heaven" (Matt 18:3). "Whoever would save his life will lose it, and whoever loses his life for my sake will find it" (Matt 16:25). This is not of course a removal of the will as such, but its conformity to that of God, so the removal of self-will. Indeed, "God does not save us without our participation" (Pinnock 2001:166). The Philippian hymn explains the humility of Christ in terms of obedience; in the same way repentance is an emptying of will, becoming obedient to God. In fact, the act of *kenōsis* often demands a steely courage, confronting the temptation to take an easier course of events; Bulgakov comments that even in Christ, obedience of the human will to the divine was not without a battle (Gavrilyuk 2005:263). The example is that of Christ himself, who if he had been weaker, would have acted to avoid the pain and ignominy of the cross. There is then an identification with the nature of Christ in his humility and obedience. Indeed, the faith through which salvation is appropriated can be seen in these terms. This means that far from repentance and obedience to God being extra to the receipt of salvation by grace, it is an integral part of it. Paul's rebuttal of any anomianism (Rom 6) is really superfluous. Fiddes comments that the human response to God is an integral part of salvation, not just a reaction to it (Peacocke 1993:327).

Of course the act of humility is essential for any relationship; there has to be a self-limitation for the sake of relating to the other. This is of course what God did in Christ, and our response should then mirror that. Self-limitation is also a part of our relating to other people; citing Markus Barth, Yoder (1972:225) suggests that it is in reconciliation with others as a result of this that reconciliation with God occurs. However, it is as a result of the reconciliation with God that the action of the Spirit enabling this radical act is made possible. However the two aspects must be closely related.

In fact, insofar as *kenōsis* is an aspect of the image of God, a person, in conformity to that image must be humble. Morris (1974:242) comments that the fact that the father in the parable of the prodigal son ran (Lk 15:20) is striking. It is an act of humility that reflects the action of *kenōsis* in God the Father. Then in the conforming of human nature to this, a person more readily partakes in the divine nature (2 Pet 1:4), also of course kenotic, and so is saved. Ward (2001:164) explains that through the divine *kenōsis* came the possibility of *enōsis*, union with the divine, so that human nature could experience divinization. Pinnock (1996:150) notes that this process of *theōsis* was commonly held by the Fathers, especially by Irenaeus and Athanasius; he notes also Romans 5:2. The parallel here is with the *communicatio idiomatum*, the mutual effect of the divinity and humanity in Christ.

This relates to the second main theory of the atonement, and it is this in which *kenōsis* is clearest. Aulén (1950) expounds the "classic" theory as the victory of Christ over the powers of sin and death, so rising, then ascending victorious. It is in this victory that the believer can share in, thus also conquering sin and overcoming death, so receiving eternal life. It is notable that John's gospel refers several times (eg Jn 3:36) to the fact that a Christian already has eternal life, so it is not just something to be received after death. In union with Christ, a person receives his life. This is symbolised very clearly in baptism. Here the word "baptise" has application in the dyeing process, where a garment is put into the dye, but then the dye goes into the garment, producing the desired effect. Thus Paul can speak of a Christian being "in Christ", and also that Christ is in the Christian (eg Col 1:27); there is mutual "interpenetration" in the enacting of salvation.

On the surface, this would seem to have nothing to do with *kenōsis*, but on the contrary, with the exercise of the power of God. It seems to have more affinity with triumphalism, with imperial ideas, with medieval conceptions of Christ as king. Indeed, in my earlier work (Williams 1997), I did not hesitate to link this theory of the atonement with the kingly office, while the other two seemed to reflect rather the priestly and the prophetic. Certainly this picture would seem consistent with the New Testament, such as in Ephesians 4:8, and commonly in the book of Revelation. However, albeit incomprehensibly to normal human procedures, that victory was brought about through the cross, not by force. It is this seeming paradox in which Paul glories in 1 Corinthians 1:20f, contrasting the weakness of the cross with the desire for signs and wisdom. The word to Paul was indeed that "my power is made perfect in weakness" (2 Cor 12:9). Actually there is perhaps some appreciation of this point in modern thought, such as in Bonhoeffer, who stressed that God's power is not that of the world (Fiddes 1988:2), and in the use of non-violence and passive resistance as a political weapon. There is also a distinct parallel with the Exodus, the main Old Testament experience of salvation. Indeed Christ is sometimes seen as a second Moses (Lk 9:31, 1 Cor 10:1f). The Exodus involved a *kenōsis*; the Israelites had had to give up much in order to leave (Num 11:5!); without this they could never have reached the promised land.

Clearly the emphasis falls on the obedience of Christ in the passion; Käsemann sees obedience as central to Paul's theology of the cross (Richard 1982:216). It was there that the decisive victory was achieved; it was there that the decisive battle was fought (Aulén 1950:46). The resurrection is the manifestation of it (Aulén 1950:48), not the victory itself. It is "through death he might destroy him who has the power of death, that is, the devil" (Heb 2:14); that this is a text probably quoted by the Fathers more than any other of the New Testament (Aulén 1950:90), makes this point clear. In this case, the victory was achieved by Christ's self-emptying, his *kenōsis*, not through the power that raised him. With his blood, his life was emptied out (McDonald 1994:47). Incidentally, in this case, it gives a strong indication of the Christian approach to confronting wrong. Reconciliation with God is done when both give up rights, which is an aspect of *kenōsis*. God does not exact punishment from the sinner, we give up our pride and sin; both are placed on Christ.

Although the emphasis falls of the cross as the decisive act, the theory relates to his entire life of obedience. If it were only necessary for him to die, Jesus could just as well have been killed by Herod to enact atonement. Of course, that would also have lost the positive effects of his life in healings, feedings and teaching. It would also have lost the elements of pain and suffering that was in the cross, as well as the effect of Jesus' example, especially in the public manner of the execution.

Interestingly, Aulén found a natural affinity to his exposition in Irenaeus, whose thought he described as clear and indisputable, a "simple exposition of the central ideas of Christian faith itself" (Aulén 1950:33). He sees the key idea in the work of Christ as destroying sin, overcoming death and giving life, with an aspect of this in the common caricature of his belief, seen in many of the Fathers, that Christ became human so that we can be made divine (Aulén 1950:35). Significantly, he views this as the bestowal of what is real humanity; "those that fear God ... such are justly called men (*Adv. Haer.* V 9.2, cited in Aulén 1950:38). He therefore puts his stress on the resurrection rather than on the cross as in the penal substitution model, seeing death as the final battle (Aulén 1950:45).

Irenaeus' idea is commonly referred to as "recapitulation" (Letham 1993:159f), that Christ was, in his incarnation, uniting with humanity, and drawing it to salvation. It is essentially a development of Romans 5:19 (Placher 2001:39). The central concept here is of Christ as a new "head" (Latin *caput*) of humanity. Whereas the first head of humanity, Adam, misused the freedom with which he was created, and fell into sin by this disobedience, for which he died, the second head, Christ, "recapitulated" the human drama, and acquired victory by his obedience. Just as Jesus was enabled by the Spirit to be sinless, so the Spirit enabled him to recapitulate (Pinnock 1996:80). The central act is clearly the cross, but Irenaeus draws attention also to such events as the Temptations (Aulén 1950:46). Jesus then repeated and reversed the story of Adam (Lampe 1978:48), who yielded to temptation. It is probably true to say that the writer of Philippians 2:5f was deliberately making a contrast with the Adam story; Adam wanted to grasp at divinity but lost his immortality by disobedience, whereas Christ did not grasp as divinity, and therefore God exalted him. Jesus had the same choice that Adam had, but chose not to grasp at equality with God (Dunn 1989:117). It is noteworthy that Galatians 4:5 speaks of Jesus being born under the law to redeem those born under the law. He recapitulated their experience.

The theory of recapitulation was commonly held in the early Church, such as by Tertullian (Bray 1979:71). By the third century, writers even refer to Jesus' descent to Hades to redeem the best of Israel (Placher 2001:129). Calvin interprets Christ's forsakenness in terms of descent to Hades (McDonald 1994:32). Thus he adopted the problems, the humility and emptiness that is the common human lot, but then in his resurrection and glorification, carries it through to the fullness of salvation. He took our human nature fully (eg Irving, Barth, Torrance etc (Macleod 1998:223)). The resurrection is then the start of the removal of the limits that Christ had accepted, achieved through the *kenōsis* of the Spirit (Richard 1997:112). Then "he ascended, ... that he might fill all things" (Eph 4:10). "For because he himself has suffered and been tempted, he is able to help those who are tempted" (Heb 2:18). A person who is "in

Christ" participates in the experience of Christ, so dies to sin, and rises also to eternal life in Christ (Pinnock 1996:94f). Baptism and the Lord's Supper may be seen as indicating this identification, so reflect recapitulation. C S Lewis once commented that salvation was by closeness to Jesus (Pinnock 1996:105). He or she is joined by the Spirit as *vinculum amoris* to Christ, hence is saved; likewise, of course it is by this bond that a person is empowered to lead a better life. Pinnock (1996:89) comments that blasphemy against the Spirit is so serious as it is against the only power that is effective. Incidentally, this explains why the Spirit was not given until after the ascension (Jn 7:39), for only then was the experience of Jesus complete with which we could participate. In contrast, a person outside Christ recapitulates the experience and condemnation of Adam (Pinnock 1996:161).

Modern reaction to this idea will naturally be sceptical due to the seemingly imposed parallelism; thus Irenaeus speaks of the original sin, and therefore salvation through a tree, and both through the agency of women (Barry 1968:198). In particular modern hesitation follows from the general rejection of the historicity of the Genesis narrative, which Irenaeus would have accepted literally (Barry 1968:122). Nevertheless, it must be noted that the validity of the idea does not in fact depend on this; it is quite compatible with an idea that disobedience to God is the uniform human experience, that all people, even if they are not understood to have fallen *in* Adam, nevertheless have fallen, and as such are *like* Adam. This point was made by Pelagius in his controversy with Augustine who felt that the former was the correct understanding of Romans 5:12. This is of course by no means an endorsement of the rest of Pelagius' theology! Such an observation also applied to Paul in Romans 5, where he contrasts the humanity in Adam with those in Christ. Even if it is likely that Paul viewed Adam as an historical individual, the theology does not depend on it. Bonhoeffer (1967:112) can comment that recapitulation is a "magnificent conception, full of comfort".

The specific word "recapitulation", as many theological ideas, is not found in the Bible. A derivative of the Greek equivalent *anakephalaiōsis* is however found in Ephesians 1:10, where it indicates the summing up of all things, their unity in Christ. Although this is not the same idea, what a Christian does in fact do in acquiring salvation, according to Irenaeus and Aulén, is the summing up of his or her life with Christ as the head. As such, the concepts are compatible.

Lampe then draws attention to two aspects of the meaning of the idea. Recapitulation then means firstly the reversal of the effects of the fall of Adam on humanity, and secondly its union with the immortality of the Son (Lampe 1978:49). The first is subject to the objection that Adam is viewed as the head, who dragged humanity into sin by his fall, however the second is free from that idea. However the story of Adam is viewed, it is valid, in the light of the incarnation, to see the history of Christ as unique, and as a human life that is ideal as uniquely obedient to God, "summing up" what it should be. As such, salvation is indeed attainable by union with it, through the Spirit.

The extent of salvation

I always enjoy the story that I regularly tell to my African students of the black American minister who was preaching on the parable in Matthew 25:31f. He was pointing out that those who came to be judged were divided into sheep and goats, the former being those who were saved, but the latter condemned. Then he asked how it is possible to tell the difference between the two. Very easily, for the ones who are saved have short curly hair, he said, fingering his own, while the other group have long straight hair. Such a description naturally went down well with his congregation, and with my African students, when I touch my own very European hair!

The basis of judgement between those who are saved and those lost may well not be on the basis of type of hair, or even racial identity, but the whole point of the story that Jesus told is that there is indeed a judgement, and that some indeed are saved while others are indeed lost. And the point can be multiplied repeatedly in Jesus' teaching, where he spoke of the wide and narrow ways (Matt 7:13), of the rich man who was condemned to Hades (Lk 16:19f), and just as for that rich man, of the horrors of being lost, the unquenchable fire and the gnashing of teeth (Matt 8:12 etc). It is sometimes pointed out that some of the hardest words about the fate of the lost came from the lips of the one who was characterised as having the nature of love.

In fact it seems impossible to cite Jesus' support for what must be one of the most commonly held beliefs in the modern world, that of universalism. Where there is a belief in an afterlife, which is by no means held by everybody, it is commonly felt that in the afterlife everybody will just go to the same place, that there is no judgement, and so no distinction into saved and lost.

Such a belief is by no means limited to the modern world but even claims support in antiquity. The church father Origen in the third century believed, in accordance with the Greek world-view commonly held at the time, that all souls are naturally immortal, and all people will then by very nature live forever. He believed that God made a number of souls (Greek *psuchē*) in the beginning, but that there was a Fall, as described in Genesis, at which point all the souls "cooled" (Greek *psuchein*). The one who fell, or cooled, the most was the devil, the next group was the demons, then human beings, and after them the angels cooled comparatively little. The Son of God, the *logos*, did not cool at all, and remained perfect. But then he also held that at the end of time, all would be "reheated" and would be restored, even the devil.

It is in the modern world, however, that universalism has become commonly held. To cite just one example, Barth is commonly held to be universalistic due to his belief that salvation was enacted by the incarnation, when Jesus identified with humanity as a whole, which is then saved. This would be in keeping with the modern world-view, which from the Enlightenment, holds the equality of all human beings. It naturally follows from this that all are saved equally. This is in reaction to the common view throughout the Middle Ages, which held to differentiation between people, particularly between nobility and common people. This belief is of course supported by a distinction between those who are saved and those who are lost, which in itself rests on the distinction between Christians and those of other religions.

It is indeed the feeling that all are equal because of having a common humanity that lies at the root of universalism, or perhaps more exactly, that supports the hope that no matter what people have done, ultimately they will not suffer because of it. There are of course variations in this basic idea, such as that held by Tillich, that God could not permit any part of his precious creation to be lost forever. As he carefully made it, then he must also preserve it. That argument does depend on the notion that all people are indeed created by God; if on the other hand it is felt that human life arises simply due to the action of two human beings, as simply a biological process, that argument largely loses its force.

A related argument connects to the idea of providence. If God carefully looks after his creatures so diligently in the world, then surely he would continue to look after them even after death, or his care of them would have been fruitless. Again, it is by no means clear that God does indeed do that, but that it could simply be that the world just continues along the path that God gave it at the beginning. This need not be Deism in the sense that was commonly held in seventeenth century Europe, which is incompatible with a Christianity that accepts the possibility of miracles, of revelation, and particularly the incarnation, but the latter need not demand that God is directly involved in everything that is and occurs.

More than such considerations, universalism is more commonly supported by a view that God is love, and if so, could not permit anybody just to be lost. If God loves, then he must care for all, therefore all are saved. This is often associated with the very Biblical ideas that God is a Father, and so naturally cares for his children, and that God is almighty, so is totally able to save everybody. If some are not saved, so it is argued, it reflects back on either, or both, of those most cherished beliefs. Vanstone (1977:43) affirms that God's love and therefore his forgiveness is unlimited; it is not affected by *kenōsis*. Yet he continues that it is restricted by the one who receives it.

Part of the reason why universalism has become popularly held in the modern world is that with Enlightenment thinking, the authority of the Bible has become questioned. No matter that the Bible, and even Jesus, spoke so clearly of the possibility of damnation, because what is recorded in the Bible must have just reflected the beliefs of people at the time. The Bible, it is felt, does not contain absolute truth. But in any case, it is argued, there are several indications of universalism within the Bible itself. There are indeed several texts which appear to indicate such a belief in the New Testament, and a universalistic belief can be supported even more readily from the Old Testament, which appears to indicate that all would go to a single destination, *sheol*, where all the dead would stay.

However, closer examination of those passages fails to present a convincing case, as all of them can be interpreted in a different way. 2 Timothy 2:4 may well mean God's desire that all be saved, a statement that few would question, but this does not mean that the desire needs to be actualized; this is in fact an aspect of *kenōsis* itself. Then Philippians 2:11, following hard on the heels of the description of Jesus' own *kenōsis*, actually only supports the idea that at the *parousia*, the rule of God becomes absolute, and that at that point "every knee will bow"; but some may then equally reap the result of a lifelong rebellion and be lost. Even the absence of the idea of division in an afterlife in the Old Testament need not be taken to say that such a division is not present. That is an example of an "argument from silence". In fact the story of the rich man and Lazarus (Lk 16:19f), which clearly indicates a division between the two, even with a "great chasm" between them, need not be inconsistent with a view that both men, saved and lost, are in the same place; it is just that the one place is divided.

Certainly, it is really impossible to defend universalism from a consideration of the texts in themselves. They are comparatively few in comparison with those which speak of judgement, and all can be explained in a way compatible with the latter. On the other hand, there is a plethora of texts which just cannot be explained in a universalistic sense. One example is probably enough: the picture of the wide road and narrow gate (Matt 7:13) is graphic, even if sad.

It may well be suggested that support for a universal salvation can also be adduced theologically, from the idea of salvation by grace, so foundational to Protestant theology. If salvation is indeed *sola gratia*, entirely by faith, and totally independent of the deeds of a person, then how can anybody be condemned? It is this belief which, coupled with the texts that indicate a division between the saved and the lost, issues in the doctrine of predestination, which itself is then queried on the grounds of the love of God. Not only is he then said to allow some to be lost, but even positively causes that. Even if there are in practice few that say that God actually causes people to be lost, believing that he only predestines some is effectively tantamount to exactly the same thing. Christ did not only die for a limited number of the predestined "elect", but is for all, offering a real salvation to as many as accept. Barth (1957:310) in fact sees Christ as the only predestined one, but that a person then shares in that predestination in union with him.

The doctrine of predestination is notoriously difficult to reconcile with the equally Biblical teaching of human free will, but it is equally the case that if there is such a thing as real and valid free will, then a limitation of salvation logically follows. If a person has chosen to reject God and his offer of salvation right throughout his or her lifetime, how can such a person ultimately be saved unless God has over-ridden such a free choice, thus denying that it is free? It effectively means that the person is dragged into heaven contrary to his or her will. Here it must be noted that salvation is enabled through the action of Jesus in *kenōsis*, a connection which Richard (1982:231) makes, but then interprets it universalistically as union with humanity. However, *kenōsis* was an action of Jesus in obedience to God, but of his own free choice, and therefore to be received by choice. It could therefore be refused, or human will was not free. Bulgakov, in his stress on *kenōsis,* stresses that God persuades, not compels (Gavrilyuk 2005:258). At the same time, the action of Christ in *kenōsis* is done as an example to be followed; certainly this is how Paul presents it in Philippians 2. But an example is really meaningless if the action that it motivates is meaningless, which it would be if salvation was going to happen anyway. Rather, as seen in the subjective aspect of the atonement, a response is essential. Thus universalism is inconsistent with *kenōsis.*

Salvation essentially by union with Christ need not demand any universalism. The union with Christ is not with humanity as a whole, which would mean that the whole of humanity was divinised, as this would mean that individual human beings are forced into heaven simply by being human. On the contrary, one aspect of the *kenōsis* that was part of the act of creation is that God granted freedom of choice, and particularly to humanity. As part of its appeal for our obedience, the Philippian hymn stresses the obedience of Christ; this makes no sense unless disobedience were a possibility. The offer of salvation is exactly that, an offer, and a person has freedom to accept it or to reject it. Incidentally, this compulsion that Christ experienced can well be seen as a part of his own *kenōsis*. He was not free not to go to the cross, except, of course, insofar as the act of *kenōsis* itself was a voluntary action. A similar situation pertains to the prophets, who experienced compulsion to prophesy (Jer 20:7f). Not of course that this compulsion is absolute; there are several examples of disobedient prophets, such as the one in 1 Kings 13, who was eaten by a lion, and of course Jonah, who suffered a similar fate with the whale!

It must be emphasized that the self-limitation of Christ does not mean in any way that his work is limited. There is no reason here for belief in a limited atonement. In fact, this belief in a limited atonement, far from being a result of the self-limitation of God, rather rests on quite the opposite; the belief is that God as fully sovereign predestines some to be saved, and therefore the effect of Christ's death was limited only to the elect. Erickson (1998:842) insists that there is total agreement that the death of Christ is sufficient for all; this of course does not mean that all will receive it. Christ's death may be seen as effective for all, but the limitation of the number of the saved which is so evident in the Bible (eg Matt 7:14), may be seen as due to the fact that the relationship with Christ, which is the means of salvation, is dependent not only on the forgiveness of sins, the negative aspect, but also positively upon the union of the sinner with Christ. This is a matter of human freewill, made possible by the self-limitation of God.

Universalism also puts a question mark over the idea of the

holiness of God, for how can a holy God have real fellowship with somebody who chooses to live in a way which is contrary to the will of God, so rejecting the standard of holiness that God puts forward?

Likewise it cuts away the ground from the Biblical appeal for people to be saved. Preaching becomes irrelevant if all are to be saved in any case. This has proved also to be a problem with advocates of predestination, who however usually say that they continue to preach out of obedience to the direct command of God. As with universalism, there can hardly be the same compulsion if the ultimate destiny of people is already settled. More practically comes an effect which is an all too conspicuous part of the modern world. If there is no belief in an afterlife, or if it is felt that all will be saved, then the belief in a final judgement also falls away, and there is no longer much incentive to do what is right. A belief in hell was a strong reason for doing good throughout the Middle Ages.

A further view which understands a limitation in the number of the saved, so quite consistent with the idea of *kenōsis*, is that of "annihilationalism" or "conditional immortality". God limits himself in relating to only those who accept him. Here, the arguments for both the traditional view and for conditional immortality are each quite persuasive. On the one hand, the former has got two millennia of existence behind it, and it must be only with extreme reticence that such a view is thrown out. Essentially, this view notes the Biblical indication of a universal resurrection and afterlife, such as from Daniel 12:2, which does seem strange if this is just to be quickly terminated in a loss of existence. Then there are several passages which do indicate torment after death, such as the parables of Matthew 25:31 and Luke 16:19f. Jesus himself had much to say on the issue; most graphically, he talks of the worm that does not die, and the fire which is not quenched (Mk 9:48).

On the other hand, proponents of annihilationism do suggest that nearly all the references can be understood in terms of extinction rather than conscious suffering. The very nature of the worm is to enable the destruction of the body, and that of fire is to destroy. They may well be permanent, but this does not mean that they are permanent for a particular individual; once the body is totally consumed, it is ended, even if the worm and the fire keep on going.

In fact there are only two occasions in the New Testament which would seem to speak of unending torment in an unequivocal way. Both are found in the book of Revelation (14:11 and 20:9), which must itself give rise to caution as to their understanding. The book of Revelation is hardly one to be interpreted in a straightforward literal way, but employs pictures and figures to convey its message (a genre known as "apocalyptic", quite common at the time of the New Testament).

Boyd (2001:321) concurs that universalism is not really an option for those who accept Biblical authority as normative. He feels that from a Biblical perspective, it is really only possible to accept the traditional teaching of a permanent hell of conscious torment, or the increasingly popular view of annihilationalism or of "conditional immortality". He observes that several noted and well-respected evangelical scholars are adopting the latter, but also that the idea of hell which has been quietly neglected for so long due to the obvious difficulty of presenting it, has made something of a comeback. His approach is then to try to present a theory which adopts the features of both views, something similar to the way in which the Trinity might be presented as paradox, or in physics, the nature of light as particles and waves. He actually takes the view of Karl Barth that hell could be seen as positive nothingness, *das Nichtige*, so that it is the final result of a person's conscious choice of selfishness and inwardness, and that in the culmination of this lies the torment, but in the culmination of this comes the lack of contact with anything else, which amounts to the same thing as extinction, seeing that existence must involve interaction with things and other people.

A view which rejects universalism but accommodates the awareness that there have always been several people who are good, but who are not Christian, is that of "inclusivism" (cf *inter alia* Pinnock 1996:198f). This suggests that salvation is not "exclusive", limited specifically to Christians, but includes others, often called "latent" or "anonymous" Christians. In particular, advocates of this look at the Old Testament, which tells of several people who were saved, notably, of course Abraham, specifically reported as saved by faith (Rom 4:3). Yet these could not be saved by an awareness of the gospel, and made no commitment to Christ. The suggestion is then that the same could apply to some adherents of other religions. Very emphatically, this stand is not "pluralism", a belief that other religions are viable means of salvation, parallel to Christianity, but that salvation is always and only through Christ, even if unknowingly.

This view could well find support from a kenotic understanding of salvation. On the one hand, Jesus is described in his *kenōsis* as obedient and as humble. If a person, formally outside Christ is obedient to God according to his or her understanding, and in an attitude of humility, then there is an identification with Christ. But the Philippian hymn very specifically says that Jesus did not grasp at equality with God, so did not act according to his status; he did not presume on a specific relationship with God. In the same way, a person would then not be saved by an appeal to a specific relationship to God, so a Christian commitment, but, as Christ still be acceptable to God. Nevertheless of course, Jesus was exalted just because he was Son, and a person could only be saved by a relation to God, whether or not this was appealed to.

Chapter 12

A kenotic theology of healing

A number of years ago, many were deeply disturbed by the fact that the well-known Anglican, David Watson, contracted cancer. He had been instrumental in bringing many to faith, and in deepening the commitment of others, especially in university contexts, but despite long, repeated and believing prayer for his recovery, he died. He relates the story of his battle in a little book, *Fear no evil* (Watson 1984). What was striking is that he had embraced a mild charismatic view, and accepted the gifts as of continuing validity, including that of healing. He recounts the visits for prayer of John Wimber of the Vineyard Fellowship, who had seen many healed (Watson 1984:50f, cf also Wimber 1987:147f). Even more dramatic was the case of Kathryn Kuhlman, who had by all accounts a remarkable healing ministry (Kuhlman 1962). She too died of cancer; how ironic when so many had testified that their cancer had been healed through her ministry.

The tragedy of the deaths of Watson and Kuhlman is heightened by the fact, and I use the word deliberately, that Christian healing does occur. The prayers made for David Watson were not just wishful thinking but based on the experience that God does sometimes heal in answer to prayer. There are just too many remarkable stories of healing to simply dismiss it as spurious. Moreover these are not just claims, but there are many that have been investigated thoroughly, verified to the full capability of modern science. One example is that at Lourdes, where many claims of healing are made, most of which cannot be verified, but where investigation by the Roman Catholic authorities has revealed a number which have no other explanation than of the direct intervention by God; Wimber (1987:10) notes the stringent criteria that are applied. Fitch (1974:252) records medical attestation of the healings through Kathryn Kuhlman; he also refers to Martin Lloyd-Jones, who was a medical doctor before he had an extremely influential and effective career in the ministry. MacNutt, who has developed a theology of healing, testifies that he did this as a result of seeing it work (1977:91). He did not pray because of a belief that God heals, but believes because of the experiences that he has had.

For many, it is sufficient evidence that the Bible, especially in the New Testament, describes many healings. However some explain the difference between this and modern experience, or perhaps the lack of it, by a suggestion of dispensationalism (cf Wimber 1987:10), that God acts in different ways in different times or "dispensations"; healing was only for the time of the apostles. This suggestion however falls foul of the admittedly diminishing number of healings (Wimber 1987:42) that were reported in the early centuries of the Church; they did not simply cease to occur. Kelsey (1973:191f) suggests historical reasons why the Church gradually ceased to practise healing; he then relates characteristics of the modern world-view which still militate against the practice. It is a tragic story, and ironic when many modern churches claim to seek to base their beliefs and practices on the New Testament church.

Of course there has been no shortage of those who have

questioned the Biblical account; a recent example is Bultmann, who, from the perspective of existentialism, viewed the miracle stories as myths to encourage people to make the decision to authentic living. He believes that modern people, however, are not impressed by such stories, and so the Bible should be "demythologised". Bultmann, and others, were reacting to the fact that in the questioning of the Bible comes the doubting of the faith that is based on it. This of course does reflect the fact that in contrast to the New Testament, healing has not been a common modern experience. More especially, the fact of evil and suffering, of which sickness is a part, is one that has resulted in the questioning, and even the loss of Christian faith for so many. Even if very correctly, God is portrayed as love, many just cannot understand how he can stand by when people suffer, such as the pain of cancer. Their pain is exacerbated when at the same time God is preached as all powerful, and quite able to solve the problem.

This however does have another side to it; when there is an experience of God's power in healing, it can be a tremendous affirmation of the truth of the Christian faith. Every healing is a proclamation (MacNutt 1974:56). It is therefore imperative that, if healing is a continued possibility for the Church, it is practised as much as possible. Not only is it a simple matter of compassion for those who are afflicted by disease and other bodily problems, but it would further the expansion of the gospel. The latter is itself a matter of compassion if the Biblical witness to the reality of the result of disbelief is accepted, and then also a plain matter of conformity to the mind of God, "who desires all men to be saved" (1 Tim 2:4).

It is evident that this is not happening. People are not conforming to God's mind, and seem to require repeated admonitions to do just that. One such appeal is in Philippians 2:5, where Paul is explaining why people should think in that particular way. He appreciated that if a person understands the reason for an action, he or she is more likely to do it. Then he is explaining what Jesus did on his road to the cross, for again, if a person understands how it is possible for salvation to occur, it is more likely to be accepted. And the same is true of healing; although there must always be an element of mystery, the more that is understood, the more likely it becomes that the experience will be a reality. It is not satisfactory, if with such as Erickson (1998:857), the only explanation offered is "a supernatural force". Warrington (2003:45) says that while the fact of healing is not in dispute, the explanation is lacking.

It is here that the experience of Jesus in his *kenōsis* can provide such an explanation. In what he did in his incarnation, and particularly in his suffering on the cross, comes the possibility not only of salvation, but of healing as a facet of this. Erickson (1998:853) adds the stimulating thought that if disease is one effect of sin, it cannot be totally dealt with while excluding the spiritual aspect of dealing with sin.

Indeed, not only have there been sufficient experiences of healing to indicate that it is not just a myth, but, with qualifications, it may be accepted as a reality, but also that it should occur because it is a part of salvation. If it is true that salvation is a reality, that salvation should not be limited to the giving of eternal life to a spiritual soul after death, but should affect the present. Indeed it was the dualistic distinction between matter and spirit that contributed to the decline in the practice of healing, and indeed still does. Nevertheless, the Bible, particularly in the Old Testament, portrays a human being rather as a unity (Wimber 1987:59); in this case salvation should affect every aspect, body, mind and spirit. Even more significantly, the very facts of creation, and then of the incarnation, are God's affirmation of the value of the material, and that salvation should affect it.

These actions of God are actions of his *kenōsis*. Particularly the second was done for the sake of salvation; in this case the idea of *kenōsis* could throw more light on the two fundamental issues connected with Christian healing:

how is healing possible; what is the mechanism involved?
why is healing not universally received?

A kenotic theology of healing

It is natural to relate healing to the work of the Spirit, whom I have described as *vinculum amoris*, the bond of love (Williams 2004). The essential concept here is that healing can occur when the Spirit links the sick person to the ultimate source of life and health, God himself. It is therefore an aspect of salvation (MacNutt 1974:50). Sanders (1998:96) observes that a conversation with Jesus often preceded his healings; this would establish a relationship.

Then I have also linked the mechanism of healing to the three-fold "office" of Christ (Williams 1997:266-74). Having identified three main modes, a mechanical method of orthodox medicine, the exercise of a distinct *charisma* by a few specifically endowed individuals, and the result of a prolonged exercise of what MacNutt (1974:309) has referred to as "soaking" prayer (also Watson 1984:109), a method available to anybody (cf Jn 14:12); Pentecostals make such a distinction (Warrington 2003:47). I related these to the action of Christ as, respectively, priest, prophet and king. In this case, they should not be seen as exclusive alternatives, but complementary aspects of an overall method of Christian healing.

It is then not a big jump to relate both ideas together in a further approach to a theology of healing, as an aspect of *kenōsis*. This is by no means contrary to the earlier work, but complements and expands the earlier ideas as a means to a more complete understanding. To put the idea in a nutshell, the essential theology that can be proposed is that in the kenotic experience of Christ, described most completely, but not exclusively, in Philippians 2:5-11, he identifies with the human experience of weakness, which includes sickness, and therefore in the overcoming of *kenōsis*, he overcomes it. Then this is available to Christians insofar as they are related to Christ by the work of the Spirit. This is a slight development of the understanding of the kingly office of Christ; as *Christus Victor* (Aulén 1950), he overcomes the effects of sin, which includes disease, in his resurrection. This was a "spiritual body", but this was still physical, real humanity, indeed humanity as it should be; the adjective "spiritual" does not refer to any immateriality, but to its power and motivation (Williams 2004:232).

Healing is then a sharing in the resurrection life of Christ through the Spirit. Indeed, the whole process of *kenōsis* that Jesus went through, from incarnation through to final glorification, was enabled by the Spirit. It must then follow that the healing that he did was done not by his divinity (Storms 1996:307, Williams 2004:6), which had been limited in his *kenōsis*, but by the power of the Spirit, which related him to his Father and so empowered him. He was anointed and filled by the Spirit for his ministry at his baptism. Therefore, as Turner (1996:32) notes, it was by the Spirit that Jesus cast out demons (Matt 12:28). Luke 5:17 relates that on one occasion, the power of the Lord was with Jesus to heal.

The connection between healing and *kenōsis* becomes clear in some of the Biblical accounts of healing. Wimber (1987:137) draws attention to the humility that Naaman showed (2 Ki 5:12); without which healing did not occur. He also notes the emphasis placed on humility in the story of the healing of the centurion's servant (Matt 8:5f). It is this kenotic emptying that is necessary for a full relationship with God, in order to receive the resurrection life that heals. The faith that is often seen to be present in healing is then more clearly understood as the humility that is a willingness to receive. Indeed, one aspect that is commonly necessary in healing is an accepting of limitation, and the need to rest (Peck 1997:186). The Genesis narrative describes the first sin (and therefore disease) in the Fall, which resulted in loss of harmony with God, as due to pride, the antithesis to humility.

Can it then be suggested that the emptying provides an explanation for the sensations of energy, heat or electricity, that sometimes accompanies the process of healing (eg Wimber 1987:148, Foster 2000:139), as when heat flows to something at a lower temperature, or electricity to a lower voltage? Woolmer (1997:223) speaks of a sensation of the flow of "golden liquid light". Often the one who heals reports a feeling of tiredness (MacNutt 1977:43). Jesus testified that power had gone from him (Mk 5:30, where the key word is *dunamis*, and not *exousia*, authority).

Disease is in any case a lack, manifesting as disfunction or weakness. It is likely to be caused by lack, such as of harmonious relationships with others (Wimber 1987:77f). What is needed is that the lack is filled, that a person be made whole, which is indeed a normal way of referring to healing. Wimber (1987:38) notes that wholeness is a root idea of *iaomai*, which is a common word denoting healing.

Human ability to heal is then by the same process. Firstly, a person through whom God heals must be a child of God by adoption, by relating to Christ, and receiving his life. He or she then participates in the *kenōsis* of Christ, healing through the link with God that the Spirit gives, just as Christ himself did. This implies that the ability to heal, as a Christian, is not a natural human ability. This of course does not mean that such "non-medical" healing is inherently impossible for others, who may well have a human ability. This could be expressed in reconciliation, or in helping in a psychological way, which can well have bodily effects. Even the possession of a psychic ability must not be excluded in principle. However, healing which is specifically Christian can only be done through the Spirit.

On the one hand this could be by the granting of a specific gift, a *charisma*. Here the healer reflects the prophetic role of Christ, so that just as he commanded the sickness by the authority of God through the Spirit, so does the healer. On the other, healing occurs by the so-called "soaking" prayer, enabling the transfer of spiritual life to the sick. Here it is notable that Jesus was aware of the power going from him when he was touched by the woman with an issue of blood (Lk 8:44). Sometimes there is an experience of a transfer of pain (Woolmer 1997:197). The Spirit anticipates the resurrection life that will be received fully at the *eschaton*, and imparts that to the one who is sick.

As is prominent in the Biblical accounts, faith plays a pivotal role in healing, a feature that makes a lot of sense when it is understood in terms of a relationship to Christ. This is then not, as often thought, merely intellectual acceptance, belief in Christ; hence, as Erickson (1998:855) correctly observes, healing does not depend on cognitive trust. One can imagine the delight with which MacNutt (1974:131) recounts the story of a preacher who as a sermon illustration against the possibility of healing, mimicked the practice of healers and laid hands on a line of people; he was devastated when all were healed!

Irenaeus

Not surprisingly, because healing is an aspect of salvation, the mechanism of healing also relates to the ideas of the early Christian Father. Indeed, I have been indebted to him in other respects, mainly in his insightful treatment of the work of the Son and Spirit as the "two hands of God" (*Adv Haer* 4.20.1 (Pinnock 1996:58) cf

Williams 2003). Both Persons' work is essential for Christians, each complementing the other. The atonement is not just achieved by the death of Christ on the cross, but is effective through the Spirit linking that event to the Christian. This same point is clear in the possibility of healing, for if healing is possible by the work of Christ, it is only applied to the Christian by the Spirit. Neither work is effective alone, unless the Spirit applies it.

In this case, however, the aspect of Irenaeus' thought which is most applicable is his presentation of "recapitulation". As a Christian is united with the history of Christ, of course through the Spirit, and therefore is saved, he or she may also be healed. This may be seen in the spirit as in the traditional idea of salvation, but also more widely, such as in the body or the mind. As an example of the last, MacNutt (1974:96) cites the great success of Christian action against drug dependency, citing a 70% success using "spiritual" methods in contrast to the 5% by secular techniques (also Laurentin 1977:189). This is a restoration of wholeness; full humanity is of course a healthy humanity.

The sickness of Christ

But is it valid to say that Jesus bore this experience of sickness, achieving a victory over it in which Christians can share? Unlike many, if not all of those who followed him, there is no record that Jesus ever shared in the human experience of being sick. Paul suffered from a "thorn in the flesh" (2 Cor 12:7), Timothy from "frequent ailments" (1 Tim 5:23), and there are many other instances. Despite the claim of some, notably of the so-called "prosperity emphasis", such as Kenneth Hagin, who believe that a Christian has a right to perfect health and can claim healing, the evidence is to the contrary. Yet there is no indication that Jesus actually experienced this himself. Not that the absence of reference in the New Testament is any proof that Jesus was not sick; silence is no evidence! Indeed, it may well be suggested that as part of the assumption of a full humanity came disease and pain. Certainly the New Testament witnesses to the fact that Jesus really suffered, whether from tiredness, thirst, or no doubt in countless other ways. Suffering is essentially a lack of harmony, and it is this which the Genesis story describes. Disease is the same, a lack of harmony in the working of the body, and naturally dealt with through the Spirit, who generates unity, disentangling disorder (Wimber 1987:135). In this case, Jesus may not have been sick as such, but shared in the disharmony that sometimes manifests as sickness. This is the same point made by such as Pannenberg (1968:358) who go further by saying that a sinful nature is an integral part of being human. Nevertheless, the repeated witness of the New Testament (eg Heb 4:15, 1 Pet 2:22) is of the sinlessness of Jesus; it was not an integral part of his humanity.

However, despite the connection that is made, especially in the Old Testament, between sin and sickness, sinlessness did not in itself guarantee perfect health. Even if the connection is valid, and may indeed account for much of the sickness that afflicts a sinful humanity, it is definitely not always the case that a person's sickness is a direct result of his or her own sin. Jesus clearly denied that connection in the story of the man born blind (Jn 9:1f). It is quite possible for a person to suffer sickness as a result of somebody else's sin, which was the explanation of the disciples, or even simply by being in a sinful world (Erickson 1998:854). What may be affirmed in the life of Jesus is that the fullness of the Spirit should have enhanced the quality of his health, and he should also have been aware of the possibility of accidents. His sinlessness would also shield him from many of the problems that are lifestyle generated. Then a short life should have prevented the degenerative ailments of old age. Perhaps it could be affirmed, as with sin, that he could have experienced sickness, but did not. This however is not known definitely.

Thus far is in reference to the first stage of the *kenōsis* of Christ, his nature as a full human being, participating in the humanity of those round him, and of us, who are subject to disease. More than this, it hardly needs to be pointed out that Jesus became incarnate among the poor, and the poor of an oppressed people. A couple of years ago, the South African president and the minister of health engendered considerable controversy by an assertion that AIDS was caused by poverty. Although it is clear that it is the result of an infection by the HI virus, the point made was valuable in that a situation of poverty accelerates the onset and development of the full-blown disease, which a measure of affluence enabling a good diet and drug therapy can at least retard. It may also be suggested that the hopelessness of a situation of poverty is conducive to the promiscuity that spreads the infection. Indeed, poverty opens up those entrapped in it to disease both by the unhygienic situation that often accompanies it, and by the weakness that goes with an inadequate diet and which stops the inevitable infections being quickly defeated by the body. This is of course not to deny that affluence brings its own health problems due to over-indulgence and stress, but it must be quickly pointed out that for most these are a matter of choice; one does not have to over-eat! But the diseases of poverty are largely inescapable, and it is into such a situation that Jesus became incarnate.

But the Philippian hymn says more than just his incarnation, but refers to his experience as a *doulos*, a slave. What ill-health does is in fact is to make us slaves. We become servants of the ailment. It causes us to lose the freedom that we ought to enjoy, it prevents our actions by draining our strength. It is these effects that are important to us, not just the disease itself, and it is those phenomena that Jesus indeed participated in. More than this, the slavery of Jesus was also a participation in the sickness of society. It is this "structural" sin that results in oppression, and in so much suffering, which in itself often causes and aggravates physical sickness. Jesus experienced the effects of ill-health both on an individual and a societal level.

The final stage of the *kenōsis* of Christ was his death. It is significant that Moltmann (1985:89) then makes a connection between that passage and Isaiah 53, which is itself used as a text with reference to healing, being cited by Matthew 8:17 as an explanation of the ability of Jesus to heal. This link is however disputed (eg Wimber 1987:155, König 1986:94); Erickson (1998:857) thinks that it means no more than Jesus was sympathetic, and so moved to heal. However, if sin is the ultimate cause of disease, then healing is possible in the atonement; Jesus died for all the effects of sin. This statement does not mean that the atonement removed disease; König (1986:94) stresses that Jesus died for sin, which means that his death did not enact healing, but rather made it possible. Otherwise he would have had to have been sick on the cross, so that disease could die with sin. Nevertheless, what is clear is that in the cross the bodily functions of Jesus were affected; not only was he wounded, suffering from the scourging, but suffered extreme thirst and many other symptoms of bodily malfunction. These may not have caused his death, indeed it is often remarked that he, unlike us, chose to die in that he "yielded up the spirit" (Matt 27:50), but he certainly experienced bodily suffering. Docetic ideas of the impassibility of Jesus and of his only appearing to suffer and die were rebuffed even in the early centuries. The body is material, but is not thereby essentially evil; otherwise a real incarnation would have been an impossibility. The other side of this affirmation of the goodness of the body is that suffering, the pain of the body is not good, and therefore healing itself is good and to be sought (MacNutt 1974:64).

But then Jesus overcame these effects, rising from the dead, an event which also shows the essential goodness of the material body. He became a victor over sin, and so all its effects, especially overcoming the death that is often the result of ill-health again both of the individual and of society. He then finally ascended to glory. Here it is noteworthy that Irenaeus' view links salvation not to Jesus' death but also with his life and resurrection. In the events of his passion he proclaimed his Lordship, as indeed stressed in the Philippian passage (2:10). Such a message is reinforced every time a person's life is changed in their union with Christ, whether in salvation, in its effects in a change in lifestyle, or, of course, in healing.

It is then in the union with him that is enabled by the Spirit that we too can conquer the effects of sin in ill-health, again both of the individual and of society. This understanding incidentally explains what can be a puzzling feature of healing, that it is often delayed by a period of time after prayer (MacNutt 1974:142); the resurrection did not immediately follow after the cross. Wimber's experience was that a cancerous tumour often grew after prayer before it died (Watson 1984:57).

Very dramatically, even the effects of slavery itself, as a human institution, were indeed dealt with through what Jesus did on the cross, a punishment that was indeed much later abolished by Constantine when he adopted Christianity. But even if slavery lasted far longer, Christian faith had already blunted its effects, as the little story of Onesimus and his master Philemon (Philm 1f) demonstrates. In a Christian atmosphere, even slavery can be a benefit! Then of course, much later it was Christian convictions that prompted the campaign at the hands of Wilberforce to abolish it completely.

A limited healing

Just as salvation is not received by all, many are not healed. Even if healing is a reality, it is not always experienced, not even by Christians, or even by the more "spiritual", "saintly", or effective in doing God's work. The early claims of Pentecostals have been abandoned (Warrington 2003:45). Such a statement must be seen in the context of MacNutt's claim to see positive results in the majority of cases that are prayed for; he cites a figure of three quarters of those with emotional or physical ailments who are healed or noticeably improve (1977:22); Wimber (1987:188) gives an even higher figure. Nevertheless, again this is not total. Incidentally, the fact of improvement draws attention to the point that healing, whether "spiritual" or medical, can well be a long-term process (cf Wimber 1987:131). It is, after all part of salvation, so of sanctification, which is normally a process. Both this and healing then require patience, and may well cease due to lack of persistence. Nevertheless, not all are healed, although it is interesting to read the testimony of Woolmer (1997:192) that in the healing campaigns of Fred Smith, even those who were not healed were blessed.

Here it is common to relate such "failure" to God's sovereign will. It is suggested that some are not healed simply because God chooses not to heal them. Quite correctly, healing cannot be presumed upon or claimed, unless it is known that it is indeed God's will, in which case prayer can validly be made in the name of Jesus (Warrington 2003:48). It may still be requested, even if some, such as MacNutt (1974:205), advise against adding the prayer "if it is your will" to requests for God to act. It seems to hinder faith (Foster 2000:228). Indeed, many practitioners of divine healing claim awareness of God's will (a word of "knowledge" (1 Cor 12:8)?) (eg Wimber 1987:181,185); they then refuse to pray for those that God does not want to heal. It would, after all, be disobedience. MacNutt (1974:127) even recounts that Kenneth Hagin, the "father" of the prosperity emphasis, which teaches that health and wealth may be claimed, has occasionally been interiorly prevented from praying for some who were sick. Incidentally, here, such knowledge may also be of an underlying cause of a disease, which itself then has to be dealt with if the physical healing is to be received completely (MacNutt 1974:307). The situation of some not receiving healing when others are, if not quickly qualified, is, however, intolerable for many; why does God reject some, seemingly arbitrarily? Of course the pot has no rights over the potter (Rom 9:21), but is that all?

It must be pointed out immediately that the acts of *kenōsis*, from creation to the cross, were all acts of God's sovereign choice. He freely chose to limit his freedom! In power he chose to be weak. It should then not be seen as strange if he chooses that some people also share in his weakness. Such a desire to identify has always been a part of Christian devotion; even the ascetic rejection of pleasure has been explained as a desire to share in God's impassibility (Taylor 1992:136). However, I wonder if any have chosen sickness for this reason, although flagellation and the receipt of the *stigmata* comes close to this.

The very limitation of the numbers being healed is however consistent with *kenōsis*. God limits the exercise of his ability in this way as well as in others, such as in the creation of a limited number of species. Perhaps such limitation, as the free will that gave the possibility of sin, is also for a greater good? Notably in Augustine, evil has been explained as being consistent with the love and goodness of God insofar as it has resulted in a blessing greater than would have occurred if it did not occur. Certainly some have found that in the struggle against sickness comes a blessing. Even pain can be good, such as when it warns of problems, and if the theory of evolution is accepted, is one of the most creative elements in the universe (Elphinstone, in Taylor 1992:196); nevertheless he quickly points out the more obvious negative side; fear of pain is, for example, often the main reason for choosing other than the most moral of possible choices (in Taylor 1992:201). It is wonderful that the experience of so many Christians is that while God does not necessarily take away pain and suffering, he so often does bring a good result from them (Rom 8:28). Physical healing may not be the greatest good for a person (MacNutt 1974:250). Tozer even wrote that "it is doubtful if God can bless a man greatly without hurting him deeply" (Watson 1984:121).

Human free will

God's limitation of sovereignty was to enable human free will. God is one who offers, but does not compel (Watson 1984:114). "Mr Pentecost", David du Plessis, once said that "the Spirit is a gentleman" (Bennett & Bennett 1974:99); his services are available, but he does not force himself onto us. This freedom means that some choose not to accept salvation, and may well give further reasons why a particular person is not healed. Firstly, it could well be that healing is offered to that person, but it is not received. There could be several reasons why this is the case; foremost is a lack of faith, something commonly connected to healing in the Biblical accounts. If a person does not believe that healing is a possibility, it is not likely to be appropriated. It is not surprising that healing is more likely in a church where it is actively practised, so where it is expected. Then if there is a holding onto the sin that is a cause of that disease, again, healing is unlikely to be effective. Some even do not really want healing, they enjoy being sick and the attention that results from it; hypochondria is not that uncommon!

Secondly, an aspect of God's *kenōsis* is that he has chosen to act by means of agents, who themselves have free will. Indeed, even the initial action of creation was through the Son (1 Cor 8:6), but then the giving of salvation likewise was by the Son, who himself experienced *kenōsis* in the process. Humanity is then the agent of God in the rule of the world, being granted dominion as God limited himself (Gen 1:26). Then in their disobedience, God did not speak directly, but sent prophets as his agents. It is quite consistent with this that when God heals, it is usually by human agents, and not directly. This then means that on the one hand a person who is offered the *charisma* of healing does not accept it, maybe even not recognising the offer, and secondly that a particular healing is not performed by the healer, again perhaps not recognising it, but secondly possibly refusing it. Even if the healing authority of Jesus' disciples is the same as that of Jesus, so through the Spirit, the practice is very often not (cf Warrington 2003:46).

The right to health

One of the problems that we have with the matter of healing is our belief that health is ours as of right. There is an increasing tendency to run to the doctor or to take medication at the slightest pain or weakness. Moltmann (1985:270f) has strongly rejected such a notion. As part of an inherently limited creation we should expect and accept imperfection, so that our bodies would not be expected to operate perfectly all of the time. For him health rather lies in a positive attitude to reality; in practice this would tend to result in better health in any case.

What is noticeable in the progress of *kenōsis* was that it was a progressive surrendering of rights. The act of creation as autonomous immediately involved the restriction of God's rights over it, especially as humanity was given dominion over it. This meant that God was restricting his right to intervene even when things happened which were not to his liking, for otherwise the freedom and authority of the creation, and specifically of humanity would be compromised. Even if God could intervene, he chose not to. Here the loving heart of God is doubly afflicted, both when he sees the suffering of creation and when he could actually do something about it, but in love chooses not to. At least not directly; Christian theology has identified in the cross the action of a loving God to deal with sin and its effects without compromising the free will that made the sacrifice of the cross necessary.

Likewise his very suffering was a renunciation of his right to comfort, seen time after time in his earthly life, and his death even a renunciation of his right to life. Both of these are also taken as rights in the modern world, but can not be presumed upon by Christians. There is no justification in the experience of Christ for such a belief.

Eschatological completion

Perhaps the wonder of the Philippian hymn is the second part, the end of *kenōsis* in Jesus' resurrection and glorification. Here it must be immediately added that just as *kenōsis* comes to an end at the *eschaton*, so all are healed at that point, in the resurrection. Hans Küng wrote that "God's kingdom is creation healed" (Watson 1984:106). All become whole in God's action in recreation and restoration, but only then (Wimber 1987:157). We may have to wait (Warrington 2003:46). It is only then that salvation becomes complete, the kingdom comes, healing is total and wholeness arrives (cf Erickson 1998:858). Cullmann speaks of healing as a proleptic deliverance of the body (Pinnock 2001:134). The work of the *Holy* Spirit itself becomes whole, complete. The work of the Spirit in the present is always partial, a foretaste or firstfruits (eg Eph 1:13) of the completed work at the *eschaton* (1 Cor 13:10). Even Jesus' resurrection was partial, not full glory. Thus again, even if healing may always be totally received as part of the eschatological resurrection, the re-creation of the body, it may or may not be received in the present, subject to God's will. It can never be received as of right, but may be as an act of grace. In a sense all healing before that time is an exception. A Ugandan Christian who had had the lower half of his face blown away in an ambush testified that "God never promises us an easy time. Just a safe arrival" (Watson 1984:141).

There has been some discussion as to what name was given to Jesus as his exaltation (Phil 2:9). Here there is a reasonable consensus that it was the name of "Lord" (Fee 1999:99). On the one hand this reflects the end of *kenōsis* in that the limitation of divinity had come to an end; *kurios* is the Greek equivalent, such as in the Septuagint, for the divine name in the Old Testament, the *Tetragrammaton*. In the completion of the act of atonement the need for this limitation had been fulfilled. On the other hand, the restoring of the divine name indicated the assumption of the full authority of Christ over the creation which had been limited in *kenōsis*. Therefore, "every knee shall bow ... every tongue confess that Jesus Christ is Lord" (Phil 2:11). In the assumption of the lordship of Christ comes the restriction of other choice. In the removal of choice comes also the removal of its effects, and healing becomes absolute. He exerts his authority as lord over what was wrong, and re-creation follows.

Again, such re-creation is not a total act, but there is a continuity with the past. As in the resurrection of Christ, with holes in his hands into which Thomas could have placed his fingers (Jn 20:27), the scars would remain (cf Rev 5:6), but they would no longer matter. Even here, God still respects the choices that he gave to people.

Not that the eschatological solution to pain is the totality of God's action, which is more often indirect, such as prompting people to change the activity which contributes to pain and disease. They do however retain the right to suffer if they desire! He may also act directly, such as providing comfort and strength to the afflicted and even perhaps heal. The very fact that healing does occur, but not always, is then an indication that human health is not an absolute right. God has limited his rights, and as *imago Dei*, our rights are limited; he has limited his choice, and as *imago Dei*, we are not always able to do what we would choose to do.

Conclusion

It must always be a tragedy when somebody does not receive what they could, whether healing or salvation in the wider sense. It is always a disaster when people suffer unnecessarily, but unfortunately all too common; James (4:2) says, "you do not have, because you do not ask".

However, perhaps the major issue is the fear that prevents many from praying for the sick, fear of failure, fear of appearing foolish. This is foolish in itself if the claims of such as MacNutt are valid; there will be a lot of embarrassment in heaven! But this fear is at base a result of pride, a pride that is totally contrary to the humility that Jesus manifested in his *kenōsis*! How can we who claim to be the *douloi* of Christ be too proud to follow in the path of compassion for the sick in which he trod?

Chapter 13

Accepting *kenōsis*

It cannot be fitting that a book that deals with the idea of self-limitation just gets bigger and bigger. It has itself to be limited! In the case of Jesus, he limited himself in *kenōsis* just so that he could relate to people, and it was the same motive that lay behind dividing what was originally a single book into two. The danger that accompanied the *kenōsis* of Christ's divinity was however that it would then not be perceived, and indeed, just as at the time of Jesus himself, and throughout the history of the Church, many people today find it hard to accept that he was in fact fully divine. Thus the danger of splitting the book into two, a theoretical and a practical volume, is that on the one hand people do not appreciate the reason behind an ethic of self-limitation, but on the other, that they do not perceive that the fascinating study of the *kenōsis* of God should impact upon their lifestyles.

But it must. As I pointed out in the sister volume to this book, the main Biblical passage that describes the self-limitation of Christ is part of an ethical appeal. Indeed, the very title of that book, *Have this mind* (Williams 2007), is taken from the first phrase of the kenotic hymn of Philippians 2:5f. Sproul (1986:46) says that for a Christian, following Christ must be the only absolute. White (1979:109) writes that "the imitation of Christ is the nearest principle in Christianity to a moral absolute." He notes that it is basic to the appeals of both Peter and John (1979:192,202), but examples in other writers can be readily adduced. For Mark, discipleship is Christological (Richard 1982:109). So if Christ's very existence was kenotic, so should be the lives of those who seek to follow him.

Apart from Philippians 2, Adams (1986:105) adds that the command to self-denial occurs explicitly six times in the gospels (eg Matt 16:24), but that the concept is everywhere in scripture. He particularly cites 2 Corinthians 5:15 and Romans 14:7 (1986:109f). White (1979:193) also observes how important the idea of the meekness of Christ was to Peter. Davis (1993:201) cites 1 Peter 2:21f, indicating that the Christian life is a voluntary submission.

Imitation of God

It cannot then be right for a book that deals with the self-limitation of God to close without pointing out that if self-limitation is characteristic of the very nature of God, it should then be characteristic of God's people. If the Christian ideal is to be in the image of God as completely as possible, this then includes self-limitation. A kenotic ethic follows from the imitation of a kenotic God (Murphy & Ellis 1996:174). If the essence of the Christian life is union with God in Christ (Yoder 1972:116), it must be kenotic, because Christ's very incarnation was kenotic. Moreover, if the means of salvation, God's answer to evil, involves *kenōsis*, it naturally follows that the Christian life which counteracts evil is similarly kenotic; if God is not coercive, then neither should we be (Murphy & Ellis 1996:247f). The response to God's grace is a natural gratitude, and an appreciation of the sacrifice of Christ naturally calls forth sacrifice. Wiersbe (1997:33) cites the well-known story of the missionary C T Studd, who, in response to the sacrifice of Christ for him, insisted that "no sacrifice can be too great for me to make for Him." More than this, there is a strand of Christian tradition which sees the sufferings of Christians as a participation in those of Christ; Paul even speaks of making up "what is lacking in his afflictions for the sake of his body" (Col 1:24). This follows from the idea of union with Christ which is basic to the idea of recapitulation. The sufferings and sacrifice of Christians are then redemptive (Murphy and Ellis 1996:248).

It was appropriate that the means of salvation, the enabling of the restored relationship between God and people, should be by Christ's *kenōsis*. Indeed, all relationship must involve a measure of self-limitation if it is in any way mutual, although even using an implement can be said to be kenotic, simply because it involves a measure of choice, which means the limitation to that action rather than another, and to that tool rather than another. God's creativity is therefore inevitably kenotic, because it involves choice. Whether to create implies rejection of the option not to create, what to create implies the rejection of other possibilities that could have been created. These are ethical choices. In this case, salvation would also be kenotic, because it is also creative (2 Cor 5:17).

When what is created has the ability to respond rather than simply to react, so has life, the *kenōsis* of the creator deepens, as the creator must limit himself further if the created has any freedom of choice. Again, this involves ethics on the part of the creator, as he must decide whether to react to the actions of the created, and if so, how. Then inevitably, the created has to make ethical choices in the use of the measure of freedom that is given. Then if there is to be any real relationship between creator and created, this too involves choice, so is kenotic.

Indeed, whenever there are more than two beings with any

313

ability to choose, any relationship between them demands their self-limitation. Even the decision to ignore the other is kenotic, but how much more if the relationship is positive. Civilization demands that every person yield up a measure of his or her autonomy for the sake of living together (Peacocke 1993:241); the debate is always how to balance the needs of the community with the freedom of the individual. Societies have ranged from the totalitarian, where the freedom of the individual is minimal, to the other extreme, crystallized in capitalist ideology, where, following the belief of Adam Smith, the belief is that if all follow their own self-interest, the society as a whole will benefit. Yet even in the second extreme, it is inevitable that people have to limit themselves, simply by virtue of living together. They have to make choices, and therefore be limited; and the very existence of choice is ethical.

The establishing and the maintenance of relationship are therefore automatically kenotic; thus in order to re-establish the relationship with people that had been lost due to sin, God limited himself in Christ. The essence of sin was the opposite of *kenōsis*, so the elevation of self, so the remedy for sin is self-limitation. On the one hand, God in Christ limited himself, and on the other, people limit themselves in repentance and acceptance of grace.

Of course, the reason lying behind the grace of God, the means of salvation, is his love. Some have defined grace as unmerited favour, which is of the essence of love. It follows that a Christian ethic is one of love, which is encapsulated in what has been called the great commandment, to love God and neighbour (Matt 22:37f). Likewise Paul describes it as the more excellent way (1 Cor 13). It is hardly surprising that it is the great characteristic of a specifically Christian ethic; the Greek term *agapē* was very little used before Christianity, but reflects the nature of both God's action and human response. But it was little known as it is so unnatural for people without Christ, only coming into full expression by God's act, as a fruit of the Spirit

(Gal 5:22). And central to this love is *kenōsis*, self-giving; they are two sides of the one coin (Peacocke 1993:123).

However, even if relationship inevitably demands self-limitation from its essential nature, this self-limitation must be qualified, which is where the ethical issues often arise. On the one hand, the majority of issues involve the balancing of competing claims. As soon as there are two beggars, a decision has to be made, on some basis, as to which is supported, if at all, and in what proportion, if both. And are there conditions attached? But before decisions of that nature, hard though they are, comes the one which is essentially kenotic, that of the choice to limit oneself for the sake of the beggars.

It is here that an ethic based on the imitation of Christ becomes most demanding, for the Philippian hymn lifts up as the ideal the example of Christ who gave himself to the uttermost, taking the form of a slave, humbling himself even to accepting death on the cross (Phil 2:6-7). And all for the sake of relationship with people. What Paul is advocating is extreme, radical; it is not surprising that accepting such an ethic is hard, yet Murphy and Ellis (1996:118) do not hesitate to state that "self-renunciation for the sake of the other is humankind's highest good." Although they refer to Hick's view that the change from self-centredness to other-centredness is the primary goal of all major religious systems of ethics, they immediately make reference to Philippians 2 as the epitome of such an attitude.

Thus a Christian ethic of the imitation of Christ involves the adoption, by a free choice, of the role of a slave. While the work of Christ has enabled redemption from the situation of slavery to sin (Rom 6:17), Christians are then called upon to relinquish that freedom in obedience to their Lord. A slightly different view is that of Martin (1990:62f), who has suggested that salvation is not so much redemption to the status of freedom, but a transfer of ownership from one master to another. In this case, a Christian is still a slave, but to

God. He rejects Deissman's belief that salvation is paralleled by the custom of purchase by a god. However, this pushes the example from contemporary culture too far. The fact of appeal and command to Christians (eg Rom 6:13) indicates that they were not slaves, but are being urged to accept slavery voluntarily; Paul says that he made himself a slave of his own free will (1 Cor 6:17,19). Certainly this is the implication of his example in Galatians 4; a Christian is no longer a slave by nature, but is adopted as a child of God (also Rom 8:14f). Paul urged Philemon to receive Onesimus as a brother, because they were both sons of God (Philm 16). The Spirit then witnesses to us of our new relationship to our Father (Gal 4:7), a thought implicit in Jesus' calling his disciples no longer slaves, but friends (Jn 15:15). Likewise Paul's parallel with marriage in Romans 7 indicates that both the relationships of slavery and marriage ended with death, which was experienced in union with that of Christ.

Ethics, the means of correct relationship with others, are then inevitably kenotic. Effective community demands *kenōsis*. However, it must be pointed out here that the rightness of a kenotic ethic does not lay in its effectiveness. A Christian ethic is often denounced as impracticable or as an impossible ideal. Although the ethics outlined in Jesus' teaching, especially those in the Sermon on the Mount, have been universally admired, they have equally been rejected as unworkable in the real world of sinful imperfection. Bismarck famously doubted that the world could be ruled in that way (Thielicke 1966:350). Nevertheless, many, most famously Mahatma Gandhi, have found power in a policy of passive resistance (Murphy & Ellis 1996:133).

Many attempts have been made to qualify Jesus' words; perhaps the best known is the view that the ethics of Jesus may be seen as the ideal, only applicable eschatologically, but that there is a need of an interim ethic to suit the present reality. However that would reduce the underlying idea of ethics from the imitation of God to a form of utilitarianism. Most importantly, there is no indication in Jesus' words that he saw it only as an ideal or only for the future. Certainly there has been no shortage of Christian groups, from the very beginning, who have tried to live according to the Sermon on the Mount. The significant difference from the Old Testament is the presence of the Spirit, who enables such radical conduct. Of course this also implies that Christian ethics are kenotic, simply because the nature of the Spirit is self-effacing, so kenotic.

On the other hand, a kenotic ethic must be influenced by the expectation of the future. If Jesus experienced what he did for the sake of his future glory, it follows that our current life can also be conducted in the light of the expectation that we have.

The prevalent modern worldview has perhaps two dominant characteristics. Firstly, even though Pinnock (2001:116) points out that change rather than the stability assumed in the Middle Ages is the dominant idea, there is a rejection of any self-limitation, and secondly, that of living in the present, of wanting things immediately. A Christian world-view, that of *kenōsis*, is then totally antithetical to this, not only rejecting the need of getting, but of being prepared to be patient in anticipation of the future. This second is then complementary to the first.

A kenotic ethic does not elevate the ideal of self-renunciation because it is good in itself. A kenotic ethic is not world-rejecting, is not ascetic for its own sake, but so that greater good may come. Murphy and Ellis (1996:193) point out that just as the *kenōsis* of Jesus was the means to a final victory, so a kenotic ethic is ultimately the one that is finally successful. In fact, even though it is common to speak of self-limitation, or self-renunciation, the kenotic ethic must carry the added nuances, firstly that limitation is temporary, and that it is not an absolute surrender. If the kenotic theory of the incarnation had stressed those points, maybe it would not have been so decisively rejected, and in that case, therefore, a kenotic ethic as central to a Christian lifestyle would have been more acceptable.

Nevertheless, if indeed the ideal for humanity is to be most closely in the image of God, and if the nature of God is essentially kenotic, it does follow that the fullest expression of humanity is in the practice of *kenōsis*. Perhaps some indication of this can be seen in the area of marriage. While recognizing that God does call some people to a celibate life, and that obedience to that calling is the path to the life that God intends for them, it is clear that God did create humanity in such a way that marriage is the norm. But in both cases, the way to the full expression of humanity is kenotic, whether it is the deliberate abstaining from the sexual relationship for the sake of the relationship to God, which is what Paul was called to (1 Cor 7:8,28f), or in marriage, in which each partner must limit themselves for the sake of the other. In either case, the choice is valid if done in obedience to God, which was why Jesus himself adopted *kenōsis*. Indeed, it is when people yield themselves most fully to God that they become most fully human. Examples of this are in the life of prayer, which is most meaningful and effective when done in deliberate *kenōsis*, yielding to the will of God.

Being a Christian also then enables the transcending of sexual differences. Christians are therefore baptised rather than being circumcised, not only because it more adequately demonstrates the new life in Christ, the aspects of forgiveness, receipt of eternal life and of consecration to Christ as Lord, but because it can be administered to both sexes. Paul can therefore say that there is in Christ neither male nor female (Gal 3:28). Ministry should then be equally possible by both sexes; it is hardly valid to argue that ministry should only be by males as representing a male Christ, if in the glorified state he is no longer restricted to the male gender but encompasses both.

More than the enhancement of the humanity of the one practising *kenōsis*, the aim of a kenotic ethic is to benefit the people that this affects. One example of this is that Murphy and Ellis (1996) are particularly concerned that dealing with others should not be aggressive. Obviously this aspect of kenotic practice manifests in pacifism, but they argue that it has other facets. A kenotic ethic should also affect the way in which society deals with offenders. Western society makes extensive use of prisons, but Murphy and Ellis (1996:141) argue that a kenotic ethic should be restorative not retributive; here, of course, it must be pointed out that the *kenōsis* of Jesus was to restore the relationship with God damaged by sin. They point out that an attitude of *kenōsis* generates character change, but the opposite hardens attitudes (1996:160). So often the result of a prison sentence results in more crime, if only by the enforced association with likeminded criminals. The suffering of prison may well harden the attitude of the prisoner, and far from helping him or her, rather results in dehumanization. Moreover, it certainly does nothing to help the one who suffered loss or injury in the crime, as well as being expensive to society as a whole.

Working out the details

Accepting the principle of *kenōsis* is one thing; working out the details is quite another. Some applications are immediately obvious, such as to the use of material possessions, and to the practice of sexuality. But obviously, as we are in a world vastly different from the one to which Jesus came, there will be aspects which are applicable to us that Jesus did not need to embrace. He lived in a country which was subject to foreign occupation by the Romans as part of their empire, and so the urge to political violence was more a part of his world than ours often is; yet he was not confronted by the complications of the existence of modern weaponry, especially of nuclear explosives. Luther makes this point when he insists that Christ

319

is not so much the example, but the exemplar (Thielicke 1966:186); we do not so much follow his actions, for that would be a different form of legalism (Thielicke 1966:185), but follow the pattern of his life, which is kenotic. The very popular WWJD, "what would Jesus do?" is a valid guide, but it is exactly that, and not "what did Jesus do?" Imitation of Jesus must be subject to qualification. Cave (1949:153) comments that the calling of Jesus was not the same as ours, and so his actions must naturally differ. The principle was the same, but the practice may well differ.

As soon as theology is applied to the world, which it must be, the details will alter. Simply because the world itself is changing, the Christian life will change. It is interesting to speculate how Jesus would come if the incarnation was in the twenty-first century; what is certain is that it would not be the same! He would still die, but almost certainly not on a cross; after all, the inhabitants of the modern world have invented other equally horrible ways to deal with people that they find disturbing their comfort. But even if the time and place, and therefore the circumstances of Jesus' life would be radically different, even unrecognizable, the principle of his life would be exactly the same. It would embody *kenōsis*, and his teaching would encourage his followers in the kenotic life.

But Jesus did not become incarnate into the modern world, and even if it is our constant hope that he will return, the manner of that return will be different; in fact it will be to end *kenōsis*! But until he does come back, it is the constant job of his servants to work out how the unchanging principle of a life embodying *kenōsis* is applied to the ever-changing situation. That was the purpose of my work in researching *kenōsis*, but the results of that are in the other volume.

Overcoming limitation

Even if self-limitation in imitation of Christ is the appropriate response for a Christian, impotence is not! This seeming paradox is resolved in that the gift of the Spirit empowers those who yield themselves to him. As the Spirit of wholeness, he makes the kenotic life whole.

This is naturally seen most clearly in Christ, who is after all our model. Although it was necessary for Jesus to become limited so that he could fully identify with humanity, he then also accepted the impotence that is part of being a human being. This meant that he was actually unable to help people in their day to day needs. Even though he was Son of God, he was not then able to heal, not able to do miracles, in fact not even able to demonstrate to people that he was divine. If he had just come and died, even if he died to atone for the sins of the world, that death would not have been effective unless people accepted in faith that Jesus had died for them. Even if salvation is entirely by grace, it is received by faith, and faith would not be exercised without a belief that he was divine. It was for that reason that he received the Spirit at his baptism, designating him a Son of God.

But more than this, the gift of the Spirit empowered Jesus in his ministry while on earth. Jesus did not do his works by being divine, but by the Spirit. Feinberg (1980:42) points out that in all of Jesus' life he was dependent on the Spirit, and that while his actions were his, they were done through the Spirit, even the sacrifice on the cross (Heb 9:14). He adds that they cannot therefore justify any doctrine of merit or works; this is important as it does mean that the exaltation of Jesus was not a reward for his work. It is rather a result of the acceptance of the Spirit's action through him. Thus the descent of the Spirit on Jesus not only demonstrated that he was divine, a message underscored by the voice from heaven, but it also empowered him for his ministry. It was no accident that right after the baptism, Jesus was led into the wilderness to be tempted, not only because he had shown that he was the Son, but because he had received the power of the Spirit, and could then be tempted to abuse that power.

Then right after coming back from the wilderness, he went to the synagogue at his home town of Nazareth, and quoted from Isaiah 61 (Lk 4:18f), a passage which connects the works that he did with the anointing of the Spirit. Effectively what had happened that the gift of the Spirit enabled Jesus to do what he could have been able to do if he had not limited his divinity. While being limited in his essential divinity, the gift of the Spirit then effectively reversed the effects of the *kenōsis*. To put it another way, the Spirit enabled Jesus' wholeness.

This is the same as he does in relation to Christians. Firstly the Spirit makes a relationship between the Christian and the glorified Son so that he or she receives the forgiveness for which Jesus died on the cross, then also received the eternal life that Jesus has as Son by linking him to Jesus. Here the Spirit acts as *vinculum amoris*, relating the Christian to Christ, paralleling the bond that he makes in the Trinity between Father and Son. At the same time the Spirit does what he did for Christ at his baptism, designating him or her as a child of God, although of course not by nature as was the case for Christ, but by adoption (Rom 8:15).

Thus the Spirit restores to people what was lost at the fall. The Spirit makes the Christian whole. On the one hand he gives life to Christians, making this aspect complete, but then he also empowers the Christian as well. In this case, the Spirit overcomes the limitation that people experience because they are human.

PART 5

The end of *kenōsis*

"Amen"

Chapter 14

The end of *kenōsis*

Just as an utterance ends in a full stop, or perhaps an exclamation mark, so an action comes to a conclusion. The same is true for *kenōsis*.

Kenōsis is actually not a good thing. Although it might seem from a book like this that self-limitation is entirely beneficial, this is hardly the case. If God is entirely good, it would seem to be wrong for him to limit himself at all. If everything that God has made is good, it is not right to deliberately deprive oneself of it. If God has given abilities, it is wrong not to use them. So why did God limit himself? Why did Jesus limit himself in his incarnation? Why is it that we should limit ourselves in imitation of God? Why then are these actions good? The answer must be that these are not in themselves good, but are only good if by following such action, a better result follows. Since the birth of my first son, and seeing all the distress that this caused my wife at the time, I have appreciated the truth of John 16:21 that all the pain of a birth is swallowed up in the joy of a new child. And so it is in other spheres as well. The self-limitation of God in creation is not in itself good, but by his *kenōsis* came the better result of the freedom of what had been created, and the possibility of free relationships. God gained by means of his self-limitation (Pinnock 2001:101). He will have become something more through the whole process (Richard 1982:267, citing Hodgson). Murphy and Ellis (1996:127) comment that parents commonly give up resources for their children, but gain pleasure from doing so. The *kenōsis* that Jesus experienced in his incarnation and then in his humiliation and death, can hardly be seen as good, and yet we call the day of the climax of his experiences "Good Friday", just because of the benefit that this gave to us. By means of his *kenōsis*, and only through that, came the availability of salvation.

Apart from a few masochists who seem to like suffering, even the most dedicated ascetic can hardly want the suffering that goes with self-deprivation, but it is adopted because of what is seen as a far greater good, because it is believed to be of value to the soul. And in fact even the masochist only seeks to suffer, perverse though it may seem, because he or she enjoys it; the enjoyment of the pain outweighs the actual suffering.

Examples can be multiplied. The dieter seeks a better weight by limiting food intake, another seeks fitness by the discipline of exercise. For all these, self-deprivation in itself is not good, but only good if it results in a positive benefit. So if there is no benefit, there should be no *kenōsis*, and where the benefit of self-limitation has been achieved, then it should not continue. This means that the practice of *kenōsis* should be temporary, and at some point, it should come to an end. Indeed, as *kenōsis* does mean self-limitation, then *kenōsis* itself should be limited, and come to a conclusion.

This is exactly what the Philippian hymn describes in the case of Jesus. After the depths of his *kenōsis*, and the achieving of its purposes in our salvation, the process is indeed reversed in his exaltation and glorification. But, and this is the glory of it, for Jesus the final result was beneficial; he did gain from what he had gone through. The resurrection of Jesus was just that; it was not simply a restoration, not simply a revival, a return to what the situation was previously, but to more. Hebrews 12:2 puts it even more clearly, that he went through the whole process because of the joy set before him.

What must be stressed is that this final state was contingent upon what had gone before. The two halves of the Philippian hymn are connected by a simple, but extremely significant word, *dio*, "therefore". The word is not "then", implying a simple succession of events, but causal; it was because Jesus had gone through the process of emptying that exaltation followed. And the same is then true for us as well; without our going through the process of our own *kenōsis*, we will not achieve the glory that God intends for us. Just as it was for God, just as it was for Jesus, *kenōsis* is absolutely essential for us if we are to come to glory. This should be clear from the gospel affirmation that salvation is received by grace, that there is no way in which we can earn it (Eph 2:8); this demands that we must humble ourselves, swallow our pride, and simply accept that we are in ourselves unworthy. If we are to be saved, we must go through *kenōsis*. In fact the Philippian hymn stresses the point that Jesus did not in fact exalt himself, but he himself, even though he was the Son of God, was exalted by God.

Continuing *kenōsis*

This must not be taken to mean that *kenōsis* will completely disappear. As long as anything remains, which is forever, there will be self-limitation.

Firstly, the very nature of God is kenotic, so as long as the eternal God endures, so does *kenōsis*. This follows from the understanding that God is Trinity, and so each Person, simply by the existence of the other Two, is limited. The Son is limited insofar as he is not the Father or the Spirit, and the same is true of the other Persons. If this were not true, then the Persons would be identical, and not different, so that the Trinity as such disappears.

But the immediate result of the difference between the Persons would be that they are unequal, a suggestion vehemently denied by the Church as a result of the Arian convulsions of the fourth century. Arius had believed just that, so preaching that the Son is less than the Father. This idea was vehemently rejected by such as Athanasius, who clearly realized that salvation, and so Christianity itself, demanded the full deity of the Son, so that he was equal to the Father; they were *homoousios*, of the same essence. It was towards the end of the controversy that it was realized how it was possible to affirm both the equality and difference of the Persons. This was through the inter-relation of *perichōrēsis*, the mutual self-giving of each Person to the Others. But this action in itself is a form of *kenōsis*.

In this way, self-limitation is inherent to the very nature of God, to the immanent Trinity. It is however in the so-called economic Trinity that *kenōsis* was most manifested, in the incarnation of the second Person and the humility of the Son that led finally to his death upon the cross. Likewise, the Spirit's role in the world was limited. It is these that are in the process of reversal in the exaltation of the Son and the increasing activity of the Spirit. As the historical process unfolds, there will be a move towards *plērōma*. Seemingly paradoxically, the last act is the subjection of the Son to the Father (1 Cor 15:28); however, this is not a renewed *kenōsis* as such, but the end of the distinction between the economic and the immanent Trinity. In the economic Trinity, the relationship between the Persons had necessarily been limited, but this will no longer need to be so. The final subjection of the Son is not, as Arius had thought, an indication of his essential subordination, but rather an indication of the full *perichōrēsis* that is the essence of the nature of God. The full subjection of the Son to the Father is then reflected in the subjection of each Person to the two others, and so God is "all in all".

But secondly, even that statement has to be qualified. As long as anything exists beside God, he has to limit himself. The final book of the Bible indicates that there will be a "new heaven and a new earth" (Rev 21:1), and moreover, there is no indication that these, as the first heaven and earth, will be temporary. They will exist in closer relationship to God than the first, the separation due to sin having been dealt with, so for example, "God himself will be with them" (Rev 21:3), and will directly provide the light for the new Jerusalem (Rev 22:5).

Clearly these will not experience the same limitations as in the present order. The resurrection body of Jesus was not subject to the limitations of locked doors (Jn 20:19), and the future spiritual bodies of Christians (1 Cor 15:44) will be like his (1 Jn 3:2). Yet their very existence must be a limited one, and require the continued *kenōsis* of God. Again, as he is giving light and life to the new order, that is a form of self-restriction.

Then thirdly, and most importantly for people, their existence does not only demand God's *kenōsis*, but if they continue to have free will, their freedom of choice is only possible if God continues to restrict his own freedom. Surely if humanity was created with free will, and if such a price were paid for redemption, there is no question but that free will continues in the re-creation. In this case God will continue to limit himself to make this possible.

However, this gives rise to a very significant question, for if human free will was the factor that enabled the entrance of sin into the world, and then ultimately death and the destruction of the world, what is to prevent a repetition of that? Why should people on the new earth not spoil it by sin? Will God prevent this by removing free will, and so also his own *kenōsis*?

Augustine, and many others, suggested that the horror of sin and disobedience to God was permitted by him because of the greater good that resulted from the forgiveness that was enabled by the death of Christ. Although God could have compelled obedience, it was overall better that people be given free will and that a solution to sin be enacted. As well as providing the means of dealing with sin, and the gift of eternal life which had been lost by sin, God also provided the Holy Spirit who would both guide into what is right and empower obedience to it. Of course, the essence of that obedience involved subjection to the will of God, so *kenōsis*.

As long as people have free will, the possibility remains that it would be misused, and there would be another fall into sin; this must remain a possibility even in the re-creation. However, it seems most unlikely that the present situation would just be repeated. For one thing, that would open the door to an endless repetition of a cycle of sin and redemption. In any case, unless it were somehow possible that sins in a future life could be atoned for in the death of Jesus, it would mean that the atonement would have to be repeated. In this regard, Hebrews 9:28 does indicate that Christ was offered once, and, moreover, that when he appears the second time, it is not to deal with sin. The same book then adds a warning against sinning deliberately after enlightenment, for "there no longer remains a sacrifice for sins" (Heb 10:26). Paul also has to condemn those who treated sin lightly on the grounds of the free gift of grace (Rom 6:1,15). It is tragic that although these warnings were taken very seriously in the early Church, few today seem to give any thought to the seriousness to the matter.

A further possibility is that sin committed in the new creation would immediately result in the loss of eternal life, just as Adam and

Eve suffered expulsion from the Garden, and therefore from access to the tree of life, due to the Fall. If life, especially eternal life, is only enjoyed due to a relationship with God in Christ, and sin breaks that relationship, it would follow that life would be lost. However, there is no death in the re-creation, as it had been thrown into the lake of fire (Rev 20:14, cf also Rev 21:4). Paul speaks of it as the last enemy to be destroyed (1 Cor 15:26).

Spanner (1987:149) notes that the perfection in the second creation is no guarantee of not falling, as some of the angels did fall. In any case, the Fall occurred in the perfection of Eden. He suggests that it is only the remembrance of God's love that could be effective (Rom 8:39). Unlike Adam, the redeemed had the sight of a "Lamb standing, as though it had been slain" (Rev 5:6), an ever present reminder. The devotion of the Prodigal Son to his father was surely enhanced by his experiences in the far country. As Jesus himself said, the person who is forgiven little, loves little (Lk 7:47). In this case, the *kenōsis* of the redeemed, which is the essence of obedience to God, and so of a full relationship to him, depends on the *kenōsis* of Christ himself. It is then Christ who then finally delivers the kingdom to the Father (1 Cor 15:24), the kingdom that is the obedience of every member of it. Spanner then comments that this means that God could call the original creation "very good", while it contained pain and death. Sin was a condition for final blessedness! The continued obedience of the redeemed does not of course remove their free will, which is then why God continues to experience *kenōsis*. This is however little more than theoretical, as all are obedient to him.

From another perspective, because of the experience of redemption, the relationship between the believer and God was enhanced above what it would have been had there been no sin. As every relationship is necessarily kenotic as it requires giving to the other, this then implies that there is a greater depth of *kenōsis* in God due to the fact of past redemption.

Future exaltation

Even if some of the experience of limitation in *kenōsis* will continue until the last day (Dawe 1963:154), much can be expected to be reversed, and indeed, more than reversed, in the events of the future consummation of all things. One indication of this is that "every eye will see him" (Rev 1:7); the *kenōsis* of omnipresence is reversed. Jesus did receive a spiritual body, he did receive worship, even immediately after the resurrection, but this was only at the start of the process of exaltation. Hawthorne (1983:91) observes that the word for the exaltation of Jesus is actually "hyper-exalt" and that there is only one act; this is probably because at that time, the humanity and deity are fully united and glorified together, unlike the separate *kenōsis* of the deity and humanity. The glorified body seen by John on Patmos, and the worship that he gave there, was far more that that seen and worshipped by Thomas the week after the resurrection. We can expect that the benefits of or relationship with God won by Christ are likewise only the "firstfruits" (Rom 8:23) of those that we will eventually receive. What we have received now but only in part, can be expected to be received fully then. Even those controversial *charismata* cannot really be seen as part of finality, and will therefore cease when the fullness comes (1 Cor 13:8). *Glossolalia* may well be a deeper experience of prayer than the "ordinary", but it is still a pale reflection of full communion with God, and will therefore cease with the arrival of the fullness (1 Cor 13:8).

As during the overcoming of limitation in this life, the final reversing of *kenōsis* is through the Spirit. It is an act of God on Christ, a contrast to the humiliation which was an act of Christ himself (Fee

1995:219). Zizioulas (1985:130) indicates that the role of the Spirit is to liberate the Son from the bondage of history; in removing his *kenōsis* comes restoring fullness of relationship with the Father, so full deity. Likewise the "spiritual body" that Jesus had as resurrected, and which we also will receive (1 Cor 15:44), is not so much spiritual in nature, but empowered by the Spirit (Williams 2004:136).

The gospel of John insists that we have already received eternal life, so much so that it actually repeats the affirmation three times (Jn 3:36, 5:24, 6:47). Certainly this is glorious, but there is surely no Christian who is satisfied with what has been received, what has been experienced. The Christian life must be a thirst for more, for a deeper relationship with God, for fullness. Paul must surely be typical when he longs to "depart and be with Christ, for that is much better" (Phil 1:23). He was at that point in particularly miserable circumstances, cooped up in a Roman prison, but he had most certainly experienced the wonders of what the Christian walk involves, and knew that it was just a foretaste.

This must affect every part of life. How many Christians suffer, and long to get relief of their problems, and cry to their Lord for relief! So often, as well, they get an answer, and can testify that God has indeed answered, maybe not in the way that they would have liked, but to some extent. Quite often what God does is to give the patience and the courage, and to make the situation less of a problem. But only sometimes, and every Christian must wonder why it is that God rarely does do the entire job. The affirmation that we can make is that God does in fact always meet our needs, and totally; it was something achieved in what Jesus did through his life, on the cross and through the resurrection. Salvation, not just its "spiritual" aspects, is ours. We do not have divine authority to claim in the present, because we are still limited. But it is certainly more normal for much of what salvation means to be received not in the present, which would disrupt the world that God made, but eschatologically, in the future. Total wholeness is part of what Christians can expect, part of the reversing of *kenōsis*, when we would in fact have that authority to claim! This is part of the restoration of God's image. Interestingly, Wiersbe (1997:44) suggests that there will be one disfigurement in heaven, that of the scars of Jesus. We do sometimes receive in the present, and can thank God for that, but that is more usually a foretaste of what will be received in the future.

Likewise, the salvation that is completed in the fullness of eternal life and in completeness of health is also present in the fullness of relationships. It is for this reason that there is no marriage in heaven, as there is no need for exclusivity in relationships (Williams 2004:236). Perhaps we can see this principle working out in what must be the central Christian act of worship. What we experience in the Lord's supper is a pale reflection of the eschatological banquet of the lamb. Of course, participating in the Supper can be a deep and moving experience, but nobody can really say that eating a little bread, even partaking of the wine, can seriously be called a feast! And nobody can really say that they experience the presence of Christ in a fully real and satisfying way at the communion! As other aspects, it looks forward to a fuller experience in the future. Reference to the lamb should also remind us that this includes the animals as well (Is 11:6 etc); Vanstone (1977:79) insists, in view of the place of humanity in the universe, that God's consummation cannot be restricted to it.

Then even in the increased relationship with other people that follows from a relationship with Christ, there must be a realization that there is yet more, and that eschatologically the barriers will come down, and we will be open to each other in a way that never happens in this world. Paul's picture of the inter-relationship of the members of the Church being like that of the parts of the body is apposite, but everybody knows that churches do not come up to that ideal! Whereas it is, usually at least, much better than outside the Church, there are still manifold quarrels, disagreements, schisms. It is only when "every tongue will confess" (Phil 2:11), a manifestation of the full relationship of each with Christ, that relationships with each other will be fulfilled.

It must be added here that part of the process of this exaltation was the fact that Jesus was "given the name that is above every name" (Phil 2:9) (Fee 1995:221). This is the name of "Lord" (Fee 1999:99), so stands in contrast with his slavery in his *kenōsis*, and also with the "lordship" of Caesar, which gave suffering (Fee 1995:223). The name distinguishes from others, and reveals the nature, so naturally it provides the first creed' "Jesus is Lord" (1 Cor 12:3) (Hawthorne 1983:91,93). And part of the process of our exaltation is also then that we are "given a name". The essence of a name is identification, and individuality. It is only at the point when *kenōsis* comes to an end that we finally receive the fullness of personality that God intended. In his creation, God limited himself so that creation can be free, enjoying a measure of independence. This freedom and independence is then not reversed at the end of *kenōsis*, but rather fulfilled.

It is in this that a person becomes fully and completely human, as God intended at the creation, and becomes fully in *imago Dei*. It is this which was lost at the fall, when, albeit unknowingly, *kenōsis* was in fact adopted, and humanity suffered restriction and loss. It is a restoration of this that is anticipated, full humanity, which, incidentally, must also include full healing from the disease and infirmity that was one of the side-effects of the Fall.

The resurrection and exaltation of Jesus, the start of the reversal of his *kenōsis*, was a continuation of his previous life, not a radical new start. So it is with us; our first-fruits are just that, part of what will be received. Thus Moltmann (1985:93) believes that the world will be transformed, and not annihilated as God brings history to its consummation.

Even though we might accept that *kenōsis* is good and right in the current situation, it can only be in the light of the realization that it is temporary, and only in the light of the expectation of a future fullness. Our longing must again be that of the apostle, who while rejoicing in and advocating *kenōsis*, longed for its end in the return of his Lord, crying out:

MARANATHA, Come LORD Jesus (1 Cor 16:22)!

Sources cited

Adams, J E 1986. *The Biblical view of self-esteem self-love self-image.* Eugene, Or: Harvest House.

Anderson, B W 1967. *Creation versus chaos: the reinterpretation of mythical symbolism in the Bible.* New York: Association press.

Andrews, E H 1980. *God, science and evolution.* Welwyn, Herts: Evangelical press.

Aulén, G 1950. *Christus Victor: an historical study of the three main types of the idea of the atonement.* London: SPCK.

Baillie, D M 1956. *God was in Christ: an essay on incarnation and atonement.* London: Faber & Faber.

Bainton, R H 1960. *Christian attitudes toward war and peace: a historical survey and critical re-evaluation.* Nashville: Abingdon.

Barbour, I G 2001. God's power: a process view. Polkinghorne (2001:1-20).

Barry, F R 1968. *The atonement.* London: Hodder & Stoughton.

Barry, F R 1969. *Secular and supernatural.* London: SCM.

Barry, W A 1987. *Prayer as a personal relationship.* New York / Mahwah: Paulist.

Barth, K 1957. *Church dogmatics 2(2): the doctrine of God.* Edinburgh: T & T Clark.

Barth, K 1958. *Church Dogmatics vol 3(1): the doctrine of creation.* Edinburgh: T & T Clark.

Beasley-Murray, G R [1962] 1972. *Baptism in the New Testament.* Paperback ed. Exeter : Paternoster.

Bennett, D & R 1974. *The Holy Spirit and you: a study-guide to the Spirit-filled life.* New ed. Eastbourne: Kingsway.

Berkhof, H 1979. *Christian faith: an introduction to the study of the faith.* Grand Rapids: Eerdmans.

Berkhof, L 1958. *Systematic theology.* London: Banner of truth trust.

Berger, P L 1969. *The sacred canopy: elements of a sociological theory of religion.* New York: Doubleday (Anchor).

Berger, P L 1970. *A rumour of angels: modern society and the rediscovery of the supernatural.* London: Allen Lane The Penguin Press.

Bernhardt, K-H, (with Bergman, J, Botterweck, G J & Ringgren, H) 1977. *bārā'.* in Botterweck, G J & Ringgren, H (eds) *Theological Dictionary of the Old Testament vol 2.* Rev ed. Grand Rapids: Eerdmans. 242-9.

Best, W E 1985. *Christ emptied himself.* Houston, TX: South Belt Grace Church.

Birch, B C & Rasmussen, L L 1978. *The predicament of the prosperous.* Philadelphia: Westminster.

Blamires, H 1978. *The Christian mind: how should a Christian think?* Ann Arbor, MI: Servant.

Blocher, H 1984. *In the beginning: the opening chapters of Genesis.* Downers Grove, Ill / Leicester: Inter-Varsity.

Blumenberg, H 1983. *The legitimacy of the modern age.* Cambridge, Mass: Massachusetts Institute of Technology.

Bockmuehl, M 1997. *A commentary on the epistle to the Philippians.* 4th ed. London: A & C Black.

Boff, L 1988. *Trinity and society.* Maryknoll, N Y: Orbis.

Boice, J M 1971. *Philippians: an expositional commentary.* Grand Rapids: Zondervan.

Bonhoeffer, D 1967. *Letters and papers from prison.* 3rd ed. London: SCM.

Boyd, G A 2001. *Satan and the problem of evil: constructing a Trinitarian warfare theodicy.* Downers Grove, Ill: InterVarsity.

Bracken, J A 1979. *What are they saying about the Trinity?* New York / Ramsey / Toronto: Paulist

Bray, G L 1979. *Holiness and the will of God: perspectives on the theology of Tertullian.* London: Marshall, Morgan & Scott.

Brown, R E 1970. *The Anchor Bible: the gospel according to John (xiii-xxi): introduction, translation and notes.* New York: Doubleday.

Bruce, F F 1989. *Philippians.* Peabody, Mass: Hendrickson (New International Biblical Commentary.

Bruce, S 2002. *God is dead: secularization in the West.* Oxford: Blackwell.

Brueggemann, W 1982. *Genesis: Interpretation: a Bible commentary for teaching and preaching.* Atlanta: John Knox.

Brunner, E 1952. *The Christian doctrine of creation and redemption: Dogmatics, vol II.* Philadelphia: Westminster.

Budgen, V 1985. *The Charismatics and the Word of God: a Biblical and historical perspective on the charismatic movement.* Welwyn, Herts: Evangelical press.

Carasik, M 2000. The limits of omniscience. *Journal of Biblical literature* 119(2) 221-32.

Carson, D A 1979. The function of the paraclete in John 16:7-11. *Journal of Biblical Literature* 98(4) 547-66.

Cassuto, U 1961. *A commentary on the book of Genesis.* Jerusalem: Magnes.

Cave, S 1949. *The Christian way: a study of New Testament ethics in relation to present problems.* Welwyn, Herts: James Nisbet.

Chadwick, O 1975. *The secularization of the European mind in the nineteenth century: the Gifford lectures in the University of Edinburgh for 1973-4.* Cambridge: University press.

Coakley, S 2001. Kenosis: theological meanings and gender connotations. Polkinghorne (2001:192-210).

Cochrane, C C 1984. *The gospel according to Genesis: a guide to understanding Genesis 1-11.* Grand Rapids: Eerdmans.

Congar, Y M J 1983. *I believe in the Holy Spirit Vol 3: The river of the water of life (Rev 22:1) flows in the East and in the West.* New York: Seabury / London: Geoffrey Chapman.

Cox, H 1968. *The secular city: secularization and urbanization in theological perspective.* Harmondsworth: Penguin.

Cronin, K M 1992. *Kenōsis: emptying self and the path of Christian service.* Rockport, Mass / Shaftesbury, Dorset: Element.

Davis, J J 1993. *Evangelical ethics: issues facing the Church today.* 2nd ed. Phillipsburg, NJ: Presbyterian & Reformed.

Davis, P & Kenyon, D H 1989. *Of pandas and people: the central question of biological origins.* Dallas, TX: Haughton.

Dawe, D G 1963. *The form of a servant: a historical analysis of the kenotic motif.* Philadelphia: Westminster.

Dekker, G 1997. Modernity and the Reformed Churches in The Netherlands: bargaining or surrender? Dekker, Luidens & Rice (1997:13-23).

Dekker, G, Luidens, D A & Rice, R 1997. Conclusions: a resounding gong or a tinkling bell? Dekker, Luidens & Rice (1997:279-84).

Dekker, G, Luidens, D A & Rice, R 1997. *Rethinking secularization: Reformed reactions to modernity.* Lanham, MD: University press of America.

Denton, M 1986. *Evolution: a theory in crisis.* Bethesda, MD: Adler and Adler.

Dobbelaere, K 2002. *Secularization: an analysis at three levels.* Brussels: PIE- Peter Lang.

Driver, J 1986. *Understanding the atonement for the mission of the Church.* Scottdale, Penn: Herald.

Dunn, J D G 1975. *Jesus and the Spirit: a study of the religious and charismatic experience of Jesus and the first Christians as reflected in the New Testament.* London: SCM.

Dunn, J G D 1989. *Christology in the making: an inquiry into the origins of the doctrine of the incarnation.* 2nd ed. London: SCM.

Dyrness, W 1979. *Themes in Old Testament theology.* Exeter: Paternoster.

Eichrodt, W 1967. *Theology of the Old Testament.* Vol 2. London: SCM.

Ellis, G F R 2001. Kenosis as a unifying theme for life and cosmology. Polkinghorne (2001:107-26).

Erickson, M J 1991. *The Word became flesh: a contemporary incarnational Christology.* Grand Rapids: Baker.

Erickson, M J 1998. *Christian theology.* 2nd ed. Grand Rapids: Baker.

Erickson, M J 2003. *What does God know and how does he know it? The current controversy over divine foreknowledge.* Grand Rapids: Zondervan.

Farah, C Jr c 1980. *From the pinnacle of the Temple*. Plainfield, NJ: Logos.

Fee, G D 1995. *Paul's letter to the Philippians*. Grand Rapids: Eerdmans.

Fee, G D 1999. *Philippians*. Downer's Grove / Leicester: InterVarsity.

Feinberg, P D 1980. The kenosis and Christology: an exegetical-theological analysis of Phil 2:6-11. *Trinity Journal* 1 NS 21-46.

Ferguson, S B 1996. *The Holy Spirit*. Leicester: IVP.

Fergusson, D A S 1998. *The cosmos and the creator: an introduction to the theology of creation*. London: SPCK.

Fiddes, P S 1988. *The creative suffering of God*. Oxford: Clarendon.

Field, D 2003. Questions to an open theist. *Table talk* 8

Fitch, W 1974. *The ministry of the Holy Spirit*. Grand Rapids: Zondervan.

Ford, A 1986. *Universe: God, man and science*. London: Hodder & Stoughton.

Forsyth, P T 1910. *The work of Christ*. London: Hodder & Stoughton.

Fortman, E J 1982. *The triune God: a historical study of the doctrine of the Trinity*. Grand Rapids: Baker.

Foster, R J 2000. *Prayer: finding the heart's true home*. London: Hodder & Stoughton.

Frank, D W 1986. *Less than conquerors: how evangelicals entered the twentieth century*. Grand Rapids: Eerdmans.

Fretheim, T E 1984. *The suffering of God: an Old Testament perspective*. Philadelphia: Fortress.

Gaffin, R B Jr. 1996. A cessationist view. Grudem (1996:25-64).

Gaffin, R B Jr 1996. Concluding statement (cessationist view). Grudem (1996:334-40).

Gavrilyuk, P L 2005. The kenotic theology of Sergius Bulgakov. *Scottish Journal of Theology* 58(3) 251-69.

Gaybba B 1987. *The Spirit of love: theology of the Holy Spirit*. London: Geoffrey Chapman.

Gitt, W 2006. *Did God use evolution?: observations from a scientist of faith*. *: Master books (New leaf publishing).

Gresham, J L Jr 1993. The social model of the Trinity and its critics. *Scottish Journal of Theology* 46 325-43.

Grudem, W 1994. *Systematic theology: an introduction to biblical doctrine*. Leicester: Inter-Varsity / Grand Rapids: Zondervan.

Grudem, W (ed) 1996. *Are miraculous gifts for today? four views*. Leicester: IVP.

Hall, D J 1986. *Imaging God: dominion as stewardship*. Grand

Rapids: Eerdmans / New York: Friendship Press for Commission on stewardship, National Council of the Churches of Christ in the USA.

Hamilton, B 1986. *Religion in the medieval West.* London: Edward Arnold.

Harbin, M A 1997. Theistic evolution: deism revisited? *Journal of the Evangelical Theological Society* 40(4) 639-51.

Häring, B 1973. *Faith and morality in a secular age.* Slough: St Paul.

Harries, R 1991. Human rights in theological perspective. Blackburn, R & Taylor, J *Human rights for the 1990s: legal, political and ethical issues.* London: Mansell. 1-13.

Hawthorne, G F 1983. *Word Biblical commentary volume 43: Philippians.* Waco, Tx: Word.

Helm, P 1993. *The providence of God.* Leicester: Inter-Varsity.

Hewlett, M & Peters, T 2006. Why Darwin's theory of evolution deserves theological support. *Theology and science* 4(2) 171-82.

Highfield, R 2002. The function of divine self-limitation in open theism: great wall or picket fence? *Journal of the Evangelical Theological Society* 45(2) 279-99.

Hill, W J 1975. Does God know the future? Aquinas and some moderns. *Theological Studies* 36(1) 3-18.

Hill, W J 1982. *The three-personed God: the Trinity as a mystery of salvation.* Washington, D C: Catholic University of America press.

Hodgson, L 1943. *The doctrine of the Trinity: Croall lectures 1942-1943.* London: Nisbet.

Horton, M S 2002. Hellenistic or Hebrew? Open theism and Reformed theological method. *Journal of the Evangelical Theological Society* 45(2) 317-41

Houston, J M 1980. *I believe in the Creator.* Grand Rapids: Eerdmans.

Hyers, C 1984. *The meaning of creation: Genesis and modern science.* Atlanta: John Knox.

James, M 1969. *I believe in the Holy Ghost.* London: Oliphants.

Japinga, L W 1997. The church must make its influence felt: RCA responses to modernity. Dekker, Luidens & Rice (1997:25-44).

Jeeves, M 2001. The nature of persons and the emergence of kenotic behaviour. Polkinghorne (2001:66-98).

Jeremias, J (& Zimmerli, W) 1965. *Servant of God.* London: SCM.

Johnson, P E 1993. *Darwin on trial.* 2nd Ed. Downers Grove, Ill: InterVarsity.

Johnson, P E 1995. *Reason in the balance: the case against naturalism in science, law and education.* Downers Grove, Ill: InterVarsity.

Jones, A & Tyler, D 2005. Engaging with intelligent design? Reflections on the rhetoric of Howard van Till. *Science and Christian belief* 17(2) 223-32.

Kelsey, M T 1973. *Healing and Christianity.* London: SCM.

König, A 1982. *Here am I! A Christian reflection on God.* Grand Rapids: Eerdmans / London: Marshall, Morgan & Scott.

König, A 1986. Healing as an integral part of salvation, in de Villiers, P G R (ed) *Healing in the name of God.* Pretoria: University of South Africa.

König, A 1988. *New and greater things: re-evaluating the Biblical message on creation.* Pretoria: University of South Africa.

Kuhlman, K 1962. *I believe in miracles.* London: Oliphants.

LaCugna, C M 1993. *God for us: the Trinity and the Christian life.* San Francisco: Harper Collins.

Lamoureux, D O 2007a. Robert A. Larmer on intelligent design: an evolutionary creationist critique. *Christian Scholar's Review* 37(1) 77-90.

Lamoureux, D O 2007b. Gaps, design and "theistic" evolution: a counter reply to Robert A. Larmer. *Christian Scholar's Review* 37(1) 101-16.

Lampe, G W H 1978. Melito and Irenaeus, in Cunliffe-Jones, H (ed) *A history of Christian doctrine.* Edinburgh: T & T Clark. 40-50.

Larmer, R A 2006. Intelligent design as a theistic theory of biological origins and development. *Christian Scholar's Review* 36(1) 47-61.

Larmer, R A 2007. Intelligent design and theistic evolution; a reply to Denis O. Lamoureux. *Christian Scholar's Review* 37(1) 91-100.

Laurentin, R 1977. *Catholic Pentecostalism*. London: Darton, Longman & Todd.

Lederle, H I 1988. *Treasures old and new: interpretations of "spirit-baptism" in the charismatic renewal movement*. Peabody, Mass: Hendrickson.

Letham, R 1993. *The work of Christ*. Leicester: Inter-Varsity.

Lyon, D 1985. *The steeple's shadow: on the myths and realities of secularization*. London: SPCK (Third Way books).

McDonald, H D 1994. *New Testament concept of atonement: gospel of the Calvary event*. Cambridge: Lutterworth.

McGrath, A 1992. *Making sense of the cross*. Leicester: Inter-Varsity.

McGrath, A E 1997. *Christian theology: an introduction*. 2nd ed. Oxford: Blackwell.

McDonald, H D 1994. *New Testament concept of atonement: gospel of the Calvary event*. Cambridge: Lutterworth.

Macleod, D 1998. *The Person of Christ*. Leicester: InterVarsity.

MacNutt, F 1974. *Healing*. Notre Dame, Ind: Ave Maria.

MacNutt, F 1977. *The power to heal*. Notre Dame, Ind: Ave Maria.

Macquarrie, J 1974. Kenoticism reconsidered. *Theology* 77(645) 115-24.

Macquarrie, J 1978. *The humility of God*. London: SCM.

Marshall, I H 1978. *The gospel of Luke: a commentary on the Greek text.* Exeter: Paternoster.

Martin, D 1969. *The religious and the secular: studies in secularization.* London: Routledge & Kegan Paul.

Martin, D 1978. *A general theory of secularization.* Oxford: Basil Blackwell.

Martin, D 2005. *On secularization: towards a revised general theory.* Aldershot, Hants: Ashgate.

Martin, D B 1990. *Slavery as salvation: the metaphor of slavery in Pauline Christianity.* New Haven & London: Yale university press.

Martin, R P 1959. *The epistle of Paul to the Philippians: an introduction and commentary.* London: Tyndale.

Martin, R P 1983. *Carmen Christi: Philippians 2:5-11 in recent interpretation and in the setting of early Christian worship.* rev. ed. Grand Rapids: Eerdmans.

Mascall, E L 1965. *The secularisation of Christianity: an analysis and a critique.* London: Darton, Longman & Todd.

Master, J 2002. Exodus 32 as an argument for traditional theism. *Journal of the Evangelical Theological Society* 45(4) 585-98.

Molnar, P D 1989. The function of the immanent Trinity in the theology of Karl Barth: implications for today. *Scottish Journal of Theology* 42(3) 367-99.

Moltmann, J 1981. *The Trinity and the kingdom of God: the doctrine of God*. London: SCM.

Moltmann, J 1985. *God in creation: an ecological doctrine of creation. The Gifford lectures 1984-1985*. London: SCM.

Moltmann, J 2001a. *The crucified God: the cross of Christ as the foundation and criticism of Christian theology*. 2nd ed. London: SCM.

Moltmann, J 2001b. God's kenosis in the creation and consummation of the world. Polkinghorne (2001:137-51).

Morris, H M 1982. *Evolution in turmoil*. San Diego: Creation-Life publishers.

Morris, L 1965. *The apostolic preaching of the cross*. 3rd ed. Grand Rapids: Eerdmans.

Morris, L 1971. *The gospel according to John: the English text with introduction, exposition and notes*. Grand Rapids: Eerdmans.

Morris, L 1974. *The gospel according to St Luke: an introduction and commentary*. London: Inter-Varsity.

Morris, L 1976. *The cross in the New Testament*. Exeter: Paternoster.

Murphy, N & Ellis, G F R 1996. *On the moral nature of the universe: theology, cosmology and ethics*. Minneapolis: Fortress.

Murray, A 1963. *The Spirit of Christ: thoughts on the indwelling of the Holy Spirit in the believer and the Church*. London: Marshall, Morgan & Scott.

Neill, S 1984. *Crises of belief: the Christian dialogue with faith and no faith*. London: Hodder & Stoughton.

Nicholls, J A 2002. Openness and inerrancy: can they be compatible? *Journal of the Evangelical Theological Society* 45(4) 629-49.

Norris, P & Inglehart, R 2004. *Sacred and secular: religion and politics worldwide*. Cambridge: Cambridge University press.

Numbers, R L 2006. *The creationists: from scientific creationism to intelligent design*. Expanded edition. Cambridge, Mass: Harvard University press.

Oliphint, K S 2004. Most moved mediator. *Themelios* 30(1) 39-51.

Olson, R 1989. Wolfhart Pannenberg's doctrine of the Trinity. *Scottish Journal of Theology* 43(2) 175-206.

Packer, J I 1961. *Evangelism and the sovereignty of God*. London: Inter-Varsity Fellowship.

Pannenberg, W 1968. *Jesus - God and man*. London: SCM.

Pannenberg, W 1989. *Christianity in a secularized world*. New York: Crossroad.

Pawson, J D 1995. *Is the blessing Biblical? Thinking through the Toronto phenomenon*. London: Hodder & Stoughton.

Peacocke, A 1993. *Theology for a scientific age: being and becoming – natural, divine and human*. Enlarged edition. London: SCM.

Peacocke, A 2001. The cost of new life. Polkinghorne (2001:21-42).

Peck, S M 1997. *Denial of the soul: spiritual and medical perspectives on euthanasia and morality*. London: Simon & Schuster.

Pennock, R T (ed) 2001. *Intelligent design creationism and its critics. Philosophical, theological and scientific perspectives*. Cambridge, Mass: MIT press.

Peters, T 1993. *God as Trinity: relationality and temporality in divine life*. Louisville, Ky: Westminster / John Knox.

Picirilli, R E 2000. Foreknowledge, freedom, and the future. *Journal of the Evangelical Theological Society* 43(2) 259–271.

Pinnock, C H 1996. *Flame of love: a theology of the Holy Spirit*. Downers Grove, Ill: InterVarsity.

Pinnock, C H 2001. *Most moved mover: a theology of God's openness (Didsbury lectures 2000)*. Grand Rapids: Baker / Carlisle: Paternoster.

Pinnock, C H 2002. There is room for us: a reply to Bruce Ware. *Journal of the Evangelical Theological society* 45(2) 213-9.

Placher, W C 2001. *Jesus the savior: the meaning of Jesus Christ for Christian faith*. Louisville: Westminster John Knox.

Polkinghorne, J 2001. Kenotic creation and divine action. Polkinghorne (2001:90-106).

Polkinghorne, J (ed) 2001. *The work of love: creation as kenosis*. Grand Rapids / Cambridge: Eerdmans / London: SPCK.

Porter, W J 1995. The worship of the Toronto blessing. Porter, S E & Richter, P J (eds) *The Toronto blessing - or is it?* London: Darton Longman & Todd. 104-30.

Rahner, K 1970. *The Trinity*. London: Burns & Oates.

Renick, T M 2002. *Aquinas for armchair theologians*. Louisville: Westminster John Knox.

Richard, R L 1967. *Secularization theology*. New York: Herder & Herder.

Richard, L 1982. *A kenotic Christology: in the humanity of Jesus the Christ, the compassion of our God*. Lanham, NY: University press of America.

Richard, L 1997. *Christ: the self-emptying of God*. Mahwah, NJ: Paulist.

Rolston, H III 2001. Kenosis and nature. Polkinghorne (2001:43-65).

Sanders, J N 1968. *A commentary on the gospel according to St John*. London: Adam & Charles Black.

Sanders, J T 1971. *The New Testament Christological hymns: their historical religious background*. Cambridge: University press.

Sanders, J 1998. *The God who risks: a theology of providence*. Downers Grove, Ill: InterVarsity.

Sanders, J 2002. Be wary of Ware: a reply to Bruce Ware. *Journal of the Evangelical Theological society* 45(2) 221-31.

Sarkar, S 2007. *Doubting Darwin? Creationist designs on evolution.* Oxford: Blackwell.

Schumacher, E F 1973. *Small is beautiful: a study of economics as if people mattered.* London: Sphere (Abacus).

Silva, M 1988. *The Wycliffe exegetical commentary: Philippians.* Chicago: Moody.

Scheffczyk, L 1970. *Creation and providence.* London: Burns & Oates / New York: Herder & Herder.

Soelle, D 1975. *Suffering.* London: Darton, Longman & Todd.

Sontag, F 1991. Omnipotence need not entail omniscience. *Anglican Theological Review* 73(1) 68-72.

Spanner, D C 1987. *Biblical creation and the theory of evolution.* Exeter: Paternoster.

Sproul, R C 1986. *Right and wrong: ethics and the Christian today.* London: Scripture Union.

Storms, C S 1996. A third wave response to Douglas A. Oss. Grudem (1996:305-8).

Stott, J 1984. *Issues facing Christians today.* London: Marshall Pickering.

Stott, J R W 1986. *The cross of Christ.* Leicester: Inter-Varsity.

Tasker, R V G 1960. *The gospel according to St. John: an introduction and commentary.* London: Tyndale.

Taylor, J V 1992. *The Christlike God*. London: SCM.

Temple, W 1963. Readings in St John's gospel. London: Macmillan.

Thaxton, C B 1989. A word to the teacher. Davis & Kenyon (1989:153-62).

Thielicke, H 1966. *Theological ethics Volume 1*: Foundations. Philadelphia: Fortress.

Thomas, T A 1970. The kenosis question. *Evangelical Quarterly* 42 142-51.

Thompson, J 1994. *Modern Trinitarian perspectives.* (New York / Oxford: Oxford University press

Tinker, M 2001. Last supper / Lord's supper: more than a parable in action. *Themelios* 26(2) 18-28.

Torrance, T F 1996. *The Christian doctrine of God, one being three Persons.* Edinburgh: T & T Clark.

Trueman, C 2005. The unspeakable arrogance of doubt. *Themelios* 31(1) 1-6.

Turner, M 1996. *The Holy Spirit and spiritual gifts: then and now.* Carlisle: Paternoster.

van den Brink, G 1993. *Almighty God: a study of the doctrine of divine omnipotence.* Kampen: Kok Pharos.

Vanstone, W H 1977. *Love's endeavour, love's expense: the response of being to the love of God.* London: Darton, Longman & Todd.

von Rad, G 1962. *Old Testament theology: vol 1: the theology of Israel's historical traditions.* Louisville: Westminster John Knox.

von Rad, G 1963. *Genesis.* 2nd ed. London: SCM.

Vriezen, Th C 1960. *An outline of Old Testament theology.* Wageningen: Veenman & Zonen.

Ward, K 2001. Cosmos and kenosis. Polkinghorne (2001:152-66).

Ware, B A 2002. Defining Evangelicalism's boundaries theologically: is open theism evangelical? *Journal of the Evangelical Theological society* 45(2) 193-212.

Warrington, K 2003. The path to wholeness: beliefs and practices relating to healing in Pentecostalism. *Evangel* 21(2) 45-9.

Watson, D 1984. *Fear no evil: a personal struggle with cancer.* London: Hodder & Stoughton.

Wellum, S J 2002. Divine Sovereignty - Omniscience, inerrancy and open theism: an evaluation. *Journal of the Evangelical Theological Society* 45(2) 257-77.

Wendel, F 1965. *Calvin: the origins and development of his religious thought.* London: Collins (Fontana).

Westcott, B F 1958. *The gospel according to St. John: with introduction and notes.* London: James Clarke.

Westermann, C 1974. *Creation.* Philadelphia: Fortress.

Westermann, C 1984. *Genesis 1-11: a commentary.* London: SPCK.

Wheeler Robinson, H 1928. *The Christian experience of the Holy Spirit.* London: Nisbet.

White, R E O 1979. *The changing continuity of Christian ethics vol 1: Biblical ethics.* Exeter: Paternoster.

Wiersbe, W W 1997. *The cross of Jesus: how Christ understood his crucifixion.* Leicester: Crossway.

Williams, D T 1997. *The office of Christ and its expression in the Church: prophet, priest, king.* Lampeter: Edwin Mellen.

Williams, D T 2001. *New Century Trinity.* Lincoln, NE: iUniverse.

Williams, D T 2003. *The "two hands of God".* Lincoln, NE: iUniverse.

Williams, D T 2004. *Vinculum amoris: a theology of the Holy Spirit.* Lincoln, NE: iUniverse.

Williams, D T 2007. *Have this mind: following the example of Christ.* Lincoln, NE: iUniverse.

Williams, J R 1971. *The era of the Spirit.* Plainfield, NJ: Logos International.

Wimber, J with Springer, K 1987. *Power healing.* San Francisco: Harper & Row.

Woolmer, J 1997. *Thinking clearly about prayer*. London: Evangelical Alliance / Crowborough: Monarch.

Wright, R K M 1996. *No place for sovereignty: what's wrong with freewill theism*. Downer's Grove, Ill: InterVarsity.

Yoder, J H 1972. *The politics of Jesus*. Grand Rapids: Eerdmans.

Yong, A 2002. Divine omniscience and future contingents: weighing the presuppositional issues in the current debate. *Evangelical Review of Theology* 26(3) 240-64.

Zimmerli, W 1978. *Old Testament theology in outline*. Edinburgh: Clark.

Zizioulas, J D 1985. *Being as communion: studies in personhood and the Church*. Crestwood, NY: St Vladimir's seminary press.

Other books by the author:

All of the following books are available FREE from the author as a PDF file. Contact dwilliams@ufh.ac.za.

New Century Trinity. 2001.
> An exposition of the traditionally accepted doctrine of the Trinity in the context of the worldview of the start of the twenty-first century

Parables of Salvation. 2002.
> Not an academic work! Two hundred short talks using visual aids as used in High schools and in children's meetings.

Christian Approaches to Poverty. 2001.
> A discussion of seven specifically Christian methods of combating poverty. The author suggests that a correct Christian approach is a synthesis of all seven

Pictures of the Spirit. 2003.
> How does a person understand the Spirit? Only by illustration! A discussion of the ways used in Scripture, such as the dove and fire, with a few further suggestions from the modern world.

The "two hands of God": imaging the Trinity. 2003.
> If humanity is really in the image of God, it follows that the goal of human activity, and its method, is based upon the understanding of the Trinity. The principle is applied in several examples, such as marriage, poverty, and concern for the environment.

Vinculum amoris: a theology of the Holy Spirit. 2004.

> Written for students, the book takes as its starting point the idea of Augustine that the Spirit is the "bond of love", seeking to generate and strengthen relationship. The principle is applied in the various aspects of the Spirit's work.

Have this mind: following the example of Christ. 2007.

> Taken from the well-known "hymn" of Philippians 2:5f, the book suggests that correct human action is of self-limitation in imitation of Christ. Examples are provided for several ethical issues, such as war, sexual ethics, and the environment

Print versions of all the above are readily available from the publisher, iUniverse (www.iUniverse.com), or from other outlets, such as Amazon, or Barnes and Noble. South African sources such as Kalahari only list some titles

Two other books are available, but only in the print versions:

The Office of Christ and its expression in the Church: Prophet Priest King. Lampeter: The Edwin Mellen Press 1997.

Capitalism, Socialism, Christianity and Poverty. Johannesburg: von Schaik 1998.

The author has also written a chapter in another book:

Towards a unified theory of the atonement, in Tidball, D, Hilborn, D & Thacker, J (eds) The atonement debate: papers from the London symposium on the theology of atonement. Grand Rapids: Zondervan 2008 228-46.

Contact the author for a full list of what is also available in journals

David Williams was born and brought up in England, but while reading engineering at Cambridge paid two visits to Africa, first to South Africa, and then to a mission station in Zambia. Being impressed by the needs of Africa, he did a year's post-graduate teacher training in England, where he met his wife, Gill, before coming to Southern Africa with a missionary society. They spent a period in a mission High school in Swaziland, then several years ministry in township High schools in Durban. David was then called to be minister of a non-denominational church north of Johannesburg, where he also did the first part of his doctoral studies with UNISA. On completion of this, he accepted his present post, lecturing in theology at Fort Hare, soon completing his doctoral thesis, "The call of Jeremiah". He is now full professor. He is active as a "tentmaker" missionary, involved in several ministries in the area around the University. He has full ministerial recognition by the FIEC in the UK and the Baptist Union in South Africa. He has four children; the eldest is working at VW (South Africa), the second is teaching in Somerset West, the third and fourth are working in the UK.